GEORGIA OUTDOORS

GEORGIA OUTDOORS

BY
VICTORIA
AND
FRANK LOGUE

JOHN F. BLAIR, PUBLISHER
WINSTON-SALEM, NORTH CAROLINA

DESIGN BY DEBRA LONG HAMPTON
COMPOSITION BY LIZA LANGRALL
ALL PHOTOGRAPHS AND MAPS BY THE AUTHORS
PRINTED AND BOUND BY R. R. DONNELLEY & SONS

Cover photograph—
Sunset through the door of a tent
at Brickhill Bluff Camp, Cumberland Island

Library of Congress Cataloging-in-Publication Data
Logue, Victoria, 1961—
      Georgia outdoors / by Victoria and Frank Logue.
         p.   cm.
      Includes index.
      ISBN 0-89587-131-9
      1. Outdoor recreation—Georgia—Guidebooks. 2. Outdoor
recreation—Georgia—Directories. 3. Georgia—Guidebooks.
I. Logue, Frank, 1963–   . II. Title.
GV191.42.G4L64 1995
796.5'09758—dc20   95-471

*T*his book is for our daughter, **Griffin Logue**, who made the project fun.

*I*t is also dedicated to **Lowell Bouma** and **H. Jarold Weatherford**, our mentors at Georgia Southern. Their jobs were to teach us linguistics and German, but they also taught us to believe in ourselves.

Northwest Mountains

Northeast Mountains

Metro Atlanta

Historic Heartland

Classic South

Presidential Pathways

Magnolia Midlands

Plantation Trace

Colonial Coast

REGIONS AS THEY APPEAR WITHIN SECTIONS

NW Northwest Georgia Mountains

NE Northeast Georgia Mountains

A Metropolitan Atlanta Area

PP Presidential Pathways

HH Historic Heartland

CS Classic South

PT Plantation Trace

MM Magnolia Midlands

CC Colonial Coast

TABLE OF CONTENTS

INTRODUCTION

When we planned our year of traveling around the state to gather experiences and information for this book, we already felt we knew Georgia well. Frank had lived in Georgia since the age of six and Victoria since she was 15, other than our two years of living in Virginia. We both graduated from high school here. Since meeting at Georgia Southern College in 1982, we had traveled extensively on vacation and while working for the *Warner Robins Daily Sun* and later the *Rome News-Tribune*. We had paddled the state's rivers in our canoe, hunted its game lands, water-skied on its lakes and hiked and camped in its forests and parks, but Georgia still had more to offer us.

Georgia was the jumping-off point for our six-month-long thru-hike of the Appalachian Trail in 1988. But even as its trails led us away from the state, they offered us a road back. After writing several successful books about the Appalachian Trail and backpacking, we decided to write the book we wish we had on our shelves, a guide to the outdoor recreation opportunities in the largest state east of the Mississippi River—Georgia.

Georgia Outdoors describes things to see and do at more than 275 state- and federal-owned areas. For each of these sites, we give a general description which includes the history of the area, a listing of its amenities, fees and hours of operation, directions to the site and a list of nearby attractions. To keep the guide comprehensive in its coverage of publicly owned areas, we have included state historic sites and national historic sites whose main focus is educational, though some of these areas also offer recreation.

In this book, you will find some well-known, oft-visited areas, including the prairies of Okefenokee National Wildlife Refuge, the miles of pristine beach at Cumberland Island National Seashore and acres of water at the Corps of Engineers' Lake Sidney Lanier. But some less-explored areas are here to discover as well. Providence Canyon State Conservation Park is Georgia's much-photographed "Little Grand Canyon," but its back-country trail to the floor of the canyon is seldom used. The cypress-filled lake at George L. Smith II State Park pours its blackwater through a millhouse and over a dam far from the beaten paths of some of the state's most popular parks. For day-use visitors, Blackbeard Island National Wildlife Refuge offers a beautiful beach and trails to freshwater fishing and wildlife viewing without the crowds of daytime visitors on the beach at Cumberland Island.

This book is arranged by category, not geography. If you are headed to the coast, for example, and want to find places to see and stay in that part of the state, head to the appendix to find an alphabetical listing of places grouped into nine geographic regions.

The biggest surprise in working on this book was how much variety can be packed into similar packages. Each of Georgia's state parks offers a comparable array of facilities, including campsites, cottages, picnic shelters and even golf courses. But it is the differences that stand out as you visit the parks. The barrel-shaped cabins at Unicoi, Pioneer Village at General Coffee and the impressive handicapped-accessible facilities at Lake Richard B. Russell are among the many unique features that give the parks their own personalities. And as there are minor distinctions that make each state park stand out as individual, there are differences among the state historic sites, national park units and national forest recreation areas that make each site special.

To explore these differences and collect the information that forms the bulk of this book, we hit the road in our mini-Winnebago, "Harry the Truck." It gave our now four-year-old daughter, Griffin, a home on the road and a place to play while we crisscrossed the state on a year-long adventure. With many of the parks and lakes located close together, we only turned over 10,000 miles during many days on the road. Visiting parks, forests, lakes and refuges was grueling at times, but we're not complaining. Somebody had to hike those trails, paddle those lakes and sleep in those campsites, and we were fortunate for it to be us. It was a tough job personally testing playgrounds in all of the state parks, but Griffin took to her task with the energy of, well, a three-year-old.

"Harry the Truck" became our time machine as we traversed the length and breadth of the state and delved into its history as well. At Kolomoki Mounds State Historic Park and Etowah Indian Mounds State Historic Site, we traveled back to our state's pre-Columbian past. From atop the great temple mounds, we could picture these sites as centers of civilized culture that far predated European interaction.

On Georgia's colonial coast, we visited a reproduction of Fort King George, which once guarded an ill-fated corner of the British Empire.

At Elijah Clark State Park, we saw the graves of Colonel Elijah Clarke (the original spelling) and his wife, Hannah, near log cabins reconstructed to resemble their homestead. Known as "the Hero of the Hornet's Nest," he stung the British with a Revolutionary War victory at Kettle Creek.

As we traveled forward in time, we followed in the footsteps of General William T. Sherman's Union troops as they battled south to Atlanta and then marched to the sea. We pulled for the Confederate victors at Pickett's Mill State Historic Site but shared the North's shock and grief as we viewed row upon row of prisoners' graves at the former Camp Sumter in Andersonville National Historic Site.

We imagined a golden time and place for the young Martin Luther King, Jr., as we explored "Sweet Auburn" at Atlanta's national historic site named for the civil-rights leader and Nobel laureate.

Finally, we came to the tiny town of Plains, which shone brightly in the media spotlight as native son Jimmy Carter successfully ran for the presidency in 1976.

Like a rare gem, each of these special places has a character to be discovered not just in one hurried look, but by carefully exploring its many facets. At Cloudland Canyon State Park, we have hiked down to the falls with crowds of springtime visitors to see the water splashing into a deep, fern-rimmed pool, then returned in the heat of summer to find no water going over the falls at all. But perhaps that most special of visits came on a bitterly cold morning with rime ice in the trees. The calm of the canyon was shattered again and again by the crashing thunder of chunks of ice breaking free in the glare of the sun and falling to explode on the rocks below. The trail was too dangerous to traverse, but the incredible bass notes of the ice explosions vaulted the rock walls to reach us at speaker-busting volume on the rim of the canyon. We didn't see any other people in the park that day, and enjoyed the primeval music in solitude.

Through our travels in time and space, we came to know and appreciate Georgia more deeply. In every region, corner and hollow, we found a lot of new places we want to return to again and again.

GEORGIA OUTDOORS

STATE PARKS

Long a popular tourist stop on
U.S. 441, Tallulah Gorge
is Georgia's newest state park.

The canoe slices through the blackwater, barely rippling the stillness of the morning. The water takes on a tobacco color when the paddle digs in. Each time the paddle is pulled out for another stroke, the blackness overtakes the tobacco and the canoe is thrust forward.

We've already seen two alligators by the time the road and boat basin at Stephen C. Foster State Park disappear from view. We share the trip with many bugs, to be sure. But they are kept at bay by "bug dope," and no one else seems to have ventured out to share the swamp with us yet. This is Clinch County, which has fewer people than the Okefenokee has alligators. Solitude comes easy on a winter weekday. It's just a quiet paddle away.

Georgia boasts 45 state parks scattered throughout the state. From Cloudland Canyon in the extreme northwest corner to Seminole in the southwestern corner, Crooked River at the southeastern corner, Black Rock Mountain in the northeast and everywhere in between, Georgia's diverse landscapes are open for recreation and exploration.

If you like lakes, rivers and streams, you'll find a lot to love in Georgia's parks. Every park has a lake or stream (though Panola Mountain's lake and Providence Canyon's stream are seen only by hikers). All but seven have lakes with easy access for boating and/or fishing. Picnicking, hiking, biking, water-skiing and swimming are offered all around the state. Each park has its own unique personality to discover.

PARK HOURS AND RATES

All parks are open year-round from 7 A.M. to 10 P.M., with the exception of Panola Mountain, Providence Canyon and Stephen C. Foster, whose hours are listed by the parks. All unregistered guests must leave the parks by closing time. The office hours are daily from 8 A.M. to 5 P.M.

A ParkPass is required for all vehicles entering Georgia's parks. The $2 pass is valid for one day and is good for more than one park visited on the same day. Lodge, cottage and campground guests pay the fee only for the first night of their stay. Wednesdays are free days for day-use visitors in the parks.

An Annual ParkPass may be purchased for $25 at any park. Seniors (62 years and older) may buy their Annual ParkPass for $12.50. All daily and ParkPass fees are used for repair and maintenance in the parks.

A. H. Stephens, Fort McAllister and Kolomoki Mounds are historic parks. There, museum, fort, home and grounds tours are by a per-person admission fee. An annual historic-site pass (detailed in the section on historic sites) is valid for these tours.

Park facilities—including lodge rooms, cottages, picnic shelters and group shelters—have rates that are subject to change and are not listed in this book. A current list of rates and reservation information is available from each park or by calling 404-656-3530 between 8:30 A.M. and 4:30 P.M. from Monday through Friday.

CAMPING

Park campgrounds are open from 7 A.M. to 10 P.M. Registration at the park office is required and may not be completed after 8 P.M. Checkout time is 1 P.M. There is a 14-day maximum stay for each visit. The site must be occupied each night. Visitors may not hold a site for another party arriving later. Reservations for a two-night minimum stay are accepted by some parks. These reservable sites are often not in prime locations, such as on a lakeshore, though exceptions are noted with the park descriptions.

Each site is limited to a pup tent, two cars and one of the following: a motor home, a large tent, a pop-up trailer, a travel trailer or a pickup with a mounted camper. If the site is large enough to accommodate it, a boat trailer is also permitted.

Large, organized groups must stay in the pioneer camping area or group camps. Campers under 18 years of age must be accompanied by an adult who accepts responsibility for them. Quiet hours are in effect after 10 P.M. Pets are allowed, but they must be kept on a leash and accompanied by an owner at all times.

During the busy months, campground hosts are on duty to answer questions about the park and nearby attractions. These are volunteers who live out of their motorhomes in the park while

A statue of A. H. Stephens
in front of his home
at the State Historic Park
named for him
in Central Georgia

performing a vital service for visitors. If you would like to volunteer to be a host, call 404-656-6539 for more information.

COTTAGES

More than half of the parks have cottages for rent. The cottages have kitchens equipped with a refrigerator and stove, as well as cookware and eating utensils. Towels, blankets and bed linens are also included. All of the cottages are heated and many—all of the cottages in south Georgia—have air conditioning. Many have decks or porches and fireplaces; no firewood is provided.

Reservations are taken up to 11 months in advance for cottages. A one-night deposit is required to hold the reservation and must be paid within seven days of calling the park. Deposits will be refunded if you call the park at least 72 hours in advance.

There is a two-night minimum stay in cottages from June 1 through Labor Day, with a one-week minimum stay during that time if the site is not reserved at least one month in advance.

Check-in time is from 4 P.M. to 10 P.M. Reservations are not held after 11 A.M. on the second day unless you call the park and leave word that you are still coming. Check-out time is 11 A.M.

Cottages are not for use by groups, including family reunions and civic groups. Group shelters are provided in many parks for group use. Maximum occupancy varies with the arrangement of the cottage. Generally, there may be up to two persons in each double bed. As with campgrounds, an adult must accompany guests under 18 years of age. No pets are allowed in the cottage areas.

PICNIC AREAS

The picnic tables and grills located by the dozens in every park are free for use on a first-come, first-served basis. When not reserved, the covered picnic shelters are also available for free to early birds. If you want your group to be sure it has use of a shelter, a reservation is required. The reservations cost $25 to $40, depending on the park and the size of the shelter.

There are 36 parks offering large, enclosed group shelters. Available by reservation only, these shelters have heat and air conditioning, kitchens, barbecue pits, restrooms and parking. These shelters are typically used for family reunions, church gatherings and similar occasions. Reservations may be made up to 11 months in advance. The capacity of these shelters varies from 30 persons to 500 persons, with most shelters authorized for use by groups of 75 to 150 people. Prices range from $35 to $150 per day.

SWIMMING

Beaches with no lifeguard are free and open year-round. At pools and where lifeguards are present at swimming beaches, a $1 to $2 per-person fee is charged. Registered lodge or cottage guests and children under two years of age swim free. Some parks also offer a seasonal pool pass, with rates varying from $15 to $30 for adults and children and $40 to $60 for families of up to six people.

GOLF

Georgia Veterans, Hard Labor Creek and Little Ocmulgee have 18-hole golf courses, with another course in the planning stages for Lake Richard B. Russell. Nine-hole courses are located at Gordonia-Alatamaha and Victoria Bryant. Passes for unlimited play in a weekend are sold, as are annual greens passes, good at all five state courses. Special rates are offered to seniors.

OTHER FACILITIES

Pedal boats, canoes, johnboats, bicycles, horses (Franklin Delano Roosevelt State Park only) and horse stalls (Hard Labor Creek State Park only) may be rented from some parks. Not all parks offer rentals, and no park offers all of the above. Tennis courts may be used free of charge. A current price list is available by calling 404-656-3530.

SPECIAL PROGRAMS

During the summer, interpretive specialists lead nature hikes and campfire programs and teach courses on outdoor skills such as canoeing and backpacking. Living-history demonstrations are also given in some parks. Check the park office for a current schedule of events.

FOR MORE INFORMATION

Georgia State Parks and Historic Sites, Department of Natural Resources, 1352 Floyd Tower East, 205 Butler Street, Atlanta, GA 30334.

CS

An outbuilding at the A. H. Stephens home now houses the State Historic Park's museum.

Liberty Hall, the focal point of this sprawling state park, was home to Alexander Stephens, vice president of the Confederacy. Stephens and Confederate president Jefferson Davis could not see eye to eye on many issues of importance to the Confederacy, and Stephens spent much of his term as vice president at his Georgia home. He named his home Liberty Hall because any stranger passing through the area was "at liberty" to stay the night in what his servants dubbed the "Tramp Room."

Stephens, known as "Little Aleck," arrived in Crawfordville in 1834 to study law at Liberty Hall under Williamson Bird. Stephens purchased the home in 1845, after Bird's death, and slowly made improvements. In 1875, he tore down the main structure and rebuilt in the Victorian style. The recently restored home is very much as it was during Stephens's lifetime and includes

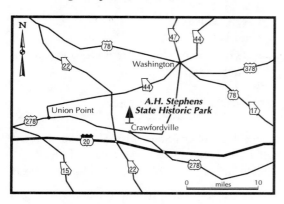

many original pieces of furniture. The law library and an adjoining room were used by Stephens's students. He also helped send dozens of area men to college.

He was imprisoned after the Civil War. During this time, while the small and always-frail Stephens's health further declined, he wrote a two-volume work entitled *A Constitutional View of the Late War Between the States*. After being released from prison, he was elected to the United States Senate, but was not allowed his seat by the still-bitter Congress. From 1872 to 1882, he did return to the House of Representatives, where he had served before secession. He was governor of Georgia at the time of his death in 1883.

The Confederate Museum is housed in a similarly styled building next to Liberty Hall and features one of the finest collections of Confederate artifacts in Georgia. Military, political and domestic items from the Civil War are all on display.

In 1994, a lily pool was built behind the museum.

Because this is a state historic site, there is a fee to see the museum and tour Stephens's home.

CAMPING

Although major renovations were made to the park in 1994, much of the work you see was done by the Civilian Conservation Corps when the park was opened during the Great Depression. The park offers 36 tent and trailer sites with electrical and water hookups. A dump station and bathhouses with hot showers and laundry facilities are also part of the camping area. There is access to Lake Buncomb, an 18-acre lake fully stocked with bass and bream.

Camp Stephens, a 120-person group camp, includes rustic cabins, a bathhouse, a ball field, assembly shelters and a fully equipped kitchen and dining hall, as well as a beach and a fishing dock on the 24-acre Lake Liberty, which is stocked with catfish.

SWIMMING

The park features a swimming pool and a concession stand. A fee is charged for swimming in the pool. During the summer months, it is in operation from 11 A.M. to 6 P.M. Tuesday through Thursday and from 11 A.M. to 7 P.M. Friday through Sunday. It is closed Monday except for legal holidays. A lifeguard is on duty during pool hours.

OTHER FACILITIES

Fishing and boating are allowed on both lakes under normal state regulations, although fishing on Lake Liberty is limited to November through March.

ANNUAL SPECIAL EVENTS

The A. H. Stephens Homecoming (April) and Christmas at Liberty Hall (December) are among the park's special events.

NEARBY ATTRACTIONS

Lake Oconee
Hard Labor Creek State Park
Robert Toombs House State Historic Site
Mistletoe State Park

DIRECTIONS

A. H. Stephens State Historic Park is located off I-20. Take the Crawfordville exit (Exit 55) and head north on GA 22 for 2 miles, then head east on U.S. 278 for 1 mile to Crawfordville and follow the signs to the state park.

FOR MORE INFORMATION

A. H. Stephens State Historic Park, P.O. Box 283, Crawfordville, GA 30631 (706-456-2602).

AMICALOLA FALLS STATE PARK AND LODGE

DAWSON COUNTY	1,020 ACRES

NE

Amicalola Falls is a 729-foot drop billed by the park as the highest waterfall east of the Rocky Mountains. The waterfall was named *Ama Kalola*, or "Tumbling Waters," by the Cherokee Indians. The lodge, cottages and camping area offer a variety of accommodations.

The reflecting pool at the base of the falls and the overlook bridge at the top offer visitors a close-up view of the "tumbling waters." Do not wander from the trail or attempt to climb

the falls. Serious injuries and death have resulted from ignoring this warning.

The park has close ties to the Appalachian Trail. The 8.1-mile approach trail leading to Springer Mountain, the southern terminus of the A.T., begins at the visitor center. More than a thousand hikers set out each year planning to hike 2,150 miles north to Mount Katahdin in

For the Cherokees, this was "tumbling waters." Today, 729-foot tall Amicalola Falls is surrounded by a 1,020-acre state park with a lodge, cottages, campsites and more.

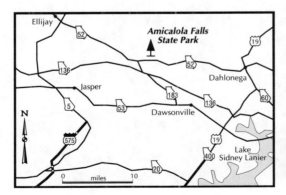

Maine. However, only 100 to 200 hikers a year achieve that goal.

LODGE

The park lodge rises above the top of the mountain to offer a impressive view of the southern end of the Blue Ridge Mountains. The 57 rooms come in five sizes, ranging from rooms with two double beds to "King Loft Suites" and an "Executive Suite." The lodge has conference facilities for groups of 10 to 200 people, with audio-visual equipment on site. The lodge features the 200-seat Maple Restaurant, with an all-you-can-eat buffet. Handicapped access and nonsmoking rooms are available. A gift shop in the lobby sells regional crafts and books, as does the visitor center at the park entrance. The visitor center also features natural-history exhibits.

HIKING

The 8.1-mile blue-blazed approach to the Appalachian Trail begins behind the visitor center near the park entrance. Two three-sided shelters are located along this trail. The first is within the park and the second at mile 7.1 on Black Mountain.

The 0.8-mile West Ridge Loop Trail is the yellow-blazed trail that begins across the road from the visitor center. A descriptive brochure with a map of the trail is available free of charge at the visitor center.

CAMPING

The 17 campsites are equipped with water and electrical hookups. The comfort station in the campground has flush toilets, showers, laundry

The 57-room lodge at Amicalola Falls State Park has a commanding view of the southern end of the Blue Ridge Mountains from its mountaintop porch.

facilities, a soft-drink machine and a telephone. Reservations are accepted with a nonrefundable deposit. Trailers 16 feet and longer are not allowed, due to the steep grade of the road leading up the mountain to the camping area.

COTTAGES

There are 14 furnished cottages in the park. The two- and three-bedroom cabins are equipped with cooking utensils and silverware, a stove, a refrigerator, linens and heating and air conditioning. Nine of the cottages are on the mountain, with the other five along Little Amicalola Creek downstream from the base of the falls. The mountaintop cottages have fireplaces.

FISHING

Trout fishing in the reflection pond and along the stream is permitted in season.

OTHER FACILITIES

There are five picnic shelters that can be reserved up to 11 months in advance for a fee. When not reserved, they are available free of charge on a first-come, first-served basis. The 78 picnic shelters and three playgrounds are also available for free.

ANNUAL EVENTS

The annual Backpacking Weekend is held in early spring and the Summer's End Tradin' Days in September. There are also Spring Wildflower Walks in April, the Fall Foliage Display in October and the Mountain Lore and Legend celebration in June.

NEARBY ATTRACTIONS

Appalachian National Scenic Trail
Dahlonega Gold Museum State Historic Site
Fort Mountain State Park
New Echota State Historic Site
Vogel State Park

DIRECTIONS

The park is 21 miles southeast of Ellijay on GA 52 and GA 400.

FOR MORE INFORMATION

Amicalola Falls State Park, Star Route, Box 215, Dawsonville, GA 30534 (706-265-8888)

BLACK ROCK MOUNTAIN STATE PARK

RABUN COUNTY   1,502 ACRES

Sheer cliffs composed of nearly black biotite gneiss give Black Rock Mountain its name. Located in the mountain country of Georgia's Blue Ridge, the park is the highest in the state, at an elevation of 3,640 feet. It sits astride the Eastern Continental Divide and offers visitors many scenic overlooks with 80-mile views of the southern Appalachians in four states. Unbelievably, even with its visitor center, campgrounds, cottages and picnic areas, Black Rock Mountain State Park is more than 90 percent undeveloped. It features five summits over 3,000 feet in elevation. Three trails take visitors into these unspoiled areas of the park.

CAMPING

The park has 48 campsites with water, cable television and electrical hookups, with two bathhouses featuring hot showers, restrooms and a washer and dryer. There are also 11 walk-in campsites without water and electricity, although they do offer a bathhouse with hot showers and restrooms. Additionally, two back-country sites with no amenities can be reached via James E. Edmonds Back-Country Trail, a loop hike of 7.2 miles. Reservations are required for the back-country site.

HIKING

There are three trails in Black Rock Moun-

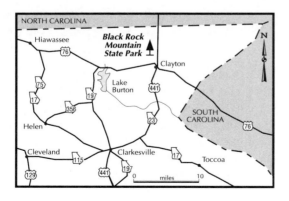

tain State Park: Ada-Hi Falls Trail, an 0.25-mile path to Ada-Hi Falls; Tennessee Rock Trail, a 2.2-mile loop that passes over the summit of Black Rock Mountain; and James E. Edmonds Back-Country Trail, a 7.2-mile loop that takes you past Black Rock Lake and across the summit of Lookoff Mountain (elevation 3,162 feet).

Tennessee Rock Trail features numbered markers and is described in an in-depth, 32-page interpretive guide available at the park's visitor center.

COTTAGES

The park rents 10 cottages—two three-bedroom cottages and eight two-bedroom cottages. Reservations can be made up to 11 months in advance, but a two-night minimum stay is required from September through May and a seven-night minimum during the summer months. Pets are not allowed in the cottages or the cottage area. All cottages have cable television.

OTHER FACILITIES

Two picnic areas and two picnic shelters are provided by the park, and picnicking is allowed only in these areas. The shelters may be reserved or used on a first-come, first-served basis.

Year-round fishing is allowed on the 17-acre Black Rock Lake, though it is restricted to the banks of the lake. The lake is stocked with bass, bream, catfish and trout. Boating and swimming are not allowed. Persons age 16 and older must have a valid state resident or nonresident license. A trout stamp is not required.

The visitor center at the park's summit features an observation deck, wildlife exhibits, a cultural-history exhibit, trail maps and wheelchair-accessible restrooms. Books, souvenirs and other items are available for purchase.

ANNUAL EVENTS

A spring wildflower program and the Junior Fishing Rodeo, both in May, and an overnight backpacking trip in the fall are among the park's special events.

NEARBY ATTRACTIONS

Moccasin Creek State Park
Unicoi State Park and Lodge
Tallulah Gorge State Park
Chattooga National Wild and Scenic River

DIRECTIONS

The park is 3 miles north of Clayton, just off U.S. 441 on Black Rock Mountain Road.

FOR MORE INFORMATION

Black Rock Mountain State Park, Mountain City, GA 30562 (706-746-2141)

BOBBY BROWN STATE PARK
ELBERT COUNTY   664 ACRES

NE

Buried beneath the waters of Clarks Hill Lake,

also known as J. Strom Thurmond Lake, is the colonial town of Petersburg. Situated where the Broad and Savannah rivers once flowed together, Petersburg was the third-largest town in Georgia at the end of the 18th century. Only Savannah and Augusta were larger. The last colonial governor, James Wright, erected Fort James here in 1773. Three years later, naturalist William Bartram visited the fort.

The town had long since been abandoned when Clarks Hill Lake began to fill in the early 1950s. Still, when water levels are low, you can see some of the foundations from this historic town. Removal of artifacts from the area is prohibited.

The park was named in honor of United States Navy lieutenant Robert T. Brown, who was killed in World War II. He was the son of Paul Brown, a United States representative from Elberton. The park is located on the 78,000-acre J. Strom Thurmond Lake, which borders both Georgia and South Carolina. Georgia prefers to call the reservoir Clarks Hill Lake. The reservoir was originally named for Revolutionary War colonel Elijah Clarke, who led the

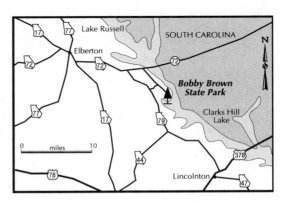

colonists in their only decisive victory in Georgia at Kettle Creek. Clarke's home is also now beneath the waters of the reservoir, but a replica can be found at Elijah Clark State Park, 30 miles away.

This reservoir, the largest man-made lake east of the Mississippi, provides more than 1,200 miles of shoreline as well as excellent fishing.

This monument is placed near the site of Colonial Fort James. The actual site of the 1773 fort is nearby, under the waters of Clarks Hill Lake.

CAMPING

There are 61 campsites at Bobby Brown, each with water and electrical hookups and picnic tables. There are two camping areas, each with its own comfort station, including heated showers, flush toilets, a washer and dryer, soft-drink machines, a pay telephone and electrical outlets. Each camping area has a dump station as well.

A boat ramp is located in Camping Area #1, where sites #3 to #13 front the water. A fish-cleaning station and enclosed picnic shelters for campers only are located in Camping Area #2, where sites #54 to #59 are on the water. A chapel is located next to Camping Area #2. From Easter Sunday through Labor Day, campers and others may attend the 9:45 A.M. services held there. Playgrounds are located at each camping area as well.

There are also two areas set aside for primitive camping, each with a covered shelter and a latrine but no electricity or water.

PICNICKING

The 40 picnic tables scattered throughout the day-use area are available on a first-come, first-served basis. A group shelter that will seat 80 can be reserved up to 11 months in advance. The heated shelter has restrooms and a stove and overlooks the water. It is connected to the day-use area by a swinging bridge.

BOATING AND FISHING

Private boats are allowed on park waters, with

no horsepower limitations. Water-skiing is also permitted on the lake. Boaters must comply with the Georgia Boating Safety Law. Launching ramps can be found at the day-use area and at Camping Area #1.

The lake is home to a large population of bass, including white, striped, hybrid and largemouth. Other game fish include bluegill, crappie and sauger. Park waters are open for fishing year-round. A fishing dock is located in the day-use area. There is also a bank fishing area in the park; if they are not registered campers, bank fishermen must leave the park by nightfall. Either a Georgia or a South Carolina fishing license may be used, as both are valid on all areas of Clarks Hill Lake. All Georgia fishing laws apply.

SWIMMING

A pool is located in the day-use area, but swimming is permitted only during the summer when there is a lifeguard on duty. The pool is closed on Mondays and Tuesdays except for legal holidays. A bathhouse is also located at the day-use area.

HIKING

A 1.9-mile hiking trail follows parts of William Bartram Trail through the park. The trail can be accessed both in the day-use area and from the loop road that circles past the camping areas.

ANNUAL EVENTS

An annual camper reunion is held each fall.

A swinging bridge over an inlet on Clarks Hill Lake connects the group shelter and the day-use area.

Because dates are subject to change, contact the park office for more information.

NEARBY ATTRACTIONS

Corps of Engineer parks on Lake Russell and Clarks Hill Lake
Elijah Clark State Park
Robert Toombs House State Historic Site
Watson Mill Bridge State Park

DIRECTIONS

The park is 21 miles east of Elberton on GA 72 and south on Bobby Brown State Park Road.

FOR MORE INFORMATION

Bobby Brown State Park, 2509 Bobby Brown State Park Road, Elberton, GA 30635 (706-213-2046)

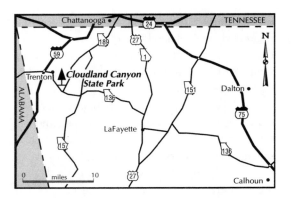

CLOUDLAND CANYON STATE PARK

DADE COUNTY   2,120 ACRES

Straddling a deep gorge carved into the western corner of Lookout Mountain by Sitton Gulch Creek, Cloudland Canyon is a favorite among hikers and campers. The ridges and valleys here range from 800 feet to 1,980 feet in elevation and offer the visitor beautiful panoramas and rugged geology. The most spectacular view of the gorge is of Cloudland Canyon, which can be seen from the parking lot in the picnic area. There are two waterfalls at the bottom of the canyon, where Daniel Creek cascades over layers of sandstone and shale into clear pools below.

HIKING

There are two major trails in the park. A 4.5-mile loop trail takes you around the western rim of the canyon, and a 6-mile back-country trail leads to two primitive camping areas. Side trails off West Rim Trail take you past the waterfalls.

CAMPING

There are 75 tent and trailer sites in the park, all with water and electrical hookups, tables and grills. There are two camping areas, each with a comfort station with hot showers and a washer and dryer.

There are also 30 walk-in sites without water or electricity, though they do offer picnic tables and a comfort station with hot showers. The primitive campsites, which can be accessed only by the back-country trail, offer no facilities.

Organized groups can reserve the four pioneer camping areas, which include water and latrines. There is also a 40-person group camp that offers four bedrooms with bunk beds, two bathrooms with showers, a fully equipped kitchen with commercial-size appliances and a dining and meeting hall. Campers must bring their own linens, pillows, etc.

COTTAGES

The park rents 16 two- and three-bedroom cottages that sleep eight and ten people, respectively. All cottages are heated and air-conditioned and include fireplaces and screened porches or decks. Reservations may be made up to 11 months in advance, but a two-night minimum stay is required most months. A five-night minimum stay is required from June through Labor Day. No pets are permitted.

PICNICKING

There are 75 picnic sites and four picnic shelters located throughout the park. The shelters may be reserved but otherwise are available on a first-come, first-served basis. A day-use group shelter is available for groups of up to 200 people. The facilities there include a kitchen with an inside grill, restrooms, a barbecue pit and a dining hall. There is a fee to reserve the shelter.

OTHER FACILITIES

The pool located in the day-use area is open from Memorial Day through Labor Day from 11 A.M. until 6 P.M. It is closed Mondays and Tuesdays except for legal holidays. The lighted tennis courts in the park are open year-round for day and evening use. A concession stand is located in the parking area near the overlook.

ANNUAL EVENTS

The park sponsors a wildflower program in April and an overnight backpacking trip in October. Confirm dates through the park office.

NEARBY ATTRACTIONS

Chickamauga and Chattanooga National Military Park
Chief Vann House State Historic Site
James H. "Sloppy" Floyd State Park

DIRECTIONS

The park is on GA 136 some 8 miles east of the town of Trenton and I-59.

FOR MORE INFORMATION

Cloudland Canyon State Park, Route 2, Box 150, Rising Fawn, GA 30738 (706-657-4050)

CROOKED RIVER STATE PARK

ST. MARYS   500 ACRES

Perched on Elliot's Bluff overlooking the salty Crooked River, this park is home to a variety of coastal woodland wildlife, including deer, bobcats, feral hogs, foxes and osprey. Cumberland Sound is 8 miles downriver. The numerous good fishing spots near the park make the ramp here popular with area fishermen.

The park's location near I-95 makes the campground popular with campers heading to and from Florida. A swimming pool, a miniature golf course and a picnic area overlooking the salt marsh are among the park's day-use attractions.

CAMPING

There are 62 tent and trailer sites in the wooded camping area, including 19 pull-thru sites. Each site is equipped with water and electrical hookups. The two comfort stations are equipped with showers, toilets and laundry facilities. There is also a campfire ring. A pay phone is adjacent to the campground host's site.

The park's two pioneer camping areas can be reserved for use by organized groups.

COTTAGES

There are 11 rental cabins in the park. Cottages #1 to #5 are on Elliot's Bluff overlooking the Crooked River. The six other cottages are a short distance away on the same park road. The kitchens are equipped with utensils. Linens are also provided. No pets are allowed.

Cottage guests swim free at the park pool.

BOATING AND FISHING

There are no horsepower limits for the waters bordering the park, though all boats must be in compliance with the Georgia Boating Safety Law. Legal fishing is permitted year-round. No license is required for saltwater fishing. A fishing dock is located alongside the boat ramp.

SWIMMING AND MINIATURE GOLF

The park's Olympic-size pool is open in season Tuesday to Thursday from 11 A.M. to 6 P.M. and Friday to Sunday from 11 A.M. to 7 P.M. A small fee is charged. The pool is closed on Mondays except legal holidays.

The adjacent 18-hole miniature golf course is open when the pool is open. A nominal fee is charged.

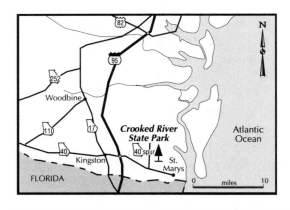

RVs in the
morning light
at the campground
in Crooked River
State Park

PICNICKING

There are 75 picnic tables and five picnic shelters along the river. There is also a picnic shelter that can accommodate 80 guests, available by reservation only. The five other shelters may be reserved but are available on a first-come, first-served basis when not reserved.

HIKING

There are three short nature trails through the park's coastal woodlands. The longest is the 1.5-mile Palmetto Trail. A map is available at the park office.

ANNUAL EVENTS

Wildflower Day (March) and the Arts and Crafts Show (September) are among Crooked River's annual events.

NEARBY ATTRACTIONS

Cumberland Island National Seashore
Okefenokee National Wildlife Refuge
Jekyll Island

DIRECTIONS

From Exit 2 off I-95, go 4 miles east to GA Spur 40. Turn left. You will reach the park after 4 more miles.

Crooked River State Park, 3092 GA Spur 40, St. Marys, GA 31588 (912-882-5256)

ELIJAH CLARK STATE PARK
LINCOLNTON   447 ACRES

CS

Clarks Hill Lake, with 71,000 acres of water and 1,200 miles of shoreline, is this park's big attraction. To help you enjoy the lake, Elijah Clark boasts 165 campsites, more than any other state park. Views of the lake from the 20 cottages in the park are also a big plus. History plays an important role here. The park features reproductions of log cabins, complete with tools and furniture from the 1780s. Living-history demonstrations and tours are offered on weekends through the summer.

Elijah Clarke was a Revolutionary War colonel who led the colonists in their only decisive victory in Georgia, at Kettle Creek. His main contributions to the war were a successful

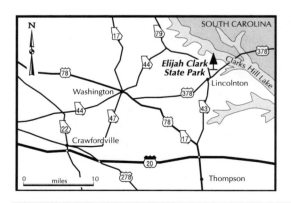

blockade of British-held Augusta and an ongoing guerrilla campaign that held the British at bay. His success at the second siege of Augusta earned him the rank of brigadier general. By the end of the Revolution, he had attained the rank of major general of the Georgia Militia.

Following the Revolutionary War, Clarke accepted a commission as major general of the French army. His brief attempts to assert French control over Louisiana were unsuccessful. Clarke and his troops set up the Trans-Oconee Republic on the banks of the Oconee River in Indian territory. He became a thorn in the side of his former commander in chief, George Washington, who sent the militia that Clarke once commanded to overtake the republic. The Georgia Militia destroyed the Trans-Oconee settlements, and Clarke returned home to Wilkes County, where he died in 1799. The remains of Elijah and his wife, Hannah, were moved 10 miles south from Graball to their current location in the park when the reservoir was to flood the original grave site.

Elijah's son, a fellow Revolutionary hero and two-time governor of Georgia, dropped the *e* from the family name, which explains the park's current spelling.

Also located within the park is Dooly Spring, once used by the John Dooly family, who lived in a cabin across the road from the spring. Colonel Dooly was murdered in his home by a group of Tories.

CAMPING

There are 165 tent and trailer sites with water and electrical hookups. Eighty-three of the campsites are on the water. There are six bathhouses located throughout the camping area. Each bathhouse has hot showers, flush toilets and laundry facilities. A dump station is also provided.

COTTAGES

There are 20 two-bedroom cottages, each equipped with heat and air conditioning, linens and a kitchen with dishes and cookware. No pets are allowed. The maximum stay is two weeks. Reservations may be made up to 11 months in advance.

BOATING AND FISHING

Private boats may use the park's four boat ramps, but there are no docking facilities at Elijah Clark. There are no horsepower restric-

tions on Clarks Hill Lake, where water-skiing is permitted. There are no rental boats or canoes in the park.

Clarks Hill Lake is home to a large population of bass, including white, striped, hybrid and largemouth. Other game fish include bluegill, crappie and sauger. Either a Georgia or a South Carolina fishing license is valid for any area of the lake.

SWIMMING

The free swimming beach is open year-round. There is no lifeguard on duty, so swimming is at your own risk.

PICNICKING

There are 121 picnic tables, five picnic shelters and one group shelter at Elijah Clark. The

Reconstructed cabins house a Colonial-era museum at Elijah Clark State Park.

21

picnic shelters may be reserved in advance for a small fee and are available on a first-come, first-served basis when not reserved.

The 60-person weatherized group shelter has a kitchen, a barbecue pit, tables and chairs. It is available by reservation only.

HIKING

The 0.7-mile Hannah Clark Nature Trail features an easy ramble along a stream through a wooded forest.

OTHER FACILITIES

The log cabins near the visitor center are open for tours on Saturday and Sunday from 9 A.M. to 5 P.M. Living-history demonstrations from Georgia's colonial period are given in the park at various times during the year. Check the park office for a current schedule.

Miniature golf and a nearby playground round out the park's recreational amenities.

ANNUAL EVENTS

Old Timers Day in October and the Log Cabin Christmas in December are among the park's annual events.

NEARBY ATTRACTIONS

Clarks Hill Lake
Bobby Brown State Park
Mistletoe State Park
Robert Toombs House State Historic Site

DIRECTIONS

The park is 6 miles northeast of Lincolnton on U.S. 378.

FOR MORE INFORMATION

Elijah Clark State Park, 2959 McCormick Highway, Lincolnton, GA 30817 (706-359-3458)

FLORENCE MARINA STATE PARK
FLORENCE   173 ACRES

PP

Florence Marina dominates the northern end of Walter F. George Lake on the Chattahoochee River. Formerly a private recreation area, the land was donated to the Georgia Department of Natural Resources in 1986 by the W. C. Bradley Company. The park offers a natural deepwater marina with a handicapped-accessible deepwater fishing pier, boatslips and a boat ramp.

Walter F. George Lake sprawls over 45,190 acres and boasts 640 miles of shoreline. Within 2 miles of the park is the site of Roanoke, which was attacked and burned by Indians. Information on the prehistoric paleo-Indian period and the area's early settlers and their encounters with the Creek Indians can be found within the Kirbo Interpretive Center, which features displays of artifacts found in the park. The park is located on the site of a former Indian village and the frontier river town of Florence.

CAMPING

The park's 44 tent and trailer sites offer individual sewage hookups, power and water hookups, grills and picnic tables. The one comfort station offers laundry facilities, as well as hot showers and restrooms.

COTTAGES

There are eight rustic, one-bedroom efficiency units and two two-bedroom cottages available for rent in the park. Each cottage is equipped with a bath, a kitchen with a stove and a refrigerator, cooking utensils, towels and linens. The cottages are heated and air-conditioned. Pets are not allowed.

CLUBHOUSE

This modern facility overlooking the Chattahoochee River accommodates 125 people. Available for family reunions, church gatherings, etc., the clubhouse features a complete kitchen, steam tables, a large fireplace and tables and chairs.

BOATING AND FISHING

The park's 66 covered boatslips offer electrical outlets and water and may be rented on a monthly basis or overnight when available. Boat-trailer storage can also be provided for those renting boatslips. The gasoline dock can easily accommodate any size boat. All boating must comply with the Georgia Boating Safety Law.

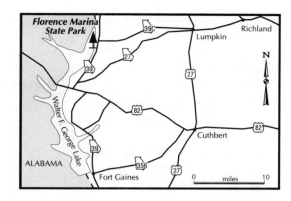

In addition to the deepwater fishing pier, Florence Marina offers two fish-cleaning stations. The lake supports bass, crappie, bream and catfish. All persons age 16 and older must have a valid resident/nonresident license.

SWIMMING

Overlooking the Chattahoochee River, Florence Marina's swimming pool is open the last two weekends in May, and Tuesday to Sunday through Labor Day thereafter. Admission is $1.25 except for children under the age of two and registered cottage guests, who swim free of charge. Lifeguards are on duty at all times.

OTHER FACILITIES

The park offers two tennis courts and a miniature golf course. There is also a trading post where guests can purchase sandwiches, soft drinks, ice and fishing and picnic supplies.

ANNUAL EVENTS

The park hosts a Crappie Tournament (March), an Easter Egg Hunt, Alligator Day (June), Astronomy Evening (November) and Haunted Halloween (October). Since dates are subject to change, confirm with the park office.

NEARBY ATTRACTIONS

Providence Canyon State Conservation Park
Eufaula National Wildlife Refuge
Corps of Engineers parks on Walter F. George Lake

DIRECTIONS

Florence Marina State Park is located 16 miles west of Lumpkin at the end of GA 39C.

FOR MORE INFORMATION

Florence Marina State Park, Route 1, Box 36, Omaha, GA 31821 (912-838-6870 or 912-838-4244)

FORT MCALLISTER STATE HISTORIC PARK
BRYAN COUNTY   1,690 ACRES

For Federal forces trying to take Savannah during the Civil War, Fort McAllister blocked the side door to that city—the Ogeechee River. The low, earthen fort weathered seven assaults during the war and withstood everything the United States Navy could batter her with. On December 13, 1864, General William T. Sherman's 15th Corps marched down the route now followed by GA 144 into the park. Sherman's troops stormed the fort. The general would later refer to the fight as "the handsomest thing I have seen in this war." The Federals charged into the fort fighting hand-to-hand. When the dust settled, 16 Southerners were dead and 54 wounded, while the Northern losses were 24 dead and 110 wounded. Savannah was doomed to fall into Federal hands.

Giant live oaks now shade the battle site, which offers a fine view of the Ogeechee River and the surrounding salt marsh.

THE FORT AND MUSEUM

The fort has been restored to its 1863–64 appearance. Visitors can walk in and around the best-preserved earthwork fortification in the former Confederacy. By reservation, guides dressed in Civil War uniforms will interpret the

fort. Visitors can go inside the earthworks to see how the men who were stationed here lived during the war.

The museum explains the role of the fort in the war and Sherman's strategy for taking Savannah. The theater beside the museum offers an audio-visual presentation to orient visitors to the history of the site. An entry fee is charged for the museum and fort.

CAMPING

The camping area is on Savage Island, over a mile from the main park area. Each campsite is equipped with electrical and water hookups, a picnic table and a grill. The two bathhouses have hot showers, flush toilets and a coin-operated washer and dryer. The camping area is equipped with a pay phone, a dumpster and a dump station. A bonus to fishermen and other boaters is the camping area's boat ramp and boat dock on Redbird Creek, reserved for registered campers. There is also a nature trail that loops to the shore of Savage Island and back.

A primitive campsite is located between the main park and Savage Island. It can be reserved by organized groups by contacting the park office.

BOATING AND FISHING

A public boat ramp is located on the Ogeechee River just outside the park entrance. Water-skiing is permitted. All boats must comply with the Georgia Boating Safety Law.

Saltwater fishing on the Ogeechee River is allowed, with no fishing license required.

Other popular activities are crabbing and shrimping.

PICNICKING

A high bluff over the Ogeechee River offers 50 picnic tables and grills, a playground and restrooms and makes for a memorable picnic spot. The two picnic shelters can be reserved for group use and are available on a first-come,

A cannon with earthworks in the background at Fort McAllister State Park.

first-served basis when not reserved. There is a large, enclosed group shelter on the road behind the park office. This area is available by reservation only.

NEARBY ATTRACTIONS

Skidaway Island State Park
Wormsloe State Historic Site
Fort Morris State Historic Site

DIRECTIONS

Take Exit 15 off I-95. The park is 10 miles east of the interstate on GA Spur 144.

FOR MORE INFORMATION

Fort McAllister State Historic Park, 3894 Fort McAllister Road, Richmond Hill, GA 31324 (912-727-2339)

FORT MOUNTAIN STATE PARK
MURRAY COUNTY   2,532 ACRES

An ancient rock wall is the source of this park's name. This mysterious wall zigzags 855 feet across the southern face of the mountain's crest in serpentlike fashion. It is bordered on both sides by sheer cliffs. The wall, which sits on the highest part of the mountain, is said to have been built by Indians as either a fortification against hostile tribes or a place for ancient

ceremonies. It is now listed on the National Register of Historic Places.

The land on which the wall rests was donated to the state of Georgia in 1934 by Ivan Allen. Under the presidency of Franklin Delano Roosevelt, the area was developed by the CCC, and a stone lookout tower was built in the vicinity of the wall.

The park rests on two mountain peaks near the most prominent peak of the Cohutta Mountains, at the southwestern terminus of the Blue Ridge Mountains. It is located at an elevation of 2,800 feet in Chattahoochee National Forest near the Cohutta Wilderness Area

HIKING

There are a number of hiking trails within Fort Mountain State Park. A very short path leads to Cool Springs Overlook, with its beautiful vista of the Cohutta Wilderness Area. The 0.7-mile Big Rock Nature Trail ambles along the stream which flows from the park's 17-acre lake. One of the more popular trails is Old Fort Trail,

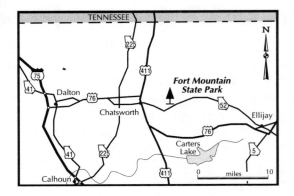

Griffin Logue sits on her father's shoulders to point out a bird from this handicapped-accessible viewpoint on the Gahuti Trail in Fort Mountain State Park.

which leads 1.8 miles to the rock wall, the stone tower and overlooks. There is also Lake Loop Trail, a 1.2-mile loop trail around the lake. For backpackers, there is an 8.2-mile back-country hike that offers four overnight camping areas available by permit only. Most of the trails are rated moderate to difficult because of the mountainous terrain.

CAMPING

Two family campgrounds within the park offer 70 tent and trailer sites with water and electrical hookups. Each area has a comfort station with hot showers and restrooms. There are also four walk-in tent sites without electricity and five "squirrel's nest" camping platforms without electricity or water. Pioneer camping is available for groups.

COTTAGES

There are 15 rustic cabins available for rent within the park. The cottages have fireplaces and two or three bedrooms and sleep eight to 10 people. Each cottage is fully equipped and also has a grill and a picnic table. They are rented on a reserved basis to families.

PICNICKING

Scattered throughout the park are 117 picnic tables, as well as seven shelters that can be reserved. There is also an 80-person group shelter available for rent. Most picnic tables have grills.

OTHER FACILITIES

Fishing is allowed year-round in the 17-acre

spring-fed lake, but during park hours only. Fishing is allowed only from the bank, not from the beach or from pedal boats. Georgia fishing laws apply. The only boats allowed on the lake are the pedal boats that can be rented at the beach during the summer.

The beach is open for swimming during daylight hours only. No fee is charged. Swimming is at your own risk, as no lifeguard is on duty.

A miniature golf course is located in the day-use area and is open during the summer as well.

ANNUAL EVENTS

The park offers a wildflower hike in the spring and overnight backpacking trips in October and November. During the summer, the park naturalist schedules programs Wednesday through Sunday. Check with the park office for specific dates and times.

NEARBY ATTRACTIONS

Chief Vann House State Historic Site
New Echota State Historic Site
Cohutta Wilderness Area
Carters Lake

DIRECTIONS

Fort Mountain State Park is located 7 miles east of Chatsworth off GA 52. Take Exit 136 off I-75.

FOR MORE INFORMATION

Fort Mountain State Park, 181 Fort Mountain Park Road, Chatsworth, GA 30705 (706-695-2621)

FORT YARGO STATE PARK AND WILL-A-WAY RECREATION AREA
WINDER   1,850 ACRES

The most important feature of Fort Yargo State Park is Will-A-Way Recreation Area. Opened in 1971, this camp was built with the intention of serving people with disabilities. It was the first recreation area of its kind to be opened in a state park anywhere in the nation. Will-A-Way is home to the State Camping Program for disabled people, a state-funded operation serving the developmentally disabled. The program has involved close to 30,000 people since 1975, at which time it was chosen as one of the top 13 innovative programs in the nation for the developmentally disabled.

The park offers a variety of recreational opportunities for its visitors. Camping, swimming, picnicking, fishing, boating, miniature golf, tennis, horseshoes and softball are among the possibilities. Most of the recreational facilities can be reached via the main entrance off GA 81, but two other areas—Day-Use Areas B and C—are accessed at separate entrances off GA 81.

The namesake of the park, Fort Yargo, can be viewed at Day-Use Area C, located along a dirt

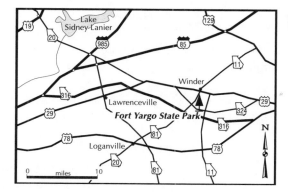

road marked by a historical marker for the fort. Built in 1762, Fort Yargo is one of four blockhouses, or forts, constructed by the Humphries brothers, Georgia pioneers. This stockade of hand-hewn logs is the only building left standing of the original four. Built 3 miles southwest of Jug Tavern (now Winder), it sits behind a chain-link fence but can be viewed more closely during historical programs. The other three forts were located in Talassee, Thomocoggan (now Jefferson) and Groaning Rock (now Commerce).

WILL-A-WAY RECREATION AREA

The Will-A-Way complex contains three interrelated areas: a day-use section, a group camp and three cottages.

The group camp can accommodate 250 people and features 20 cabins, programming facilities and a central dining hall. Nearly surrounded by the lake that Fort Yargo State Park encompasses, Will-A-Way is fully accessible to people with disabilities. It is available year-round to special

available to the public year-round. P... permitted, and reservations are r...

PICNICK...

Fort Yargo feature... it comes to picni... nated picnic... five picni... small f... sh...

...g...s. Two comfort stations provide hot showers and pay phones. Reservations for the summer months are accepted up to three months in advance for sites #5 through #13 in Campground #1 and for site #37 in Campground #2. Most of these sites are on the shore of the lake. Numbers 13 and 37 are pull-thrus and cannot be reserved for tents. A nonrefundable deposit of two nights' camping fees is required when making a reservation.

Seven walk-in sites are available to campers with tents who are seeking a little more privacy. Campers park in a central lot and walk to their site, which is equipped with a tent pad, a picnic table, a lantern post and a fire ring. All sites have access to a comfort station. A pioneer campsite is also available for group camping.

COTTAGES/CABINS

Three handicapped-accessible cottages are

ets are not
quired.

...NG

...s a variety of options when
...cking. There are several desig-
... areas along the shore of the lake,
... shelters that can be reserved for a
... ee and two large group shelters. The group
... lters, which must be rented, contain kitchen
facilities, picnic tables and restrooms.

DAY-USE AREAS

There are three day-use areas at Fort Yargo
State Park. Day-Use Area A features the most
recreational opportunities, with miniature golf,
a playground, a beach, a bathhouse, a group shelter, picnic shelters, picnic tables, a nature trail
and boat rentals. Day-Use Area B features a
group shelter, a picnic shelter and a boat ramp.
Day-Use Area C contains a picnic shelter and
the old fort.

BOATING AND FISHING

Private boats are permitted on park waters,
although there is a restriction that limits horsepower to 10. Use must be in compliance with
the Georgia Boating Safety Law. Two boat ramps
are available for public use. Johnboats, canoes
and pedal boats can be rented through the park.

Fishing in park waters is open year-round.
Anyone 16 years of age or older must have a
valid resident/nonresident license.

SWIMMING

The lake is open for swimming year-round.
Swim at your own risk, as no lifeguard is on duty.
A bathhouse is provided at the beach for changing and showering. Swimming is allowed at the
beach only.

OTHER FACILITIES

The park offers two tennis courts, which are
located just past the office.

NEARBY ATTRACTION

Lake Sidney Lanier

DIRECTIONS

Fort Yargo State Park is located 1 mile south
of Winder on GA 81.

FOR MORE INFORMATION

Fort Yargo State Park, P.O. Box 764, Winder,
GA 30680 (404-867-3489 or 404-867-5313 for
the Will-A-Way office)

FRANKLIN DELANO ROOSEVELT STATE PARK

PINE MOUNTAIN   10,000 ACRES

Sprawling over Pine Mountain in west-cen-
tral Georgia, Franklin Delano Roosevelt State

Park is a hiker's dream come true. The 23-mile Pine Mountain Trail runs the length of the park, and there are six shorter loop hikes as well. Camping, fishing, swimming and more are also offered in one of Georgia's largest parks.

Pine Mountain was dear to the heart of President Roosevelt, who visited nearby Warm Springs 41 times seeking treatment for polio from 1921 until his death in 1945. His Little White House is located just 12 miles from the park in Warm Springs. Roosevelt made many excursions to Pine Mountain during those years. You can enjoy the former president's favorite picnic area, Dowdell's Knob, where there is a commanding view from Roosevelt's old stone grill. At 1,395 feet in elevation, the knob was named for Lewis and James Dowdell of Virginia, who settled this area in 1828.

The Civilian Conservation Corps built a stone swimming pool, cabins, lakes and the park office during Roosevelt's administration. The CCC holds a reunion in the park each September.

Also of historical note is the Franklin Delano Roosevelt Memorial Bridge, located at King's Gap. This natural break in the Pine Mountain barrier was the site of an early settlement on the stage route between Newnan and Columbus. The King's Gap post office functioned here from 1829 until 1856.

COTTAGES

Along the shore of Lake Delano and on the wooded hillside nearby are 21 cabins with either one or two bedrooms, a fireplace, picnic tables and a grill. The cottages sleep a maximum of eight and can be reserved up to 11 months in advance. Pets are not allowed in the cottages.

CAMPING

There are 140 tent and trailer sites with water and electrical hookups, many along the shore of Lake Delano. The five comfort stations offer flush toilets, hot showers and washers and dryers. There is one sanitary dump station in the park.

Two group camping areas are available along Lake Franklin. The smaller camp has room for 75, while the larger camp offers facilities for 120. Pioneer camping is also available to groups in four areas of the park for a small fee.

HIKING

There are six loop trails ranging in length from the 1-mile Delano Trail to the 7.8-mile Big Poplar Loop. If you are looking for a longer hike, Pine Mountain Trail is perhaps middle Georgia's finest footpath. It follows the crest of the

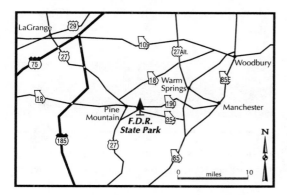

mountain from one side of the park to the other. Passing among ferns and laurels and by waterfalls and beaver dams, Pine Mountain Trail has a lot to offer. The trail crosses GA 190 seven times, making shorter hikes easy to set up.

FISHING

Year-round fishing on Lake Delano is open to children and to persons over 16 years old who have a valid fishing license. Private boats are not permitted on the lake, but boats can be rented from 8 A.M. to 5 P.M. daily. Bank fishermen who are not staying in the campground or a cottage must leave the park by 10 P.M.

SWIMMING

Liberty Bell Pool is open during the summer, with a lifeguard on duty. The pool is closed on Mondays except for legal holidays. A concession stand and a baby pool are offered. There is a small fee for the pool.

OTHER FACILITIES

An enclosed shelter with heat and air conditioning is rented to large groups. The shelter has a small kitchen and barbecue grills.

Picnic shelters are available for a small fee by reservation. When not reserved, they are open on a first-come, first-served basis.

Horses are available for trail rides in the park. The stables do not provide overnight boarding of private horses.

The amphitheater provides a range of regular musical events. Check with the park office for a current schedule.

ANNUAL EVENTS

There is an FDR birthday program in January and a memorial program each April 12. The CCC reunion takes place each September, and the 46-mile Ultra Marathon is held in November. For more information, check with the park office.

NEARBY ATTRACTIONS

Callaway Gardens
Little White House State Historic Site
West Point Lake

DIRECTIONS

The park is located on GA 190 some 5 miles east of Pine Mountain off U.S. 27.

FOR MORE INFORMATION

Franklin Delano Roosevelt State Park, 2970 GA 190, Pine Mountain, GA 31822 (706-663-4858)

GENERAL COFFEE STATE PARK
COFFEE COUNTY   1,510 ACRES

The living-history pioneer village located in this park adds an interesting dimension to what

Farm tools hang on the wall of a shed in General Coffee's Pioneer Village.

might have been an average state park. The agricultural history of Coffee County is brought to life each year during peak season by cabins representing the pioneer period, farm animals, outdoor exhibits and a recently opened museum. The theme was made possible by the donation

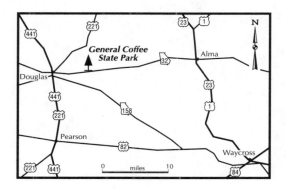

of the Meeks Log Cabin in 1976 by Stanton Meeks, Sr., of Nicholls, also in Coffee County. The cabin is the anchor of the living-history area.

The land for the park was donated to the state by the citizens of Coffee County in 1970. The park was named in honor of General John Coffee, a local planter, United States congressman and military leader. The Seventeen-Mile River winds its way through the park. Six small lakes—Dent, Gum, Turkey, Dan, Jake and Gar—can be found along the river. The endangered indigo snake and gopher tortoise can be spotted along the river and its lakes as well.

Future plans for General Coffee State Park include cottages, a group lodge, paved roads, a bridge and an interpretive trail. Currently, Burnham Cottage can be rented by the bedroom or in its entirety. Burnham Cottage was formerly a bed-and-breakfast and has now been given cottage status by the park.

CAMPING

The park offers 51 campsites, all with electrical and water hookups, tables and grills. There are two camping areas, each with a comfort station that provides hot showers and flush toilets. A playground is located at each camping area, as is a pay telephone. Tent and Trailer Site #1 has a dump station.

There are also two pioneer camping areas with spaces for tents, primitive latrines, grills and tables. These areas are available to Scouts and other organized groups. A foul-weather shelter is located in each area. Advance reservations are requested for pioneer camping.

GROUP FACILITIES

A 180-person group shelter is located at General Coffee State Park. The shelter features fans and/or heaters, an indoor barbecue grill, a stove, a refrigerator, a sink and restrooms. There is also a barbecue shelter behind the group shelter.

An outdoor amphitheater located at the park can be used for programs, weddings and other events. Reservations should be made through the park.

OTHER FACILITIES

Picnicking facilities include six picnic shel-

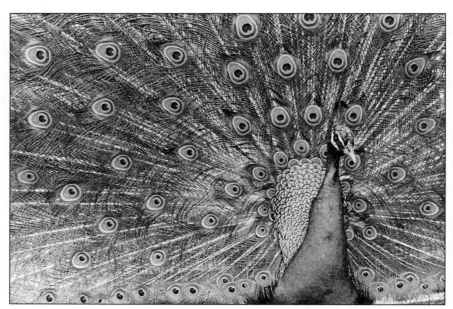

A peacock strutting in General Coffee State Park's Pioneer Village

ters located throughout the park. The shelters can be reserved but are otherwise available on a first-come, first-served basis. Picnic tables and grills are also located throughout the park.

The Seventeen-Mile River and a four-acre lake are available for fishing. Persons 16 years of age and older must have a valid resident or nonresident license.

An archery range is available to the public, although you must register at the park office to receive the key and to sign the liability waiver forms.

The park operates an Olympic-size swimming pool, a baby pool and a concession stand from Memorial Day through Labor Day. The pool is open from 11 A.M. until 6 P.M. Wednesday through Sunday and is closed Monday and Tuesday except for legal holidays.

A nature trail can be accessed from three different points as it winds through the park: Picnic Shelter #4, the swimming pool and Tent and Trailer Area #1 between sites #13 and #14.

ANNUAL EVENTS

The park features a fishing rodeo in the summer, Pioneer Skills Day and an archery demonstration and clinic in the fall. Archery competitions are held year-round.

NEARBY ATTRACTIONS

Little Ocmulgee State Park
Banks Lake National Wildlife Refuge
Laura S. Walker State Park
Reed Bingham State Park

DIRECTIONS

The park is located 6 miles east of Douglas on GA 32.

FOR MORE INFORMATION

General Coffee State Park, Route 2, Box 83, Nicholls, GA 31554 (912-384-7082)

GEORGE L. SMITH II STATE PARK
TWIN CITY   1,355 ACRES

CS

Tea-colored water rushing over the dam under Watson Mill is the main feature of this enchanting park. The mill, which is a combination millhouse, covered bridge and dam, was built alongside the 412-acre lake in 1880. Boating and fishing in the large millpond dotted with cypress trees are among the park's most popular activities. You can rent a boat or canoe at the park to explore the pond or bring your own,

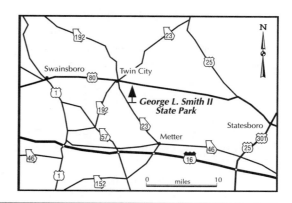

although motors over 10 horsepower are not allowed.

Black tupelo, eastern redbud, magnolia bay and water oak are among the trees found in the park, which boasts abundant wildlife. The 3-mile nature trail offers the opportunity to explore the park on foot.

The park was named for a noted legislator from Stillmore who died in office in 1973.

CAMPING

The 25 campsites are on the shore of the lake. Each site has electrical and water hookups, a picnic table and a grill. The bathhouse has showers, toilets and a coin-operated laundry. A dump station is provided.

PICNICKING

There are 60 picnic tables in the park, which also has two large picnic shelters that can accommodate up to 100 people and two smaller shelters that can accommodate 50 people, available by reservation up to 11 months in advance. When not reserved, the picnic shelters are available on a first-come, first-served basis.

An enclosed group shelter for 50 with heat and air conditioning and a barbecue shelter are also available for rent up to 11 months in advance.

BOATING AND FISHING

Private boats with motors no larger than 10 horsepower are permitted on the lake.

Johnboats and canoes can be rented from the park. All boats must comply with the Georgia Boating Safety Law and must be off the lake by sunset.

Legal fishing is permitted year-round. A fishing pier is provided. All persons over age 16 must have a valid Georgia fishing license.

HIKING

Deer Run Hiking Trail is a 3-mile loop through the forested section of the park. It passes by a millpond, a spring and a tortoise habitat along its route. An 0.7-mile dirt road cuts across the loop just off the center, making two shorter loops possible. At the trailhead, located about 100 yards along the road after crossing the dam, a map of the route is cut into a wooden sign.

ANNUAL EVENTS

A fishing tournament each May and an arts and crafts festival each October are among the park's events. Contact the park office for more information.

NEARBY ATTRACTIONS

Magnolia Springs State Park
Gordonia-Alatamaha State Park

DIRECTIONS

The park is 4 miles southeast of Twin City on GA 23.

FOR MORE INFORMATION

George L. Smith II State Park, P.O. Box 57, Twin City, GA 30471 (912-763-2759)

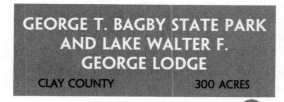

GEORGE T. BAGBY STATE PARK AND LAKE WALTER F. GEORGE LODGE

CLAY COUNTY   **300 ACRES**

PT

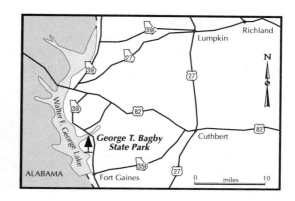

Seventy square miles of water are the main attraction at this park, which offers many ways to enjoy Walter F. George Lake. The marina, the boat ramp and the beach all provide access to the 45,000-acre lake. Boating, fishing, water-skiing and swimming are among the favorite activities at the park.

The lake was created when the Corps of Engineers built the lock and dam in 1963. The lock provides access to the Chattahoochee River for both pleasure boats and barge traffic. It takes 28 million gallons of water to lower a boat through the lock to the river below.

The lake was named for a Georgia state senator who served for 34 years. Born on a tenant farm in southwest Georgia in 1878, Walter F. George was very active in legislation concerning vocational education, among other things.

The state park was named for a former director of the Georgia State Parks. George T. Bagby also served in the Georgia House of Representatives for 19 years and worked as director of the Georgia Game and Fish Commission and

deputy commissioner of the Georgia Department of Natural Resources.

THE LODGE

The 30-room Lake Walter F. George Lodge was built in 1989. It has meeting rooms for conferences of up to 200 people, a restaurant, two tennis courts and a swimming pool. There are also five two-bedroom cottages alongside the lake. The cottages have heat and air conditioning, fully equipped kitchens and linens. No pets are allowed in either the lodge or the cottages. To reserve a cottage or a room in the lodge, contact the park office.

BOATING AND FISHING

Private boats can use the boat ramp in the park. There are no motor restrictions on the lake. Water-skiing is permitted. All boats must comply with the Georgia Boating Safety Law. The 34-slip marina in the park offers slips on a daily or monthly basis. The marina also sells fuel and other boating and fishing supplies.

The lake is open year-round for fishing. A fishing license is required for persons age 16 and older.

HIKING

There are 2.5 miles of trails in the park. The interpretive center and the lodge have a nature-trail map with an identification chart of some of the plants hikers will see on the 1.1-mile nature trail.

SWIMMING POOL AND BEACH

The pool by the lodge is open daily in season from 7 A.M. to dusk. The beach house and the sand beach are open Wednesday to Sunday from 11 A.M. to 6 P.M. from Memorial Day to Labor Day. The beach is free.

OTHER FACILITIES

The park offers 50 picnic tables along the lake and a picnic shelter for group use. When not reserved, the shelter is available on a first-come, first-served basis. There is a playground in the day-use area.

A family group shelter is also available by reservation. Fully enclosed and air-conditioned, the shelter has a full kitchen and a smokehouse. It accommodates up to 150 people.

ANNUAL EVENTS

The park hosts a Fourth of July FunFest and holds a photo contest each summer. The Bass Tournament and the Tennis Tournament are scheduled for Labor Day.

NEARBY ATTRACTIONS

Kolomoki Mounds State Historic Park
Corps of Engineers parks on Walter F. George Lake
Florence Marina State Park
Providence Canyon State Park

DIRECTIONS

The park is located 3 miles north of the town of Fort Gaines on GA 39.

FOR MORE INFORMATION

George T. Bagby State Park, Route 1, Box 201, Fort Gaines, GA 31751 (912-768-2571)

GEORGIA VETERANS MEMORIAL STATE PARK

CORDELE   1,322 ACRES

This popular park is a permanent memorial to United States veterans. It was given to the state by the Crisp County Commissioners in 1946 in memory of Georgia war veterans. The park is shielded and surrounded by Lake Blackshear, formed by the backwater of the Crisp County Hydroelectric Dam, the first county-owned hydroelectric project in the country. In

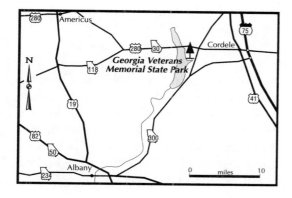

the nation, it was dedicated to teaching safety to youth. After the flood in 1994, the camp was used by Mennonite Disaster Services to provide relief to area residents.

The park's museum features a number of planes of historical importance. The B-29 bomber here saw service in the South Pacific during World War II. Another plane, the F-84F Thunderstreak, is an example of one of the free world's most powerful bombers—an atomic bomb carrier. Also displayed in the park are artillery pieces and tanks, including Sherman and Patton tanks.

The indoor museum depicts the history of the wars the United States has taken part in from the Revolution through Vietnam.

GOLF

Alongside U.S. 280 at the north end of the park are an 18-hole golf course, a driving range and a clubhouse with a snack bar. The golf course is open Tuesday through Sunday, as well as on Monday for some legal holidays. Carts are available for rent. Greens fees can be paid by the day, month or year. Tee times can be reserved for weekend and holiday play by calling the course at 912-276-2377.

CAMPING

The park has 82 tent and trailer sites, 29 of which are on the shore of Lake Blackshear, with another 30 sites in sight of the water. There are three bathhouses with flush toilets, hot showers and laundry facilities. There are also two picnic

1994, floodwaters ripped a 1,200-foot chunk of the dam loose and washed it downstream. The dam was scheduled to be repaired and the lake impounded again in the summer of 1995.

Georgia Veterans Memorial State Park was the site of a Spanish-Indian battle in 1702. Joseph de Zuniga, the Spanish governor of Florida, sent a force of more than 800 Spaniards and Apalaches northward into Georgia in an expedition against the British and their Creek allies. Forewarned by the Indians, Anthony Dodsworth and other traders at Coweta (near present-day Columbus) marshaled about 500 Creek warriors and lured the invaders into an ambush at the Flint River, striking the first blow for the English in controlling the Mississippi.

The park once featured "Camp Safety Patrol," established in 1951. Lying along the southern border of the park, the camp was sponsored by the safety education division of the Georgia Department of Public Safety and the Georgia Department of the Veterans of Foreign Wars. The first school patrol safety training camp in

shelters near the lake in the camping area. A fishing pier and a boat ramp are located adjacent to Camping Area #1. There are dump stations in Camping Areas #1 and #3.

A pioneer camping area is available by reservation to organized groups.

COTTAGES

The 10 two-bedroom cottages are on the shore of Lake Blackshear between the museum and the swimming pool. The heated and air-conditioned cabins come with linens and fully equipped kitchens. No pets are allowed in the cottages.

BOATING AND FISHING

Lake Blackshear offers 7,000 acres for boaters and anglers to explore. Private boats can use the park's three boat ramps; there are no restrictions on motors. There are two fishing piers and two boat docks in the park. Water-skiing is permitted. All boats must comply with the Georgia Boating Safety Law, and persons over 16 years old must have a valid fishing license.

PICNICKING

There are 100 picnic tables and five picnic shelters to choose from. The three open shelters may be reserved for a small fee and are available on a first-come, first-served basis when not reserved. The two winterized group shelters are available by reservation only.

SWIMMING

You can take your pick of the park's swimming pool and beach, located near each other on a peninsula jutting into Lake Blackshear; this peninsula forms the bulk of Georgia Veterans Memorial State Park. The swimming pool and beach are open from Memorial Day through Labor Day. Bathhouses are located at both the beach and the pool. There is a playground between the pool and the cottages.

OTHER FACILITIES

A model-airplane strip is located in the field behind the aircraft and ordnance displays. Contact the park office for more information on using these facilities.

ANNUAL EVENTS

In keeping with the focus on Georgia's veterans, the park holds events to commemorate Independence Day, Memorial Day and Veterans Day.

NEARBY ATTRACTIONS

Andersonville National Historic Site
Jimmy Carter National Historic Site
Providence Canyon State Conservation Park

DIRECTIONS

The park is located on U.S. 280 some 9 miles west of Exit 33 off I-75.

Georgia Veterans Memorial State Park, 2459-A U.S. 280W, Cordele, GA 31015 (912-276-2371)

GORDONIA-ALATAMAHA STATE PARK

REIDSVILLE   **280 ACRES**

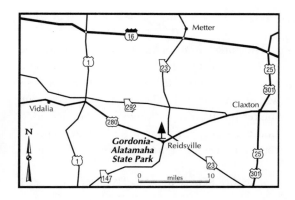

This park packs a lot of recreation into a relatively small space. Located in the town of Reidsville, Gordonia-Alatamaha uses every bit of its 280 acres for some form of recreation. There is a nine-hole golf course with a recently completed clubhouse, a swimming pool, a 12-acre lake, a campground, a tennis court, a miniature golf course, a playground and a picnic area with picnic tables, grills and four picnic shelters.

The park gets its name from the Gordonia-Alatamaha tree, or G. Franklin tree. This small tree was first identified by John and William Bartram in 1765. It has not been observed in its wild state since 1790. However, seeds and cuttings were preserved in the Bartram botanical gardens in Philadelphia, and the species has been perpetuated. The Gordonia-Alatamaha is distinguished by its deciduous leaves and flowering branches.

Loblolly bays, or Gordonia trees, can still be seen in the park.

BRAZELL'S CREEK GOLF COURSE

This nine-hole golf course challenges golfers with fairways laid out among rolling hills in a mixed terrain of forest and wetlands. The course plays 3,034 yards from the white tees and 2,500 yards from the red tees. The golf course and the driving range are open from 8 A.M. to dusk and are closed Mondays except for some legal holidays. The recently completed clubhouse has a pro shop and a snack bar. Pull carts and golf carts can be rented at the pro shop. Greens fees can be paid by the day, month or year. Tee times can be reserved for weekend and holiday play by calling 912-577-6445.

CAMPING

The 23 campsites are all near the lake and have electrical and water hookups, a picnic table and a grill. The bathhouse has showers, toilets and a coin-operated laundry. A dump station is provided.

PICNICKING

The park has 50 picnic tables and grills. The four open picnic shelters can be reserved and are available on a first-come, first-served basis when not reserved. The large, enclosed group shelter has its own parking lot, heat, air conditioning, stove, refrigerator, tables and chairs. It can be rented by contacting the park office.

BOATING AND FISHING

Johnboats can be rented at the park office, but private boats and gasoline motors are not allowed on the lake. Pedal boats are rented Tuesday to Sunday from May through Labor Day.

The 12-acre lake is open for legal fishing year-round. All persons over age 16 must have a valid Georgia fishing license.

SWIMMING

The pool opens in May on the weekends and is open Wednesday to Sunday from June through Labor Day. Swimming is permitted when the lifeguard is on duty. Contact the park office for a schedule of times.

OTHER FACILITIES

The park also has a tennis court, a miniature golf course and a playground.

ANNUAL EVENTS

The park holds a Wildflower Day each April and a fireworks display on the Fourth of July.

NEARBY ATTRACTION

George L. Smith II State Park

DIRECTIONS

The park is in the town of Reidsville on GA 280.

FOR MORE INFORMATION

Gordonia-Alatamaha State Park, P.O. Box 1047, Reidsville, GA 30453 (912-557-6444)

HAMBURG STATE PARK
WASHINGTON COUNTY   750 ACRES

A 1921 gristmill and 225-acre Lake Hamburg, which forms behind its dam on the Little Ogeechee River, are the centerpieces of this park in the extreme north of Washington County.

Bass, bream, catfish and crappie are all caught on Lake Hamburg. The churning water below the dam is home to bream, channel catfish and crappie.

CAMPING

The park's 30 tent and trailer sites are on a large peninsula jutting into Lake Hamburg. Each site is equipped with water and electrical hookups, a grill, a picnic table and a fire ring. The one bathhouse offers showers, flush toilets and laundry facilities. A dump station and a playground are also located in the campground.

The pioneer camping area is available by reservation to organized groups.

PICNICKING

A choice of 20 picnic tables, two picnic shelters and one group shelter is available to picnickers. The picnic shelters may be reserved in advance for a fee and are available on a first-come, first-served basis when not reserved. The weatherized group shelter is equipped with kitchen facilities. It is available by reservation only.

BOATING AND FISHING

Private boats are permitted on Lake Hamburg, with a 10-horsepower limit on motors. Pedal boats, canoes, johnboats and electric motors are offered for rental in the park. All boats must comply with the Georgia Boating Safety Law and must be off the water by sundown. There are two public-access boat ramps in the park.

Legal fishing is permitted in the park year-round. The boat dock across from the country store may be used for fishing. Fishing below the dam is productive as well. All anglers over 16 years of age must have a current fishing license.

HIKING

A 1.5-mile nature trail begins in front of the country store. It follows the western shore of Lake Hamburg, forms a loop and returns by the same shoreline route to the country store.

A new trail is being built that will be approximately 5 miles long.

MILL AND MUSEUM

The water-powered gristmill is still in operation. Its museum has a display of farm tools used in Georgia's past. Cornmeal from the mill may be purchased at the country store. The meal is the main attraction in the park-run store, which otherwise offers the usual camp-store assortment of food and snacks. The museum is open from 8 A.M. to 5 P.M. year-round; the store remains open until 7 P.M. for the busiest summer months.

ANNUAL EVENT

The Fall Harvest Festival, held on the third weekend in September, is the park's main annual event.

NEARBY ATTRACTIONS

A. H. Stephens State Historic Park
Oconee National Forest
Lake Oconee

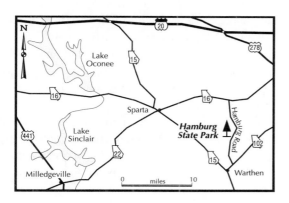

The park is 6 miles north of Warthen off GA 102 on Hamburg Road.

FOR MORE INFORMATION

Hamburg State Park, Route 1, Box 233, Mitchell, GA 30820 (912-552-2393)

HARD LABOR CREEK STATE PARK

RUTLEDGE   **5,805 ACRES**

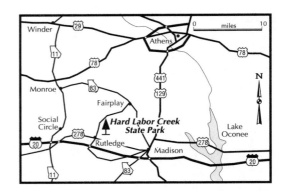

Created in 1934 by the National Park Service, this park was used to demonstrate how marginal farmland could be developed into a recreational area. Workers from the Civilian Conservation Corps built the roads, picnic areas and group facilities, planted thousands of trees and cleared the beds to create the park's two lakes—Lake Brantley and Lake Rutledge. Though the young men of the CCC certainly put in many an hour of hard labor to create this park, the creek was known as Hard Labor Creek long before work on the park began. The origins of the name have been lost to time, but it is speculated that the creek was named by slaves who tilled the fields along its banks, or by Indians who found it difficult to ford.

In the more than 60 years since the National Park Service came to demonstrate farmland reclamation, Hard Labor Creek has become one of the more popular state parks in Georgia. It now boasts an 18-hole golf course with all the amenities and even has an observatory with the largest telescope in the Southeast. The park should not be overlooked by equestrians, who can stable their horses at the park, camp nearby and enjoy the park's 15 miles of riding trails.

OBSERVATORY

Georgia State University has run a research observatory in the park since 1989. The 1,000-square-foot building houses three main telescopes—a 16-inch mirror telescope, a 30-inch mirror telescope and a telescope with an effective aperture of 44 inches. The last telescope was built by the university with a grant from the National Science Foundation. The innovative design uses nine 13-inch mirrors mounted together to act as one. It is the largest telescope in the Southeast.

The observatory is open to the public one night a month from April to October. The viewing usually begins 45 minutes after sunset when the sky is clear. During the open house, visitors have a chance to hear a guest lecture, tour the observatory and then look at some celestial body through the 16-inch telescope, which was once used at the famous Kitt Peak Observatory. It is a high-quality research-grade telescope. The length of the session varies greatly with sky conditions and the number of people in attendance. For more information, contact the Georgia State University astronomers at 404-651-2932.

GOLF

The 18-hole golf course has a driving range and a clubhouse with a pro shop and a short-order grill. The course is open from Tuesday to Sunday and on Monday during major holidays. The hours are from 8:00 A.M. to sunset during the week and from 7:30 A.M. to sunset on weekends and holidays. A tee time, required for play on holidays and weekends, can be obtained by calling up to 12 days in advance. The telephone number for the golf course is 706-557-3006.

CAMPING

The park's 51 tent and trailer sites are located alongside the smaller of the park's two lakes—Lake Brantley. All of the sites have full electrical and water hookups, a grill and a picnic table. There are four bathhouses in the campground. Some of the sites are available by reservation; contact the park office for details.

There is also a pioneer camping area available for group use. It has a pit privy and a shelter for use in inclement weather, but no water is available at the site.

Hard Labor Creek has two large camps available to organized groups. Camp Daniel Morgan can accommodate 75 campers and Camp Rutledge 120. The two camps are located on opposite shores of Lake Rutledge. Both are equipped with a dining hall, cabins and separate sleeping facilities for the staff. Groups must supply all of their own supplies, including pillows, linens, soap and toilet paper. Contact the park office for information on reserving a group camp.

COTTAGES

The park has 20 cottages for rent on a hill above Lake Brantley. Each cottage has central air, a fireplace and a kitchen equipped with an electric stove, a refrigerator and all kitchen supplies. The park also supplies linens and towels. Firewood is not provided for the fireplaces but is sold in the park's trading post. Pets are not allowed in the cottages, and there is no kennel at the park. Reservations are taken for the cottages up to 11 months in advance. Cottage guests swim free at the Lake Rutledge swimming area.

SWIMMING

The beach at Lake Rutledge is open each summer, with a lifeguard on duty. A small playground, a volleyball net, a concession stand and a bathhouse are located at the swimming area.

BOATING AND FISHING

There is a boat ramp on Lake Rutledge for

use by either the johnboats and canoes rented at the park's trading post or private boats. Motors are limited to 10 horsepower. Pedal boats can be rented at the dock next to the swimming area during the summer. All boats are limited to the hours between 7 A.M. and sunset. All boating is governed by applicable boating safety laws.

Both Lake Brantley and Lake Rutledge are stocked with bass, bluegill, catfish and shellcracker. Anyone over 16 must have a valid Georgia fishing license; licenses are sold at the park's trading post. Bank fishing is permitted from 7 A.M. to 10 P.M.

HORSEBACK RIDING

Hard Labor Creek State Park has a 30-horse stable with a riding ring, a campground and a bathhouse. The park does not rent horses, and riders must bring their own bedding, straw, water buckets and feed. Reservations are available through the park office for both the stables and the nearby picnic shelter. All horses must have proof of a negative equine infectious anemia test, to be presented at the trading post when checking into the park.

HIKING

There are 1-mile and 2-mile loop trails in the park. Hikers can also use the 15 miles of horse trails when no group rides are scheduled. Check with the park office for more information.

OTHER FACILITIES

The park has 50 picnic tables and four picnic shelters. The shelters are available by reservation for a small fee and on a first-come, first-served basis when not reserved. There is also a large barbecue pit and two group shelters, which can be reserved through the park office up to 11 months in advance.

ANNUAL EVENTS

A CCC reunion each spring and the Christmas Golf Tournament in December are among the park's annual activities. Contact the park office for more information.

NEARBY ATTRACTIONS

Oconee National Forest
Lake Oconee

DIRECTIONS

From Exit 49 off I-20, follow the signs north to Rutledge, then continue following the signs north on Fairplay Road. The park is 2 miles north of Rutledge.

FOR MORE INFORMATION

Hard Labor Creek State Park, P.O. Box 247, Rutledge, GA 30663 (706-557-3001)

A boater's and fisherman's dream come true, Hart State Park is surrounded by water, with more than 2 miles of shoreline on the 56,000-acre Lake Hartwell reservoir. The park is across the channel from the marina and 8 miles by boat from Hartwell Dam on the Savannah River.

The Lake Hartwell reservoir was built by the Corps of Engineers and opened for recreational use in 1968. The land under the lake had been farmland along the Savannah River until the dam was built.

The park, lake, town and county are all named in honor of Nancy Hart (1735–1830) a heroine of the Revolutionary War. The six-foot-tall patriot, wife and mother of eight was an expert shot. The cross-eyed heroine, sometimes disguised as a man, reportedly spied for Colonel Elijah Clarke. Her efforts as a spy are credited with giving Clarke his decisive defeat of the British in the Battle of Kettle Creek.

When a band of six Tories came to her house demanding she cook for them, she killed one and captured the others, injuring one. She was called *Wahatche*, or "War Woman," by the Indians.

A replica of her log home, with the chimney stones from her original cabin, can be seen in nearby Elbert County.

BOATING AND FISHING

The park's two boat ramps can accommodate sailboats, motorboats and houseboats of any length when the lake is at normal water level. There are seven boat docks in the park, including two that are reserved for cottage guests. Fishing, water-skiing, boating, and other water sports are all part of the lake's recreational uses.

Lake Hartwell offers largemouth bass, striped bass, hybrid bass, crappie, catfish, bluegill, bream, and walleye, among other species. Persons over 16 years of age must have a valid resident or nonresident fishing license. All state regulations apply. Bank fishermen who are not overnight guests in the park must leave by 10 P.M.

SWIMMING

There is a roped-off swimming area on the lake, with no lifeguard on duty. The swimming area has a sandy beach. Picnic tables and a bathhouse are nearby.

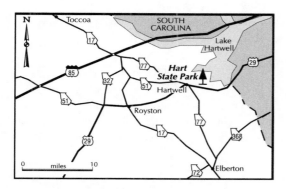

CAMPING

Each of the 65 trailer and tent sites offers electrical and water hookups, a picnic table and a grill. Many of the sites on the water are by reservation only. Contact the park to reserve a site.

HIKING

An 0.5-mile nature trail loops through the wooded middle of the park, passing within 100 feet of the lake. Five granite markers point out trees and plant species on the trail.

A chair on the beach at Hart State Park invites swimmers to take a break.

OTHER FACILITIES

The three picnic shelters are available by reservation (in person or by phone) and on a first-come, first-served basis when not reserved. Eighty-five picnic tables are also scattered around the park near the lake.

Musical events and nature lectures are given by the park at the Cricket Theater, a small outdoor stage located in the camping area; this facility is also available for organized groups. The recreational field has a volleyball court and horseshoe pits. A playground is located in a shady area on the way to the swimming area.

ANNUAL EVENTS

Annual events vary, but Confederate and Revolutionary War encampments are held regularly, giving guests a close-up view of how soldiers from those eras lived. Music programs, organized walks and special guests are scheduled. Check with the park office for details.

NEARBY ATTRACTIONS

Tugaloo State Park
Victoria Bryant State Park
Hartwell Dam

DIRECTIONS

From Hartwell, go north on U.S. 29 for 2 miles. Turn left at the sign for the park, then turn left again when you get to Hart Park Road.

Hart State Park, 330 Hart Park Road, Hartwell, GA 30643 (706-376-8756)

HIGH FALLS STATE PARK
JACKSON   995 ACRES

HH

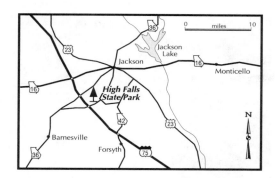

Once an industrial community with a cotton gin, a gristmill, a hotel, a shoe factory and many stores and residents, High Falls was left by the wayside when a major rail line passed the town by in the 1880s. The mill operated until 1960, but the rest of the once-thriving community became a ghost town.

Georgia Hydro Electric Company built the dam and impounded High Falls Lake in 1905. It later sold the operation to Georgia Power Company, which kept the powerhouse running until 1958.

Today, this park is a popular picnicking and sunbathing spot. Boating and fishing on 650-acre High Falls Lake are also big draws for High Falls State Park. Water streams over the dam alongside the picnic area before running under the bridge on High Falls Road. The Towaliga River splits in two after passing under the bridge and cascades over the rocks in two main stages.

Water raged over the falls in 1994 during the hard rains that caused flooding throughout southwest Georgia. The camping area was damaged, and some of the park's trails were washed away, including part of the trail to the old powerhouse. The steel bridge between the dam and the main road washed down the Towaliga River, too. By 1995, much of the damage to the park had been repaired, though the steel bridge is not being rebuilt.

CAMPING

The park offers 135 tent and trailer sites with electrical and water hookups, picnic tables and grills.

There is a bathhouse with showers, flush toilets and a laundry in Camping Area #1 on High Falls Lake. This camping area is near the swimming pool, the miniature golf course and a group shelter. There is a dump station in this camping area.

Camping Area #2, located alongside the Towaliga River, has four bathhouses and a dump station. A nature trail leads from the camping area through an undeveloped, wooded part of the park. The trail starts at the road between Loop B and Loop C, winds through the woods and meets up with the campground road next to the dump station.

Frank Logue sits on the rocky bank of the Towaliga River to get a view of High Falls.

PICNICKING

Fifty picnic tables are located throughout the park. Five picnic shelters are on the north side of the dam and river. They may be reserved for a fee and are available on a first-come, first-served basis when not reserved.

The park's 150-person group shelter is equipped with restrooms, tables, chairs, a large barbecue pit, a stove and a refrigerator. It can be rented by large groups for a fee. It is available on a reservation-only basis.

BOATING AND FISHING

Private boats can be launched at either of the park's two boat ramps on High Falls Lake. Motors are limited to 10 horsepower. From 8 A.M. to 5 P.M., boats, canoes and pedal boats are rented at the park office.

Fishing is permitted in the picnic area, from boats and in the camping areas. Fishing from the campground banks is limited to registered campground guests. No fishing is permitted between the dam and the old powerhouse.

SWIMMING

The pool is open Tuesday to Sunday from 1 P.M. to 7 P.M. Memorial Day through Labor Day. It is also open on Mondays for some legal holidays.

HIKING

There are three trails in the park. Historic Ruins Trail is a figure-eight trail on the north side of the falls. On the south side of the falls is a trail to an overlook of the falls; the section of this trail that continued from the overlook to the ruins of the powerhouse was washed away in the flood. A third nature trail loops through the wooded part of the park west of Camping Area #2.

ANNUAL EVENTS

The Forsythia Festival Crappie Tournament in March, the Fall Family Campout Weekend and the Christmas Music Concert are among the park's annual events.

NEARBY ATTRACTIONS

Indian Springs State Park
Jarrell Plantation State Historic Site
Oconee National Forest

DIRECTIONS

The park is 1.8 miles east of Exit 65 off I-75.

FOR MORE INFORMATION

High Falls State Park, Route 5, Box 202-A, Jackson, GA 30233 (912-994-5080)

INDIAN SPRINGS STATE PARK
BUTTS COUNTY   523 ACRES

Built in 1927, Indian Springs is considered one of the oldest state parks in the nation. The Creek Indians, based in this area, used the famous spring water for medicinal purposes—to heal their sick and to impart extra vigor to those who were well.

Coweta Indian chief William McIntosh built a hotel near the spring in 1819. This same hotel, located across the highway from the park,

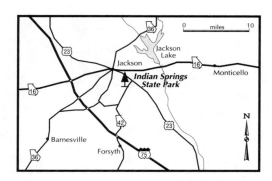

was the site where McIntosh signed a treaty that deeded all Creek lands in Georgia to the United States in 1825. Called *Tustunugee Hutkee*, or "White Warrior," by the Creeks, McIntosh was murdered by them later that same year at his homeplace in Carroll County. McIntosh had reached the rank of brigadier general in the United States Army when he fought in the War of 1812.

For the remainder of the 19th century and during the early part of the 20th century, the spring became the center of a resort area. Today, the mineral spring still pours forth from its plastic-bubble-coated niche. At certain times, a line forms from both sides of the enclosed area, as people wait their turn to fill their gallon jugs with the famed water.

CAMPING

The family camping area has 90 combination tent and trailer sites with both electrical and water hookups. There are three comfort stations,

The spring house at Indian Springs State Park is one of the many Civilian Conservation Corps projects from the 1930s that can be enjoyed in Georgia's state parks.

one in each camping area. Pioneer camping facilities are available to groups and include water and primitive latrines.

An organized group camp, Camp McIntosh, accommodates 130 people and includes dormitories, three staff quarters, a dining hall, a crafts building and an infirmary.

COTTAGES

Indian Springs offers 10 two-bedroom cottages which sleep eight people. The cottages are completely set up for housekeeping. No pets are allowed.

BOATING AND FISHING

The 105-acre Lake McIntosh is open for fishing year-round. A fishing dock and a boat-launching area are provided. As with all public waters in the state, persons 16 years of age and older must possess a valid resident or nonresident license. Fishing licenses may be purchased at the park office.

Private boats with motors of 10 horsepower or less are allowed on park waters. Johnboats may be rented at the park office. All boating must be done in accordance with the Georgia Boating Safety Law.

MUSEUM

The Indian Springs Museum is open during peak season—Memorial Day through Labor Day. It features material covering the history of Indian Springs, including the Creek Indians, the resort area, CCC work and today's facilities. The museum is closed on Mondays except for legal holidays.

HIKING

The 0.75-mile Overland Nature Trail loops through woods that were protected by the Creek Indians for hundreds of years.

GIFT SHOP

Open during peak season, the Spring Concession and Gift Shop sells Native American souvenirs, T-shirts and other items. It is closed Mondays and Tuesdays.

OTHER FACILITIES

The park offers seven picnic shelters to the public on a first-come, first-served basis; the shelters may also be reserved. A group shelter is available to large groups. Picnic tables are scattered throughout the day-use area.

The swimming area/beach located on the lake is open daily from 7 A.M. until sunset year-round. A beach concession stand and restrooms are open in season except for Mondays and Tuesdays. Swimming is allowed only within the roped area and only at your own risk. You may also rent pedal boats in this area.

The park offers an 18-hole miniature golf course in the day-use area. Contact the park office for rates and operating times.

Runoff from the dam creates this pretty waterfall in the picnic area at Indian Springs State Park.

ANNUAL EVENTS

The park offers a weekend-long astronomy program in August, a Southeastern Indian celebration in June and a Christmas at Idlewilde event in December.

NEARBY ATTRACTIONS

Jarrell Plantation State Historic Site
High Falls State Park
Piedmont National Wildlife Refuge
Oconee National Forest

DIRECTIONS

From I-75, take Exit 67 to Jackson, head southeast on U.S. 23 and then follow GA 42 to the park.

FOR MORE INFORMATION

Indian Springs State Park, 678 Lake Clark Road, Flovilla, GA 30216-9715 (404-504-2277)

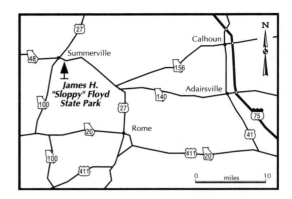

JAMES H. "SLOPPY" FLOYD STATE PARK

SUMMERVILLE   269 ACRES

Nestled at the base of Taylor's Ridge on the border of Chattahoochee National Forest, this park was named for James H. "Sloppy" Floyd, a Georgia state representative who served from 1953 until his death in 1974.

The two managed lakes within the park offer excellent fishing and add to the picturesque setting. Porch swings dot the shoreline, offering visitors a chance to sit, relax and enjoy the view.

The park manager is known in the Summerville area as "Mr. Bluebird" for his efforts to repopulate Georgia with bluebirds. The park staff is helping him in this ongoing project to restore the threatened bluebird population. Scattered around the park are numerous bluebird nesting boxes. In March and April, the baby bluebirds hatch and emerge from the nests.

The staff is also planting wildflowers to contribute to the beauty of the area.

CAMPING

Twenty-five tent and trailer sites with water and electrical hookups are located in the park. Each site has a picnic table, a grill and a fire ring. These shaded sites offer some privacy and are within walking distance of the lakes. There are pull-thru sites to accommodate large trailers. A playground, a dump station, and a comfort station with hot showers, restrooms and a washer and dryer are all located within the camping area.

Pioneer camping is available by reservation to organized groups. The pioneer camping area offers water and latrines only.

OTHER FACILITIES

Ninety-four picnic tables and four shelters are located in the park. The shelters may be reserved or used on a first-come, first-served basis.

Fishing is allowed in both lakes year-round. The lakes are stocked with channel catfish, bream and bass. There are two fishing docks. Bank fishermen who are not registered as overnight guests must leave the park premises by 10 P.M. Two boat ramps are provided. Boats are available for rent, although private boats are also permitted. Private boats may have nothing greater than a trolling motor. All Georgia fishing and boating laws apply.

There are two hiking trails. One leaves from the camping area, leads to a lake and heads both right and left following the shoreline; the second leads from the footbridge off Marble Spring Road and follows the shoreline of the other lake to the playground at the picnic area.

NEARBY ATTRACTIONS

Cloudland Canyon State Park
Chickamauga and Chattanooga National
    Military Park
The Pocket Recreation Area

DIRECTIONS

James H. "Sloppy" Floyd State Park is located 3 miles southeast of Summerville on Marble Springs Road off U.S. 27.

FOR MORE INFORMATION

James H. "Sloppy" Floyd State Park, Route 1, Box 291, Summerville, GA 30747 (706-857-0826)

JOHN H. TANNER STATE PARK
CARROLLTON   136 ACRES

Tanner Park packs a lot of recreational opportunities into a small space. It has the largest swimming beach of any of Georgia's state parks on one of its two lakes. Boating, fishing, picnicking, miniature golf, hiking and camping are among the activities offered. The park also has two large group shelters that are well suited to family reunions and other large gatherings.

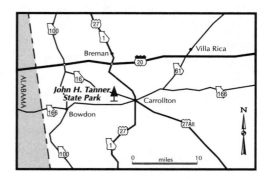

The area was developed in the late 1950s as Tanner's Beach, a privately owned recreation area. It was purchased by the state in 1971.

SWIMMING

The beach on the larger of the park's two lakes is the only area where swimming is permitted. The beach is open year-round, and swimming is free. No lifeguards are provided.

BOATING AND FISHING

Both lakes offer year-round fishing for bass, bream and catfish. Persons over 16 years of age must have a valid resident or nonresident fishing license. Minnows are not allowed as bait.

Fishing boats can be rented from the park office for use on either lake. Boats are restricted to electric motors only. Canoes and pedal boats are rented in the summer for use on the upper lake. All boats must comply with the Georgia Boating Safety Law.

CAMPING

Each of the 36 trailer and tent sites is equipped with electrical and water hookups. There are two bathhouses with restrooms, hot showers and a washer and dryer. Primitive campsites are available to organized groups.

EFFICIENCY MOTEL ROOMS

There are six motel rooms, each with its own kitchen, living room, bedroom with two double beds and full bathroom. The units will accommodate four people, but pets are prohibited. Contact the park office for current rates and reservation information.

GROUP FACILITIES

The park's lodge is fully equipped for an overnight stay by up to 40 members of an organized group.

The three picnic shelters near the beach accommodate about 45 people and have nearby grills. A fourth shelter accommodates 50 and is equipped with a refrigerator, tables and chairs; this shelter is screened-in.

A short distance from the lake with the beach is a large, enclosed shelter for up to 75 people. It has a stove, a refrigerator, a sink, tables, chairs and nearby grills. It is equipped with heat and air conditioning.

A large pavilion by the beach accommodates 200 and has nearby grills.

All of these areas can be reserved by contacting the park office.

OTHER FACILITIES

The 18-hole miniature golf course is available year-round. The upper lake has a 1-mile loop hike around it, as well as a short nature trail at the northwest end.

DIRECTIONS

John H. Tanner State Park is 6 miles west of Carrollton on GA 16.

John H. Tanner State Park, 354 Tanners Beach Road, Carrollton, GA 30117 (404-830-2222)

KOLOMOKI MOUNDS STATE HISTORIC PARK

EARLY COUNTY   **1,293 ACRES**

PT

This unusual park features one of the largest Indian temple mounds in the United States. One of seven mounds in the park, the Temple Mound was once a center of religion for the Indians of the Southeast. It was also the center of several villages and was surrounded by a number of other mounds, including two burial mounds.

The park was named for the Kolomoki Indian culture, whose residents inhabited the site from about 1000 A.D. until the end of the 13th century. But they were not the first to inhabit the site, having been preceded about 800 A.D. by Indians who combined features of the Swift Creek and Weeden Island cultures. This culture eventually developed into the Kolomoki culture, which was followed by the Lamar culture, whose members inhabited the site until the 16th century. Although the first Indians to inhabit the Kolomoki site didn't appear until 800 A.D., Indians had been present in the area since 5000 B.C.

The park also features one of largest and most elaborately constructed burial mounds in the Southeast. Built for the burial of a great leader, it includes the skeletal remains of sacrificed servants, slaves and wives, as well as bodies that had been stored in the temple awaiting burial. Radiocarbon dating indicates the mound was built about 30 A.D., plus or minus 300 years. A second burial mound can be viewed in the museum. It contains the remains of four bodies and was dated at 170 B.C., plus or minus 300 years.

Kolomoki boasts two lakes for fishing and boating, as well as a campground and a fully equipped group camp. The mounds and the surrounding area were given to the state of Georgia by the people of Early County and its county seat, Blakely, in 1933.

MUSEUM

Because it is part of a state historic site, there is a small entrance fee at the museum. The museum features displays on the area's Indian culture from 5000 B.C. until the 13th century. There is also a slide show on the excavated mound that is part of the museum. Visitors to the museum can view this burial mound as it was left by archaeologists in the 1950s. The mound was

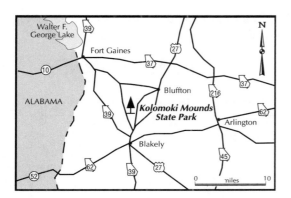

left as is to provide the public with a means of viewing the archaeological process and as an example of the construction of a mound.

A self-guided tour is available for those interested in a walking/driving tour of the seven mounds. The Temple Mound—56 feet in height—can be climbed and the entire area viewed from the top.

CAMPING

There are 20 tent and trailer sites that offer both water and electrical hookups. The comfort station offers hot showers and laundry facilities. A dump station and a playground complete the campground.

The group camp features an equipped dining hall, a swimming pool, six cabins, an infirmary, two craft shelters, a baseball field, an assembly shelter and access to Lake Yahola; the lake's dam was washed out by the floods of 1994, with reconstruction scheduled to begin in the summer of 1995. The camp is available for rental. Contact the park office for rates and reservation information.

BOATING AND FISHING

Lake Yahola and Lake Kolomoki are open to fishing year-round. Lake Yahola has a concrete boat ramp and Lake Kolomoki a fishing dock and boat-launching area. All persons over the age of 16 must have a valid resident/nonresident license, available from the park office. Bank fishing is allowed only from 7 A.M. until 10 P.M.

Private boats are allowed in the park, with a 10-horsepower restriction. Each lake offers one johnboat for rental. Boating is allowed only until sundown. All boats must comply with the Georgia Boating Safety Law.

SWIMMING

The swimming pool is open from 11 A.M. until 6 P.M. Wednesday through Sunday. It is closed on Mondays and Tuesdays except for legal holidays. A lifeguard is on duty during pool hours.

OTHER FACILITIES

The park also features a miniature golf course and a nature trail.

NEARBY ATTRACTIONS

Walter F. George Lake
Lake Seminole
Seminole State Park

DIRECTIONS

Kolomoki Mounds State Historic Park is located 6 miles north of Blakely off U.S. 27.

FOR MORE INFORMATION

Kolomoki Mounds State Historic Park, Route 1, Box 114, Blakely, GA 31723 (912-723-5296)

LAKE RICHARD B. RUSSELL STATE PARK

ELBERT COUNTY **2,700 ACRES**

Many state parks have facilities for handicapped visitors, but Lake Richard B. Russell State Park stands out for its wheelchair-accessible amenities. In addition to the usual handicapped bathrooms and ramps to buildings, this park has handicapped-access picnic tables on the lake, as well as a handicapped swimming area, where a ramp leads to a rail extending out into the park's sand beach. A portion of Blackwell Bridge Trail is also paved for wheelchair access.

Clovis points and other artifacts were discovered near the park during clearing for the lake. The 10,000-year-old site called Rucker's Bottom is one of the few Paleo-Indian sites in the state. It now lies blanketed by the waters of Lake Richard B. Russell.

The lake and park are named for Richard Brevard Russell. Over a span of 50 years, Russell served as a Georgia state legislator, as governor of Georgia and as a United States senator.

BOATING AND FISHING

Private boats are permitted in park waters, with no restrictions on horsepower. Water-skiing is allowed. There are two boat ramps and a dock in the park, with more amenities planned for the future. A rowing course was developed on the lake for Olympic and college training.

Legal fishing is permitted year-round in the park. All persons over 16 years of age must have a valid Georgia fishing license. The stocked lake is the only trout lake in the area. Bank fishermen must leave the park by dark; when the campground and cottages are completed, overnight guests will be able to continue bank fishing after the park is closed. There is a fishing dock between the beach and the picnic area in the day-use area. Canoes and pedal boats are rented during the summer.

SWIMMING

There is no charge to swim at the beach. No lifeguard is on duty, and swimming is at your own risk. The concession area at the beach is open during the summer from Tuesday to Sunday. The beach is equipped with a handicapped swimming area.

PICNICKING

Clustered near the beach are 40 picnic tables and three picnic shelters. The shelters (including

Lavonia Lake Hartwell 85 77 51 Hartwell SOUTH CAROLINA 29

N Royston 51 29 77 77 spur 17 **Lake Richard B. Russell State Park** 98 Elberton Lake Russell 72 72 77 17

0 miles 10

one handicapped-access shelter) may be reserved for a fee and are available on a first-come, first-served basis when not reserved. A short hiking trail connects the picnic area and the swimming beach.

HIKING

Blackwell Bridge Trail is a 2.2-mile round trip. The trail gets its name from the old steel bridge it crosses about 0.5 mile from the parking lot. The bridge was floated on pontoons to its present site about 11 years ago. It is the last remaining steel bridge in Elbert County.

There are benches along the trail and a picnic table by the bridge.

FUTURE PLANS

A study completed in 1994 created a plan for the park's facilities. The multiphase plan would add a camping area, a recreation center, a golf course, a 100-room conference facility, an equestrian facility, equestrian trails and a primitive camping area to the park's current amenities.

The first phase was approved by the state to begin in July 1995. Among the plans are a fish-cleaning station near the beach and a camping area with 28 sites and a boat ramp, with more sites to come later. Ten rental cottages on Coldwater Creek and added boat-ramp amenities (bathrooms, lights and docks) on Lake Richard B. Russell are also planned for the first phase of development.

The study called for a total of $30 to $40 million to be spent over the next 10 years; each phase of the project will take two to three years. All of these plans are subject to funding which will be approved in the future and is therefore subject to change. Call the park office to find out what facilities will be available at the time of your visit.

NEARBY ATTRACTIONS

Bobby Brown State Park
Victoria Bryant State Park
Hart State Park

DIRECTIONS

The park is 9 miles northeast of Elberton on Ruckersville Road.

FOR MORE INFORMATION

Lake Richard B. Russell State Park, 2650 Russell State Park Road, Elberton, GA 30635 (706-213-2045)

LAURA S. WALKER STATE PARK
WARE COUNTY   306 ACRES

A wealth of plant and animal life awaits the careful observer at this park just north of the Okefenokee National Wildlife Refuge. Endangered red-cockaded woodpeckers, alligators, gopher tortoises and carnivorous sundew and hooded pitcher plants can be found in the park, but they all take extra care to locate. One good

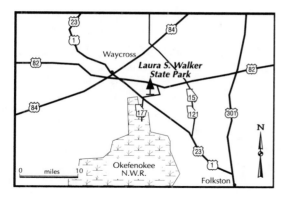

The lake is open to fishing year-round. All persons over 16 must have a valid fishing license. There is a fishing dock near the boat ramp, which is across the lake from the main park entrance. Bank fishermen who are not registered as overnight guests must leave the park by 10 P.M.

SWIMMING

The swimming pool is open Tuesday to Sunday from May 1 to Labor Day and is closed on Mondays except for some legal holidays. A certified lifeguard is on duty, and a small fee is charged. A bathhouse is located next to the pool. The lake is off-limits for swimmers, who would have to share the water with both alligators and speeding boats.

GOLF

A new 18-hole, 6,800-yard championship golf course was scheduled to open by early fall 1995. A driving range and a full-service clubhouse with a pro shop and a snack bar will open with the par-72 course.

Clinics organized by the golf pro will be held; private lessons taught by the golf pro will also be offered. Clubs, pull carts and electric carts will be available for rent at the course.

CAMPING

The park offers 44 campsites, all of which have electrical and water hookups, a picnic table and a grill. There are two bathhouses with

place for watching wildlife is along Big Creek Nature Trail.

The park is the closest camping area to the northern end of the Okefenokee National Wildlife Refuge, which makes it handy for visitors to the swamp. But the park has a lot to offer in its own right. The lake is the park's main recreational resource and is popular with powerboaters and fishermen.

The park is named for Georgia writer, teacher and naturalist Laura Walker, who loved trees and worked for their preservation. She worked tirelessly for conservation long before it was in vogue to do so.

BOATING AND FISHING

The 120-acre lake is popular with area boaters and water-skiers. It is open to boats from 7 A.M. to sunset, but use is restricted to motors of 10 horsepower or less from 7 A.M. to 11 A.M. and from 6 P.M. to sunset. Canoes are available for rent. All boats must be in compliance with the Georgia Boating Safety Law.

restrooms, showers and coin-operated washers and dryers. The camping area is equipped with a dump station.

There are two options for organized groups—a group camp for up to 120 people and the park's two primitive campsites. The group camp includes a kitchen, a staff house, a shelter for arts and crafts programs and an athletic field.

PICNICKING

The 250 picnic tables and small picnic shelters located throughout the park are available on a first-come, first-served basis. There are two screened picnic shelters available for reservation by large groups. Each is equipped with lights, tables, chairs and restrooms. Contact the park office to make reservations.

HIKING

The 1.2-mile Big Creek Nature Trail starts across GA 177 from the park entrance. An interpretive brochure about the plant and animal life along this hike is available at the park office.

ANNUAL EVENTS

The park hosts a Gospel Music Festival in April and a Rare Birds Day each October. Contact the park office for more information.

NEARBY ATTRACTIONS

Okefenokee National Wildlife Refuge
Okefenokee Swamp Park

DIRECTIONS

The park is 9 miles northwest of Waycross on GA 177.

FOR MORE INFORMATION

Laura S. Walker State Park, 5653 Laura Walker Road, Waycross, GA 31501 (912-287-4900)

LITTLE OCMULGEE STATE PARK AND PETE PHILLIPS LODGE
MCRAE   1,397 ACRES

This home-grown park was created on land donated to the state by area residents in the 1930s. The land for the park included the grounds of what had been the Shamrock Springs Health Spa. As with many other parks in the state, the roads, buildings and dam were built with the help of the Civilian Conservation Corps. A 265-acre lake was impounded on the

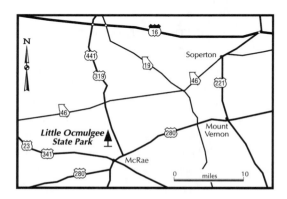

Little Ocmulgee River, and park buildings (many still in use) were built. The park opened in 1940.

The name Ocmulgee comes from the Hichiti Indian phrase *oki mulgis*, or "bubbling water." The park's sandhills, lake and swamps provide a variety of habitats for wildlife. Waterfowl, alligators, deer, gopher tortoises, opossums and armadillos are among the frequently seen park animals.

Since the park was built, it has continued to grow in size and amenities. It now boasts a lodge, a restaurant, an 18-hole championship golf course, lighted tennis courts, cottages and nature trails.

PETE PHILLIPS LODGE AND RESTAURANT

This 30-room lodge offers guest rooms with amenities including individual climate controls, telephones and televisions. There are junior suites with separate bedrooms and living areas. Many of the rooms have a view of the golf course. The lodge is named for Pete Phillips, who served for many years in the Georgia House of Representatives.

The Fairway Restaurant, located in the main lodge, overlooks the sixth tee on the golf course. The restaurant serves buffet and à la carte meals. There is a chipping/putting green next to the lodge.

Lodge and cottage reservations can be made by calling the park office.

WALLACE ADAMS MEMORIAL GOLF COURSE

This 18-hole championship golf course has a full pro shop run by a PGA professional. Lessons and club repair are offered through the pro shop. Snacks and cart rentals are also offered. The course is open throughout the week. Greens fees can be paid by the day, month or year. For more information, call 912-868-6651.

CAMPING

The park has 58 tent and trailer sites with water and electrical hookups. The two bathhouses in the campground are equipped with hot showers and flush toilets; the one nearer the entrance to the camping area has laundry facilities. There is also a dump station in the campground.

Pioneer camping is available well away from the rest of the park's attractions. A 24-person group camp is located close to the tennis courts and other day-use amenities. The group camp can accommodate up to 24 persons. Reservations are required for organized groups who would like to use either the pioneer camping area or the group camp.

COTTAGES

There are 10 cottages on the lakeshore near the fishing dock and the day-use area. The fully equipped, climate-controlled cottages include all kitchen gear and linens. No pets are allowed. Reservations may be made up to 11 months in advance.

PICNICKING

There are 91 picnic tables and seven picnic

shelters in the park. The shelters can be reserved for a small fee and are available on a first-come, first-served basis when not reserved. There is also a large family group shelter available on a reservation-only basis.

BOATING AND FISHING

Private boats are allowed to use the park's boat ramp. There is a restriction on motors before 11 A.M. and after 6 P.M., when no more than 10-horsepower motors may be used. Water-skiing is permitted, and swimming is allowed in the beach area. Canoes can be rented in the park from Memorial Day through Labor Day. There is a canoe trail at the north end of the lake.

Bass, bream and crappie are among the species found in the 265-acre lake. Fishing is allowed year-round, but all anglers over 16 years of age must have a valid Georgia fishing license. There is a fishing dock in the day-use area.

HIKING

The 2.3-mile Oak Ridge Trail forms two loops, so hikers can hike a mile-long loop or the whole trail. The trail meanders along the east shore of the lake to an observation boardwalk on the lake before looping back through the woods to the trailhead, located between the pool and the tennis courts in the day-use area.

OTHER FACILITIES

Two lighted tennis courts and a miniature golf course are located in the day-use area. The tennis courts are open year-round and the miniature golf course in the summer season.

ANNUAL EVENTS

A Civilian Conservation Corps reunion on the first Saturday in May and an Arts and Crafts Festival that same weekend are among the park's annual events.

NEARBY ATTRACTIONS

General Coffee State Park
Georgia Veterans Memorial State Park
Gordonia-Alatamaha State Park

DIRECTIONS

The park is 2 miles north of McRae on U.S. 319 and U.S. 441.

FOR MORE INFORMATION

Little Ocmulgee State Park and Lodge, P.O. Box 149, McRae, GA 31055 (912-868-7474)

MAGNOLIA SPRINGS STATE PARK
MILLEN   948 ACRES

Turtles and fish swim through the clear water while an alligator basks in the sun on the bank of the spring pond at this historic park. This

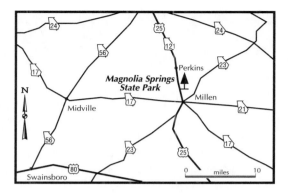

comfort station has flush toilets, showers and electrical outlets. A dump station is provided.

A pioneer camping area is available for organized groups. The cleared campsites have nearby pit toilets.

An 85-person group camp along the shore of Upper Lake can be rented by organized groups. It offers a staff cabin, an infirmary, two dorms, a dining hall with a kitchen, an open shelter and a swimming pool. Campers must bring their own linens, toilet tissue and soap. Contact the park office for more information on renting the group camp.

COTTAGES

There are three two-bedroom and two three-bedroom cottages in the park. Each cottage has a fireplace, an electric stove, a refrigerator, heating and air conditioning, kitchen utensils and linens. No pets are allowed in the cottages, and there is no kennel in the park. Reservations can be made through the park office. Cottage guests swim free at the pool by the park office.

BOATING AND FISHING

Private boats are allowed on the park lake, but motors of 10 horsepower or less must be used from 6 P.M. to 11 A.M. All boats must comply with the Georgia Boating Safety Law. Boats and motors can be rented in the park. There is a boat ramp at the south end of the lake.

Upper Lake is open to year-round legal fishing. There is a fishing dock on the lake. No fishing is allowed around the spring at any time.

idyllic setting was briefly home to Union prisoners during the Civil War. Camp Lawton was built in a belated attempt to relieve the tremendous overcrowding at Andersonville Prison. The 42-acre stockade was completed in October 1864 and evacuated the next month as Sherman's troops marched to the sea after the fall of Atlanta. Although the new stockade was built to accommodate 40,000, only 10,229 prisoners of war were ever transferred here. Remnants of the Civil War camp can be seen in the park today.

Nine million gallons of icy water bubble up from deep underground to run through the park each day. The spring-fed 28-acre Upper Lake is open for boating, fishing and water-skiing.

The Bo Ginn National Fish Hatchery and Aquarium is adjacent to the park. A bridge over the spring leads to the aquarium.

CAMPING

Each of the 26 campsites has electrical and water hookups, a picnic table and a grill. The

OTHER FACILITIES

There are 55 picnic tables and eight picnic shelters in the park. The shelters can be reserved for a fee and are available on a first-come, first-served basis when not reserved. There are two playgrounds in the picnic area by the spring.

The swimming pool, located by the park office, is open in the summer, when a lifeguard is on duty. The pool is closed on Mondays and Tuesdays except on legal holidays.

There are two trails in the park. One is 0.25 mile long and the other 1.2 miles. A trail map is available at the park office.

ANNUAL EVENTS

A fishing tournament in June and Canoe the Ogeechee River, held in October, are among the park's annual events.

NEARBY ATTRACTION

George L. Smith II State Park

DIRECTIONS

The park is 5 miles north of Millen on U.S. 25.

FOR MORE INFORMATION

Magnolia Springs State Park, Route 5, Box 488, Millen, GA 30442 (912-982-1660)

MISTLETOE STATE PARK
COLUMBIA COUNTY 1,924 ACRES

CS

Bass fishing, boating and swimming on 76,000-acre Clarks Hill Lake are some of the activities that draw visitors to this park. The lake is the largest Corps of Engineers project east of the Mississippi and one of the nation's 10 most-visited Corps lakes.

For 40 years, the reservoir was known in both South Carolina and Georgia as Clarks Hill Reservoir. However, in 1991, it was named J. Strom Thurmond Lake in South Carolina, in honor of that state's senior senator. Georgia refused to make a name change it considered costly—it would have been necessary to change signage and brochures—and unnecessary. The Georgia side remains known as Clarks Hill, after the South Carolina town near the dam.

Mistletoe's name derives from the profusion of mistletoe in the area; a nearby spot is named Mistletoe Junction. The park's most distinctive amenities are the five cottages near the camp-

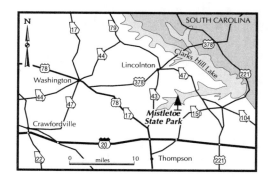

ground. Many other parks rent nice cottages, but these well-equipped, three-bedroom log homes are among the best rental cottages the state offers. They are often booked well in advance.

The land the park is situated on has long been settled. The park's two creeks were home to Savannah Indians, then Euchee Indians and later settlers who built farms here. Foundations, chimney remnants and grave sites are among the signs of early settlement still found at Mistletoe.

CAMPING

Each of the park's 102 tent and trailer sites has a good view of the lake, with over half of them right along the shoreline. These sites are equipped with water and electrical hookups, picnic tables and grills. Campsites #87 through #100 are spaced a little farther apart than the other sites and are close to the lake and a bathhouse. Reservations may be made for 10 of the sites up to 90 days in advance. None of the sites open to reservations is directly on the lake.

There are three bathhouses, each with flush toilets and hot showers, in the campground, along with a dump station and a boat ramp. There are four walk-in sites (sites #1 to #4) with a pit toilet and picnic tables.

Organized groups can reserve the pioneer camping area, which is located away from other park development.

COTTAGES

Mistletoe has 10 rental cottages to choose from.

Cottages #1 to #5 have two bedrooms and two baths. Each bedroom has its own dining area and section of porch, but shares a living room (with fireplace) and the equipped kitchen with the other bedroom.

The other five cottages are log homes with two bedrooms downstairs and a large sleeping loft above. They have a large living room/dining room/kitchen area and porches with rocking chairs facing the main body of the lake on the Little River.

Up to eight people can sleep in each cottage. No pets are allowed in the cottages or the cottage area. There is a two-night minimum stay year-round, with a one-week minimum in June, July and August. Cabins can be hard to get in the summer and should be reserved well ahead of time. Reservations are taken up to 11 months in advance; there is a one-night deposit and a small cancellation fee.

BOATING AND FISHING

Private boats are allowed to use the park waters, with no horsepower restrictions. Water-skiing is also allowed. There are three boat ramps and a courtesy dock in the park. Jet-Skis are allowed, but their operators should check the park office for special information.

The park is known for its productive fishing. Clarks Hill Lake is home to a large population of bass, including white, striped, hybrid and largemouth. Other game fish include bluegill, crappie and sauger. Legal fishing is allowed in the park year-round. Through a reciprocal agreement, either a South Carolina or a Georgia fishing license is valid on all areas of Clarks Hill Lake.

PICNICKING

There are 25 picnic tables, four picnic shelters and an enclosed group shelter in the three picnic areas. The picnic shelters may be reserved for a fee and are available on a first-come, first-served basis when not reserved. The weatherized group shelter is equipped with a kitchen, restrooms and a barbecue pit. It may be used by reservation only. A boat ramp, a dock, restrooms and a playground are located in the picnic area with the group shelter. The picnic area by the park office and the beach has a playground and restrooms.

SWIMMING

A swimming beach with a bathhouse is located behind the park office. There is no lifeguard on duty at the sand beach, which is open year-round.

HIKING

There are three trails and two spur trails to choose from, offering more than 5 miles of hiking in the park.

The longest trail is the 1.9-mile Twin Oaks Long Trail, which connects the campground and the beach. That trail is blazed with yellow paint and has an 0.3-mile spur which leads to the road by cottages #1 to #5.

The 1.2-mile Turkey Trot Trail loops through

the woods behind the maintenance office. The 0.6-mile Canyon Spur Trail connects to two sides of this loop, making a shorter hike possible.

The white-blazed Cliatt Creek Nature Trail begins across from the maintenance office and loops to Cliatt Creek and back.

NEARBY ATTRACTIONS

Clarks Hill Dam and Lake
Elijah Clarke State Park
Robert Toombs State Historic Site

DIRECTIONS

The park is located off GA 150 on Mistletoe Road, 12 miles north of Exit 60 off I-20.

FOR MORE INFORMATION

Mistletoe State Park, Route 1, Box 335, Appling, GA 30802 (706-541-0321)

MOCCASIN CREEK STATE PARK
RABUN COUNTY   32 ACRES

Located on the shores of Lake Burton, Moccasin Creek State Park offers not only excellent fishing but a central location to visit many of Georgia's mountain attractions. The park's southwestern boundary is formed by Lake Burton, which encompasses 2,800 acres of water within its 62 miles of shoreline. Moccasin Creek enters Lake Burton after flowing nearly 7 miles

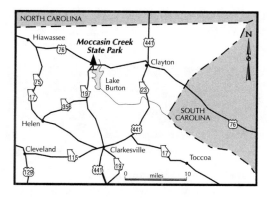

from high on the Eastern Continental Divide. The park's camping area is located on the north side of the creek and the Lake Burton Fish Breeding Station on the south.

At 2,000 feet in elevation, the park has moderate temperatures during the summer, earning it the motto, "Where Spring Spends the Summer." With 80 inches of precipitation annually, Moccasin Creek State Park is home to lush forests and a variety of wildflowers, as well as radiant foliage in the autumn.

CAMPING

The park offers 53 tent and trailer sites with water and electrical hookups. There are two bathhouses with hot showers, restroom facilities and washers and dryers. There is also a dump station in the campground. Campers may pitch their tents on the gravel pads provided.

PICNICKING

There is a small picnic area in the park, as well as an open-air pavilion. Both are located on the waterfront. There are also a few picnic tables at the fish hatchery. Picnicking is not allowed at campsites unless you are registered to camp.

BOATING AND FISHING

All powerboats except houseboats are allowed on Lake Burton. There is a public boat ramp next to the Lake Burton Fish Breeding Station on the south side of Moccasin Creek. Registered campers are allowed to dock privately owned boats at the park pier overnight. Rental boats are available at LaPrade's Marine, which is 2 miles south of the park. All boaters must comply with the Georgia Boating Safety Law.

Fishing is allowed year-round on Lake Burton. Licenses are available at the park office. Trout fishing along Moccasin Creek within the park is restricted to children 11 years old and under and holders of honorary fishing licenses. A fish-cleaning station is available for registered campers.

Moccasin Creek offers a specially designed fishing pier to wheelchair-bound and other handicapped visitors. Anyone who possesses a Georgia disability fishing license may fish from this pier, as well as along other sections of Moccasin Creek.

HIKING

Moccasin Creek State Park features a 1-mile loop nature trail, as well as a 2.5-mile hike along the creek. The hike along Moccasin Creek begins in the park and features two small waterfalls. The park is also within a 10- to 15-minute drive of the Appalachian Trail at Dicks Creek Gap and Addis Gap. Ask the park rangers for more detailed information.

OTHER FACILITIES

Volleyball, basketball, horseshoes and a playground are among the recreational opportunities in the park.

Adjacent to Moccasin Creek State Park is the Lake Burton Fish Breeding Station, administered by the Georgia Department of Natural Resources' Game and Fish Division. This station raises rainbow trout, which are used to stock lakes and streams throughout the Georgia Blue Ridge. The facility is open to the public from 8:00 A.M. until 4:30 P.M. daily.

NEARBY ATTRACTIONS

Tallulah Gorge State Park
Appalachian National Scenic Trail
Chattooga National Wild and Scenic River
Unicoi State Park and Lodge
Black Rock Mountain State Park

DIRECTIONS

Moccasin Creek State Park is located 20 miles north of Clarkesville on GA 197.

FOR MORE INFORMATION

Moccasin Creek State Park, Route 1, Box 1634, Clarkesville, GA 30523 (706-947-3194)

PANOLA MOUNTAIN STATE CONSERVATION PARK
STOCKBRIDGE   617 ACRES

Panola is a granite monadnock rising above the Piedmont at the heart of this unique park. The mountain's slopes spread out for 100 acres. It's inevitable that comparisons are made between this mountain and its much bigger brother, Stone Mountain, which can be seen from Panola. But this park was designated Georgia's first state conservation park and is listed by the National Park Service as a National Natural Landmark. That is in sharp contrast to the development on and around Stone Mountain.

On Panola, a diverse array of plant and animal life is protected from human intrusion. Spring begins in March and April with the yellow blooms of trout lilies and, later, the tiny red blooms of diamorpha, a rock outcrop plant.

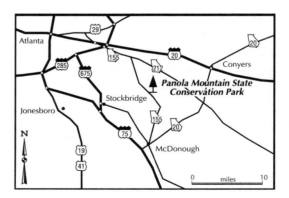

Trout lilies pop up among the granite at Panola Mountain State Conservation Park each March to herald spring.

The bloom season continues as blue-eyed grass, buckeyes and fire pinks awaken from their winter hibernation. Wildflower walks led by ranger-naturalists help visitors find and identify these and many other plants.

This wild mountain just 18 miles from Atlanta was purchased by the Nature Conservancy in 1967 and later deeded to the state for protection. The park's primary purpose is to protect the fragile ecology of rare plants and animals while interpreting its significance for visitors. The visitor center offers static displays, audio-visual programs, environmental programs and guided hikes to further this mission. The park's newsletter gives a complete listing of upcoming events and programs. Call or write the park office for more information.

In 1985, the United States Geologic Survey created the Panola Mountain Research Watershed to gather information and to research water-quality, soil and climatic changes. Input (rain and dry matter) and output are measured through the watershed's streams to determine what material is entering the watershed and how it leaves. Researchers examine the information to see how the watershed processes input such as acid rain as it filters through the park.

Panola comes from the Choctaw word for cotton. The mountain itself is off-limits to unescorted hikers, but ranger-guided hikes are scheduled daily.

There is also another side to Panola Mountain State Conservation Park. At the park entrance is a picnic area with an impressive playground, picnic tables, picnic shelters, restrooms and the mile-long Fitness Trail.

HIKING

The 3.5-mile ranger-led hike to Panola Mountain passes through the outcrop environment to the top of the monadnock. The hikes are scheduled each Tuesday through Sunday at 2:30 P.M. From Memorial Day to Labor Day, an additional hike is scheduled on Saturday and Sunday at 10:00 A.M. The hike is offered by reservation only. You must call at least 24 hours in advance to take part in a guided hike. These hikes may be canceled due to bad weather or staffing and programming restrictions. The guided hikes are for visitors who are not part of a group. Organized groups must arrange for a special guided hike.

There are two self-guided nature trails that shouldn't be overlooked. Both have broad paths and gentle terrain. The 0.75-mile Rock Outcrop Trail loops through a pine and hardwood forest to the edge of a granite outcrop with views of Panola Mountain and Stone Mountain. The outcrop's mosses, lichens and other plants can be observed from the trail without being damaged. The 1.25-mile Microwatershed Trail shows how watersheds work as it loops through an area of spring and erosion cuts which feed a small stream.

The 1-mile Fitness Trail has 16 exercise stations. It can be used for a gentle stroll or a more serious exercise hike.

PICNICKING

Twenty-five picnic tables and four picnic shel-

ters are scattered around the picnic area near the entrance to the park. The picnic shelters may be reserved for a small fee and are available on a first-come, first-served basis when not reserved. Restrooms are located in the picnic area, which also contains playground equipment and the Fitness Trail.

ANNUAL EVENTS

In keeping with the park's environmental-education focus, there are a number of annual programs, including wildflower walks, geology programs, bird walks, an environmental day and more. Contact the park office for a current listing of events.

NEARBY ATTRACTIONS

Sweetwater Creek State Conservation Park
Martin Luther King, Jr., National Historic Site
High Falls State Park
Indian Springs State Park

DIRECTIONS

From Exit 36 off I-20, the park is 18 miles southwest on GA 155.

FOR MORE INFORMATION

Panola Mountain State Conservation Park, 2600 GA 155 S.W., Stockbridge, GA 30281 (404-474-2914)

PROVIDENCE CANYON STATE CONSERVATION PARK

STEWART COUNTY   **1,108 ACRES**

Providence Canyon is the beautiful result of a worst case scenario for bad farming practices.

Georgia's "Little Grand Canyon" is an area of unique beauty. On a clear summer day on the canyon floor, you can see the light orange and salmon blooms of the rare plumleaf azalea standing out in sharp contrast to the white, pink and clay-red walls of the canyon. The brilliant blue sky beckons from beyond the green pine trees growing at the rim of the eroded landscape 150 feet above the creek.

Providence Canyon's wild, scenic beauty was man-made, but the canyon's creation was far from intentional. Poor farming practices in the early 1800s started the process of erosion. By the middle of that century, the ditch that would become Providence Canyon was only three to five feet deep. Water easily stripped away the colorful, erosion-prone soil of what geologists named the "Providence Formation" and cut its way down to the more erosion-resistant "Ripley Formation" of the canyon floor. Today, there are 16 canyons in the park, nine of which are alongside the day-use area. The spires in the canyon were created when water runoff eroded both sides of a hill, leaving only the spires behind.

The park, created in 1971 to protect the canyon's scenic beauty, offers few services compared to some of the state's other parks.

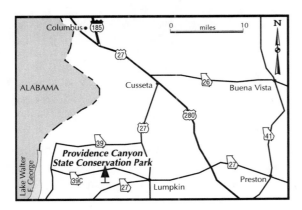

CAMPING

Primitive camping is permitted in the back country, but a permit is required. There are also two primitive campsites set aside for group use. All of these sites are located on the 7-mile Backpacking Trail.

HIKING

There are 3 miles of trail in and around the canyon, including Canyon Rim Trail. Backpacking Trail is reserved for hikers with camping permits. All of the trails start behind the park's interpretive center.

Remember, the canyon walls can be unstable. Stay on designated trails.

INTERPRETIVE CENTER

The interpretive center offers exhibits on the canyon's formation and area plants and animals. There is also a small theater with an audio-visual presentation. The center is open daily from 8 A.M. to 5 P.M. The park itself is open from 7 A.M. to 6 P.M. from mid-September to mid-April and from 7 A.M. to 9 P.M. the rest of the year.

OTHER FACILITIES

There are 65 picnic tables and two picnic shelters in the park. There is also a picnic shelter equipped with tables, chairs, a grill, a stove and a refrigerator. It can be reserved for a small fee.

ANNUAL EVENTS

The park hosts Wildflower Days in the spring and fall and a Kudzu Takeover Day each August. Contact the park office for more information.

NEARBY ATTRACTIONS

Florence Marina State Park
Kolomoki Mounds State Historic Park
Walter F. George Lake

DIRECTIONS

The park is 7 miles west of Lumpkin on GA 39C.

FOR MORE INFORMATION

Providence Canyon State Conservation Park, Route 1, Box 158, Lumpkin, GA 31815 (912-838-6202)

RED TOP MOUNTAIN STATE PARK AND LODGE

CARTERSVILLE   1,950 ACRES

This park is located on a peninsula surrounded almost entirely by 12,000-acre Lake Allatoona. The park and lake were developed jointly in the 1950s. To help visitors make the most of the lake, the park offers a marina, two boat ramps, seven boat docks and a beach. If you don't have a boat of your own, you may rent one in the park.

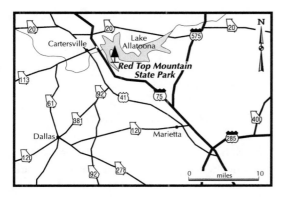

The park packs a lot of recreational facilities onto the peninsula, including tennis courts, a miniature golf course, hiking trails and picnic areas. The park's lodge has a swimming pool for lodge and cottage guests to use. If the lodge isn't what you are looking for, the park also has cottages and a tent and trailer camping area.

Red Top Mountain's name comes from the deep red of the iron-rich soil. The area was once an important mining area. Visitors to the park can find the remains of old mines on the peninsula.

LODGE

The 33-room lodge offers meeting facilities, a restaurant and a pool. For information or reservations, call the park office. No pets are allowed in the lodge, and there is no kennel in the park.

COTTAGES

The park's 18 cottages are all near the water.

They are equipped with central heat and air, fireplaces and a kitchen with a refrigerator, an electric stove and necessary cookware. Towels and linens are also provided. There are five boat docks in the cottage area for the use of registered cottage guests. Pets are not allowed in either the cottages or the cottage area.

CAMPING

The camping area has 24 sites without any hookups, 56 sites with water and electrical hookups and 12 pull-thru RV sites. The RV sites have water and electrical hookups, and there is a dump station in the RV area. There are five comfort stations in the tent and trailer camping area. Thirty of the campsites—but none of the pull-thru sites—are near the water. All sites are available for reservation by calling the park office and are otherwise available on a first-come, first-served basis.

Organized groups can use the pioneer camping area on a reservation basis. It offers a cleared area for tents, a pit toilet and a shelter for bad weather or equipment storage.

BOATING AND FISHING

Red Top Mountain is particularly well suited to boating. There are two boat ramps and seven docks in the park. There is also a marina with docking and boat-repair facilities. Boat rentals are available in the park as well. All boats must be in compliance with the Georgia Boating Safety Law.

Legal fishing is permitted in the park

year-round. Registered park guests are the only ones who may bank-fish after the park closes. Anyone over 16 must have a valid Georgia fishing license.

SWIMMING BEACH

The wading beach has a nearby concession stand, a miniature golf course, a playground and picnic shelters. There are no lifeguards on duty. No pets are allowed at the beach.

PICNICKING

The park has 150 picnic tables, seven picnic shelters and two group shelters. The picnic area along the lake near the park entrance has a comfort station. The picnic shelters can be reserved for a small fee and are available on a first-come, first-served basis when not reserved. The screened-in group shelters can be rented. Call the park office for more information or to make reservations.

HIKING

There are five trails in the park ranging from 0.75 mile to 5.5 miles in length. Near the lodge is the 0.75-mile handicapped-accessible Lakeside Trail. Homestead Trail is a 5.5-mile loop in an undeveloped area of the peninsula. Maps and information covering these two trails—along with Campground Trail, Sweet Gum Trail and Red Blaze Trail—are available at the lodge and the visitor center.

TENNIS

Red Top Mountain has two lighted tennis courts near the visitor center. No reservations are taken for these courts.

NEARBY ATTRACTIONS

Etowah Indian Mounds State Historic Site
Kennesaw Mountain National Battlefield Park
Lake Allatoona
New Echota State Historic Site
Pickett's Mill Battlefield State Historic Site

DIRECTIONS

The park is near Cartersville, 1.5 miles east of Exit 123 off I-75.

FOR MORE INFORMATION

Red Top Mountain State Park and Lodge, 653 Red Top Mountain Road S.E., Cartersville, GA 30120 (404-975-0055)

REED BINGHAM STATE PARK
ADEL   1,620 ACRES

PT

A 375-acre lake on the Little River is the centerpiece of this park. Boating, fishing, swimming and water-skiing are all popular activities on the lake. Camping, picnicking, hiking and miniature golf round out the recreation at this park on the Colquitt and Cook County lines.

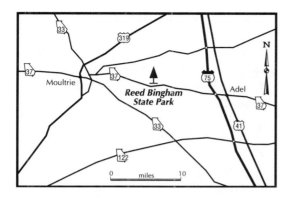

Buzzards roost in abundance in trees along the Little River in the park; the staff offers pontoon-boat rides upriver upon request.

The park is named for a Chicagoan who came to Moultrie in 1920 to work for that city's light and water department. He was an electrification pioneer in the area, working to form the Colquitt County Cooperative. Reed Bingham pushed the state legislature to form the lake to supply power and provide a new recreational resource for the area. To aid the push for the park, Bingham surveyed the land along miles of the Little River and measured the water level in different seasons. The park was named to honor his tireless efforts in working toward its creation.

CAMPING

The 47 tent and trailer sites among the Spanish moss–draped trees each have electrical and water hookups. All of the sites have picnic tables, and most have grills. There are two bathhouses and a dump station in the campground.

PICNICKING

There are 74 picnic tables and seven picnic shelters around the lake. The picnic shelters may be reserved for a small fee and are available on

This narrow island in the lake at Reed Bingham State Park is an idyllic picnic spot. It can be reached by a footbridge.

a first-come, first-served basis when not reserved. There are also four group shelters in the park. These larger, weatherized shelters are available by reservation only.

BOATING AND FISHING

Private boats may use the park's two boat ramps. There is no horsepower restriction from 7 A.M. to sunset. Water-skiing is permitted. Fishing is allowed from 7 A.M. to 10 P.M. year-round on the lake and river and below the dam. A fishing dock is provided. All anglers over 16 must have a valid Georgia fishing license.

HIKING

The park's two nature trails offer a chance to see many plants and animals, including gopher tortoises, deer, waterfowl and pitcher plants. The 0.5-mile Gopher Tortoise Trail is a loop hike just north of the camping area. The 3.5-mile Coastal Plains Nature Trail uses boardwalks and trail to connect several south Georgia habitats, such as a cypress swamp, a pitcher-plant bog and a sandhill area. Many of this trail's boardwalks were damaged during flooding in 1994. They were scheduled to be rebuilt during 1995, money and manpower permitting.

BEACH

Wading and sunbathing at the beach west of the dam are popular in the summer. No lifeguard is on duty. A bathhouse and a small playground are provided at the beach.

OTHER FACILITIES

A miniature golf course and a large playground are located near the camping area on the east side of the lake. Contact the park office for golf-course hours and fees.

ANNUAL EVENTS

A Fourth of July music festival and the Old Fashioned Games, held on Memorial Day and Labor Day, are among the park's annual events.

NEARBY ATTRACTIONS

Banks Lake National Wildlife Refuge
General Coffee State Park

DIRECTIONS

From Exit 10 off I-75, it is 6 miles west on GA 37 to the park entrance.

FOR MORE INFORMATION

Reed Bingham State Park, Box 394B-1, Route 2, Adel, GA 31620 (912-896-3551)

SEMINOLE STATE PARK
SEMINOLE COUNTY   343 ACRES

PT

Located in Seminole County on the shores of Lake Seminole, the park is yet another namesake of the Seminole Indians, a Muskhogean

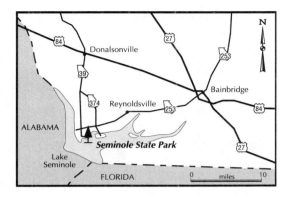

tribe that once lived primarily in what is now Florida and in the Okefenokee Swamp. The Seminoles are a mixed people, combining natives of the area, wandering Creek Indians and Negro slaves. Seminole itself is a Creek word that means "separatists," "runaways" or "wanderers."

At the confluence of the Chattahoochee and Flint Rivers, this park on Lake Seminole offers unsurpassed fishing. Among the tree stumps and grass beds is an abundant supply of largemouth, hybrid, striped and white bass. Bream, catfish and crappie are also found in Seminole State Park's waters. Adjacent to the park is the 17,000-acre Lake Seminole Wildlife Management Area—a prime area for deer, waterfowl and small-game hunting—making this park a double threat to the free time of hunting and fishing enthusiasts.

The lake was impounded in 1957 behind the 3,600-foot long Jim Woodruff Lock and Dam. Congress authorized the project in 1946 as part of a plan to improve navigation on the Chattahoochee and Flint Rivers and provide hy-

droelectric power. Before the dam was built, the water in the two rivers was about three feet deep. Now, water backs 47 miles up each of the two rivers, for more than 500 miles of shoreline.

CAMPING

The park's 50 tent and trailer sites are equipped with water and electrical hookups. The two bathhouses have hot showers, flush toilets and laundry facilities. There is a dump station in the camping area.

Organized groups may use the pioneer camping area by reservation. Running water is the only amenity at this primitive site, which is set apart from the park's developed areas.

COTTAGES

The park has 10 two-bedroom cottages. Each cottage has linens and a kitchen equipped with cookware and utensils. No pets are allowed in the cottage area. Reservations may be made up to 11 months in advance.

BOATING AND FISHING

The park offers a boat ramp and a dock to help you make the most of Lake Seminole. Private boats are allowed, with no horsepower restrictions. Water-skiing is permitted. Canoes may be rented in the park.

Anglers over the age of 16 must have a valid Georgia fishing license, as no reciprocal agreement is in effect for park waters.

SWIMMING

The beach is open year-round to swimmers. There is no lifeguard on duty, so swimming is at your own risk.

PICNICKING

There are 100 picnic tables, six picnic shelters and one group shelter in the park. The picnic shelters may be reserved in advance for a fee. They are available on a first-come, first-served basis when not reserved.

The 70-person, air-conditioned group shelter has an equipped kitchen, a barbecue pit and restrooms. It is available by reservation only.

OTHER FACILITIES

The 2.2-mile Gopher Tortoise Trail features Georgia's only native tortoise on an easy ramble through wire grass and stands of longleaf pine.

NEARBY ATTRACTIONS

Kolomoki Mounds State Historic Park
Lake Seminole
Lapham-Patterson House State Historic Site

DIRECTIONS

Seminole is located 16 miles south of Donalsonville off GA 39, or 23 miles west of Bainbridge off GA 253.

FOR MORE INFORMATION

Seminole State Park, Route 2, Donalsonville, GA 31745 (912-861-3137)

SKIDAWAY ISLAND STATE PARK
CHATHAM COUNTY   533 ACRES

This park lies along Skidaway Narrows on the western edge of Skidaway, one of Georgia's barrier islands. The tidal estuaries, salt marsh and mature forest of the park are home to a wide variety of land animals and marine life. The forest is largely composed of live oak, holly, cabbage palmetto and longleaf pine. The park's two nature trails offer visitors a chance to explore the barrier-island habitat and view wildlife.

Being close to historic Savannah makes the park popular with campers who want to explore that city by day and return to Skidaway Island in the evening.

CAMPING

There are 88 pull-thru sites in the wooded camping area. Each site has its own water and electrical hookups, picnic table, grill and tent pad. Campfires are permitted, though not on the grass tent pads. There are three comfort stations with hot showers, flush toilets and coin-operated laundry facilities in the camping area. A dump station with nearby dumpsters is also provided.

PICNICKING

A hundred picnic tables are scattered through the 10-acre wooded picnic area. There are also five covered shelters and two playgrounds in the picnic area. The shelters may be reserved and are available on a first-come, first-served basis when not reserved. There are two restrooms in the picnic area. Horseshoe and volleyball gear can be rented from the park office.

A large group shelter with heat and air conditioning, a range, a refrigerator, a grill, tables and chairs and an outside oyster-cooking shed is available for rent from 10:00 A.M. to 9:45 P.M. Contact the park office for rates and reservations.

HIKING

Ferry and Sandpiper Nature Trails give hikers a close-up look at the barrier island and the surrounding salt marsh.

The 3-mile Ferry Nature Trail loops out and back from a trailhead near Camping Area #4. A sign at the trailhead gives a map of the trail's route.

The 1-mile Sandpiper Nature Trail has a trailhead next to the visitor center. An interpretive brochure available at the visitor center describes many of the plants and animals encountered on the trail and from the observation platform. The trail passes by a Confederate earthwork fortification and the remains of an old moonshine still.

Ranger-led hikes are given during the summer. Check at the park office for a schedule of programs to be given during your visit.

BOATING AND FISHING

Though located on a barrier island, the park has no facilities for boating or fishing at this time. However, about 0.5 mile from the park, there is access to fishing along the Atlantic Intracoastal Waterway, where no license is required for saltwater fishing.

SWIMMING

The pool and the bathhouse are open from Memorial Day through Labor Day from 11 A.M. to 6 P.M. The pool is closed on Mondays and Tuesdays except for some legal holidays.

ANNUAL EVENTS

Each year, the park offers a Coastal Bird Program in April, a Seafood Delights Program in the fall and a Wild Game Cooking Program in the winter. Contact the park office for dates and information.

Wormsloe State Historic Site
Fort Pulaski National Historic Site
Fort McAllister State Historic Park

DIRECTIONS

The park is 6 miles southeast of Savannah on the Diamond Causeway.

FOR MORE INFORMATION

Skidaway Island State Park, 52 Diamond Causeway, Savannah, GA 31411 (912-598-2300)

STEPHEN C. FOSTER STATE PARK
CHARLTON COUNTY   80 ACRES

"Way down upon the Swanee River" they named a park for Stephen Foster. The little 80-

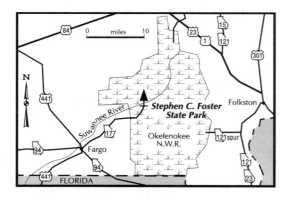

acre park, located on Jones Island inside the 391,402-acre Okefenokee National Wildlife Refuge, offers the only cottages and tent and trailer campsites in the swamp. The park also offers an unsurpassed chance to view thousands of plants and animals in their native habitats. It is estimated that 9,000 to 12,000 alligators live in the refuge, while only 8,496 people live in the county the park is located in. The refuge is also home to 64 species of reptiles, 76 species of amphibians, 50 species of mammals and 237 species of birds.

The Okefenokee National Wildlife Refuge was created in 1937 to preserve one of the nation's oldest freshwater areas. In 1974, the interior 354,000 acres were protected as a National Wilderness Area. The huge saucer-shaped depression that contains the swamp was once part of the ocean floor. Now, much of the swamp floor is filled with peat deposits up to 15 feet thick. The swamp is drained by the St. Marys River at its southeastern edge and by the Suwannee River, which leaves the swamp near the state park. The black swamp water gets its color from tannic acid released by decaying plant matter.

This 600-square-mile area of swampland was called "Land of the Trembling Earth" by the Seminole Indians. Fed by rain, small springs and streams, the swamp is only 110 to 130 feet above sea level. Its pure, fresh water forms the headwaters of the St. Marys River, which flows to the Atlantic, and the Suwannee River, which flows to the Gulf of Mexico.

To help visitors explore the refuge, the park has a boat ramp; private boats are allowed, but there is a 10-horsepower limit. The park also rents canoes and motorboats. There are 25 miles of waterways in the day-use area. For a small fee, permits are available through the Okefenokee National Wildlife Refuge for two- to five-day canoe trips. The 0.5-mile Trembling Earth Nature Trail goes through a forested section of swamp on boardwalks and has interpretive signs describing the swamp ecosystem.

In addition to the $2-per-vehicle fee for the state park, visitors must pay a $4-per-vehicle fee to enter the wildlife refuge.

Stephen C. Foster (1826–64) wrote "The Old Folks at Home" and more than 200 other songs between 1844 and 1864. His famous songs, including "Camptown Races," "My Old Kentucky Home," "Jeannie with the Light Brown Hair" and "Beautiful Dreamer," earned him a good deal of fame and a steady income, but they were not enough to support the songwriter's habits as an alcoholic. He died in the charity ward at New York's Bellevue Hospital.

TOURS

A one-and-a-half-hour tour of the swamp is available year-round. Inquire in the park office about the schedule at the time of your visit. Group tours can be reserved in advance by calling the park.

BOATING AND FISHING

Johnboats, canoes and motorboats are available for rent at the trading post. Private boats can use the boat ramp for a $1 fee but are lim-ited to 10-horsepower motors. All boats must be in compliance with the Georgia Boating Safety Law.

The refuge is open to fishing year-round. Persons over 16 must have a valid fishing license, which can be purchased at the trading post.

CAMPING

The park's two camping areas have a total of 66 tent and trailer sites with water and electrical hookups. These are the only drive-up campsites in the refuge. Each campsite has a picnic table and a grill, and each camping area has a bathhouse with hot showers, toilets and coin-operated washers and dryers. There is a dump station in Camping Area #2.

A primitive camping area is available to organized groups. Call the park office to arrange a reservation.

COTTAGES

All nine two-bedroom cottages have heat and air conditioning, a kitchen with the necessary utensils and towels and linens. Cottages can be reserved up to 11 months in advance by calling the park office. There is a two-night minimum stay. No pets are allowed.

PICNICKING

The three group picnic shelters are available for reservation. When not reserved, they may be used on a first-come, first-served basis.

MUSEUM

The museum is open daily from 8 A.M. to 5 P.M. It offers interpretive displays on the swamp's ecosystem and wildlife.

OTHER FACILITIES

A playground is located across the drive from the trading post.

NEARBY ATTRACTIONS

Okefenokee National Wildlife Refuge
Okefenokee Swamp Park
Laura S. Walker State Park

ANNUAL EVENTS

The park hosts a Reptile Weekend each May and a Man in the Swamp program each November. Contact the park office for information.

DIRECTIONS

The park is 18 miles northeast of the town of Fargo on GA 177.

FOR MORE INFORMATION

Stephen C. Foster State Park, Route 1, Box 131, Fargo, GA 31631 (912-637-5274)

SWEETWATER CREEK STATE CONSERVATION PARK

LITHIA SPRINGS   1,986 ACRES

This park was created to protect the natural character of the Factory Shoals section of Sweetwater Creek and the historic integrity of the New Manchester Manufacturing Company and town-site ruins. The area around the ruins has remained virtually untouched since the Civil War. Taking a walk along the trail to the ruins is like walking backwards into history.

Legend says that Sweetwater Creek was named for Cherokee chief Ama-Kanasta. This land was occupied by Indians from 1000 B.C. through 1000 A.D. The hills on the south side of the park are evidence of more recent Indian habitation. Known as Jack's Hills, they are named for Chief Jack, who is reputed to be buried in the area.

When the Cherokee Indians were forced from Georgia in 1832, the land was sold in a public lottery. It passed through the hands of a couple of owners before being sold to Colonel James

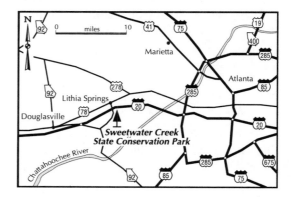

Once the center of a bustling community, the ruins of the New Manchester Manufacturing Company textile mill now lie at the heart of Sweetwater Creek State Conservation Park.

Rogers and former governor Charles J. McDonald in 1845. The two incorporated the Sweetwater Manufacturing Company and built a textile mill on the site in 1849. In 1857, McDonald reorganized the business into the New Manchester Manufacturing Company, outfitted the mill with new machinery and tripled its output. By that time, a small town had grown up around the factory.

With the beginning of the Civil War, the mill began producing a material called osnaburg for the Confederate government. Because of this contract, the mill became a viable military target. During the Battle of Atlanta, General Sherman destroyed the mill and torched the town, home to 200 people. The families were moved to Louisville, Kentucky, before being dispersed throughout Ohio and Indiana for the remainder of the war. Some of them later returned to New Manchester, only to discover it lying in ruins. No attempt was ever made to rebuild the mill.

At the end of the history trail stand the ruins of what was, at five stories, the tallest building in the Atlanta area in 1860. You can still see how the tall windows flare outward toward the inside of the wall. They were designed to allow as much natural light as possible inside the factory and thus eliminate the need for open-flame light sources.

The park, opened in 1976, offers no overnight facilities.

HIKING

There are three trails in the park.

Red Trail, or History Trail, is the most popular. It takes you along Sweetwater Creek to the sites of the New Manchester mill town and the mill itself. You can either end at the mill (a 0.5-mile walk) or continue another 0.5 mile to Sweetwater Falls. A number of loop options are possible on this trail.

Blue Nature Trail, or Non-Game Wildlife Trail, is a 2-mile hike that leads to the falls area. It intersects Red Trail at the ruins of the mill after a mile. The park's nongame wildlife and natural plant communities are featured on this hike. The trail winds through several stream coves and ridge areas that overlook the creek bed and Red Trail.

White Trail, or Non-Game Wildlife Trail Extension, is a 4-mile dogleg that completes a loop. This trail passes through some of the more remote areas of the park to the west of Sweetwater Creek and follows the creek bed to its southern boundary with the park. It then turns west and follows the Jack's Hill Lake stream. This is where you will find most of the wildflowers in the park. You will pass through areas covered with ferns, big-leafed magnolias, mountain laurel, wild azaleas and other flowers. The trail then passes through the Jack's Hill meadow area and into the old picnic loop.

OTHER FACILITIES

There are 75 picnic tables with grills in the park, along with 11 picnic shelters and one group shelter. The picnic shelters hold up to 50 people and offer a grill, water and electricity. They can be reserved for a fee and are available for free on a first-come, first-served basis when

Griffin Logue looks at a trout lily, one of the first signs of spring, alongside the Factory Ruins Trail at Sweetwater Creek State Conservation Park.

not reserved. The group shelter holds 150 and is available by reservation only.

Fishing is allowed both on the park's 215-acre lake and in Sweetwater Creek. Most common freshwater species are found in the lake and the creek. A valid resident or nonresident license is required for fishing. Private boats with electric motors are allowed on the lake but must pay a fee for launching. Canoes and johnboats can be rented from the bait shop. The Georgia Boating Safety Law applies.

Interpretive programs and walking tours are scheduled regularly. A program schedule is posted at the park office.

ANNUAL EVENTS

Among the special events at Sweetwater are the New Manchester Commemoration, the History Lecture Series, spring wildflower walks and fall foliage walks. Contact the park office for dates and times.

NEARBY ATTRACTIONS

John H. Tanner State Park
Pickett's Mill Battlefield State Historic Site

DIRECTIONS

Take I-20 west from Atlanta; exit at Thornton Road (Exit 12) and turn left. Travel 0.25 mile, turn right onto Blairs Bridge Road and then left onto Mount Vernon Road to reach the park.

FOR MORE INFORMATION

Sweetwater Creek State Conservation Park, P.O. Box 816, Lithia Springs, GA 30057 (404-944-1700)

TALLULAH GORGE STATE PARK
TALLULAH FALLS   3,000 ACRES

NE

As you look down at the river cutting through the nearly 1,000-foot-deep gorge, it's easy to imagine the view legendary tightrope walker Karl Wallenda had as he walked over the chasm on July 18, 1970, at 65 years of age. From North Wallenda Tower, you can see Oceana Falls and the lower part of the 2-mile-long gorge. From the safety of the rim, you can picture how the gorge would have looked spread out beneath you with only a cable separating you from the river rushing below. Wallenda was matching a feat accomplished in 1886 by J. A. "Professor Leon" St. John.

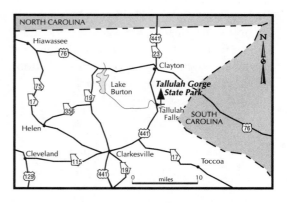

Bald eagles are frequently seen on Tugaloo Lake at the lower end of the gorge. The gorge is the only place you will find the persistent trillium, an endangered species. It is also home to monkey-faced orchids, green salamanders and several other threatened or endangered species.

Tallulah Gorge is the state's newest park. Scheduled to open in the fall of 1995, it is the result of a partnership between Georgia Power Company and the Georgia Department of Natural Resources. Georgia Power Company employees will work side by side with state park employees to interpret the park and run some of the facilities.

The river's name has many possible sources. Among the theories are that it derives from the Choctaw word *talulu*, or "bell"; that it derives from the Cherokee word *tu-lu-lu-li*, or "the frog place"; and that, according to a 1835 legend, it derives from a word meaning "terrible," in reference to the 1,000-foot falls on the river. The Cherokees knew the river as *Terrora*, which may explain the 1830s interpretation.

The 63-acre Tallulah Falls Lake and the impressive Tallulah Falls Gorge have long made this a popular stop for visitors going to and from the Smokies on U.S. 441. Now, it is an attraction in its own right. You'll want plenty of time to explore the park. There are several trails, but no safe access has been provided to the bottom of the gorge yet. Trails are planned for the future that will allow you to explore the gorge as well as the lake and the rim.

The park is being developed as this book goes to print. To get the most up-to-date information on available services, call the park office.

INTERPRETIVE EDUCATION CENTER

An impressive 16,000-square-foot building will house both permanent and changing exhibits on the culture, history, geology and natural resources of the park and the surrounding area. Displays will also give visitors background on Georgia Power Company's work and the history of hydroelectric power in the area.

Visitors will enter the center on its second floor. To give visitors who can't get into the gorge itself a feeling for the experience, a ramp spirals down through the atrium. Small display areas off the ramp will interpret the gorge as visitors get closer and closer to the floor. At the bottom of the atrium, visitors will walk through a rocky area, with trees stretching from the top of the rock wall high up into the atrium. The path leads to the center's state-of-the-art theater, which features a 20-minute film. During the film, visitors will see rock climbers scaling the gorge's rock walls, get a close-up view of some of the gorge's unique plants and animals and take a wild ride through the gorge from a kayaker's perspective.

Visitors who step out the back of the center will be able to take in a commanding view of the gorge, including Hurricane Falls.

The center is on Rock Mountain Road near the north rim of the gorge. It offers restrooms.

CAMPING

There are 50 tent and trailer sites in the campground off South Mountain Road between U.S. 441 and the interpretive center. Primitive camping will be allowed on spur trails being built off North Rim Trail. Inquire at the interpretive center for more information on these sites.

HIKING

North Rim Trail leads from the parking area at Terrora Campground to the gorge across the highway from the dam. It leads to five overlooks, including L'Eau d'Or Overlook, with its view of L'Eau d'Or Falls and Hawthorne Pool. The trail also leads to Hawthorne Overlook, with its breathtaking view of the upper gorge, including Hawthorne Pool, Tempesta Falls and L'Eau d'Or Falls. The interpretive center is uphill from this trail between Hawthorne Overlook and North Wallenda Tower.

Terrora Trail is a 1-mile trail connecting several of the natural communities of the park—rocky cliffs, lakeside, streams and fields. The trail from the parking area on Old U.S. 441 to the first overlook is handicapped-accessible.

More trails are to be built in the park in the coming years. They will include South Rim Trail, which was operated on a fee basis for many years before becoming part of the park. Many of the planned trails will be built for mixed bicycle and hiking use. There are plans to connect trails in the park to trails on adjoining national-forest land.

OTHER FACILITIES

A swimming beach, two lighted tennis courts and picnic tables are located along Tallulah Falls Lake. Legal fishing will be permitted year-round in the park for visitors with a valid Georgia fishing license.

NEARBY ATTRACTIONS

Black Rock Mountain State Park
Chattahoochee National Forest
Dahlonega Gold Museum
Moccasin Creek State Park
Traveler's Rest State Historic Site
Unicoi State Park and Lodge

DIRECTIONS

The park is on U.S. 441 in the city of Tallulah Falls.

FOR MORE INFORMATION

Tallulah Gorge State Park, P.O. Box 248, Tallulah Falls, GA 30573 (706-754-8257)

TUGALOO STATE PARK
LAVONIA   393 ACRES

Situated on a peninsula surrounded on three sides by Lake Hartwell, this park was named for the Tugaloo River, which once flowed freely nearby. The river was named by naturalist William Bartram, who spelled it Tugilo. Tugilo derives from the nearby Cherokee Indian town of *Dugiluyi*, or "Fork in the Stream." The Tugaloo River now makes up part of Lake Hartwell.

This is one of two state parks on Lake

Lakeshore sites on 56,000-acre Lake Hartwell make the campground at Tugaloo State Park popular with boaters and anglers.

Hartwell, one of the ten most-popular Corps of Engineers reservoirs in the nation. The reservoir was opened in 1963, the park two years later. The 56,000-acre reservoir provides ample fishing, boating and water-skiing opportunities.

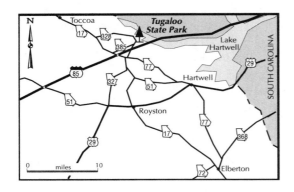

CAMPING

The park offers 120 tent and trailer sites with water and electrical hookups. There are three camping areas. The two smaller areas each have a comfort station, and the larger area has two. A dump station is located in Camping Area #1.

The primitive camping area features only fire rings, latrines and one camp shelter.

COTTAGES

The park offers 20 fully equipped two-bedroom cottages. The cabins are heated and air-conditioned and come with linens, cooking equipment and dishes. They also have fireplaces or wood stoves. Reservations can be made up to 11 months in advance.

FISHING

There are two boat ramps in the park, as well as nine boat docks for cottage guests. Private boats are permitted in park waters, with no horsepower restrictions. All boating must comply with the Georgia Boating Safety Law, and all fishermen over the age of 15 must have a valid resident or nonresident license.

OTHER FACILITIES

The park has 104 picnic tables and seven picnic shelters. The shelters may be reserved for a fee and are available on a first-come, first-served basis when not reserved. There is also a group shelter with a kitchen, available by reservation only.

Visitors may swim at the white-sand beach located in the day-use area. It is open year-round, but there is no lifeguard on duty. Both the rental booth and the miniature golf course are closed Mondays except for legal holidays. Tennis courts, volleyball courts and horseshoe pits are available at the park as well.

There are two nature trails in the park—the 0.7-mile Muscadine Trail (which leads to an observation deck over the lake after 0.2 mile) and the 0.2-mile Crow Tree Nature Trail.

NEARBY ATTRACTIONS

Victoria Bryant State Park and Golf Course

Traveler's Rest State Historic Site
Lake Hartwell
Hart State Park

DIRECTIONS

From I-85, take Exit 58 and drive north on GA 17. Follow the park signs to County Road 385, which leads 1.5 miles to GA 328. Turn left and travel 3.3 miles to the park.

FOR MORE INFORMATION

Tugaloo State Park, Route 1, Box 1766, Lavonia, GA 30553 (706-356-4362)

UNICOI STATE PARK AND LODGE

HELEN   1,081 ACRES

Located in the heart of an area of the mountains popular with tourists, Unicoi State Park has an array of amenities to tempt you. There

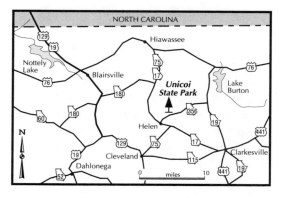

is even a smorgasbord of choices on where and how to spend the night. Five camping areas with 87 sites are convenient to Lake Unicoi and surrounding hiking trails. But if your idea of camping out is to go to a budget motel instead of a four-star resort, the park has 30 lakeside and creek-side cottages. Still too rustic? The 100-room lodge and conference center may be your style. It has more rooms to choose from than any other state-park lodge in Georgia.

Boating, swimming, picnicking and hiking are among the many recreational activities in the park. Anna Ruby Falls, an impressive 153-foot double waterfall, is near the park. To get to the falls, continue past Smith Creek Cottage Area onto National Forest Service land. There is a small fee for hiking the 0.5-mile trail to the falls, which can be accessed by a 10-mile round-trip hike from Little Brook Camping Area in the park.

The lake was drained and under repair during 1994 and 1995. It is expected to make its comeback in the spring of 1996.

Unicoi is believed to come from the Cherokee word for "new way."

UNICOI LODGE AND RESTAURANT

The 100 rooms in the lodge are comparable to commercial hotel rooms. Each room has two double beds and a private bath. The lodge rooms are connected by a breezeway to the conference center, which has a variety of meeting rooms for conferences and seminars. The restaurant offers buffet-style dining for breakfast, lunch and dinner. There are four lighted tennis courts ad-

jacent to the lodge. Call 706-878-2824 for information or reservations.

CAMPING

Unicoi offers 85 campsites and 19 sleep platforms to choose from. Its four bathhouses feature hot showers and restroom facilities.

Squirrel's Nest Camping Area has 19 platforms, which accommodate four sleeping bags each. There is a bathhouse between this area and the group activity shelter and amphitheater.

Hickory Nut Hollow Camping Area has 33 tent sites, three group fire rings and a bathhouse.

Little Brook Camping Area has 16 RV sites with water and electrical hookups. It also offers a dump station. The bathhouse along the drive in this camping area is convenient to a dozen or more of the tent sites in Hickory Nut Hollow Camping Area.

Big Brook Spur Camping Area, with 13 sites, and the adjoining Laurel Ridge Camping Area, with 23 sites, each have a group fire ring and share a bathhouse, located between the two areas.

The trading post and its nearby group activity shelter and amphitheater are convenient to all of the camping areas. In addition to the usual camp-store snacks and souvenirs, the trading post has laundry facilities and a pay phone. Check-in for the camping areas is in Little Brook Camping Area.

A group camping area is located away from the park's other facilities. It may be reserved by organized groups only.

COTTAGES

There are 30 cottages clustered in two areas. The 20 lakeside cottages include Unicoi's unique barrel-shaped cabins. Resembling an oversized wooden keg lying on its side, they rise over the sloping hillside on stilts. The other cottages are at the park's northern boundary along Smith Creek. All of these furnished cottages have kitchens and linens. No pets are allowed.

UNICOI LAKE

This 53-acre creek-fed mountain lake was on sabbatical as this book went to press in 1995. It will be restocked with fish after it is filled again in the spring of 1996. Boating and fishing will again be offered at that time. With the return of the lake will come the return of the sandy swimming beach. The beach house has restrooms with showers.

FISHING

Trout fishing on Smith Creek remained a popular activity during the lake's hiatus. The area from the lake to the cottages is productive. Many anglers venture upstream beyond the cottages onto National Forest Service land in pursuit of trout.

PICNICKING

The picnic areas on Anna Ruby Falls Road offer 70 picnic tables, seven picnic shelters and a group shelter. Shelter #7 is near the dam at the south end of the lake. Shelters #1

Round cottages are among the features that make Unicoi State Park unique.

and #2 are near the beach. The others are upstream on Smith Creek. These shelters may be reserved for a small fee and are available on a first-come, first-served basis when not reserved.

A group shelter with a kitchen and restrooms is at the beach house. It has a porch overlooking the lake. This group shelter is available by reservation only.

HIKING

The four trails in the park range in length from a 1.3-mile hike to a 10-mile round-trip hike.

Bottoms Loop Trail is marked with yellow blazes. You can make either a 1.3-mile or a 2.5-mile loop along this trail, which starts at the road leading from GA 356 to the conference center.

Unicoi Lake Trail is a yellow-blazed loop that circles the lake, passing by the lakeside cottages, the campgrounds and the beach along the way.

Unicoi/Helen Trail is a 3-mile one-way hike down to the popular tourist town.

The longest hike from the park is the 5-mile one-way hike on Smith Creek Trail to Anna Ruby Falls. This blue-blazed trail starts at Little Brook Camping Area. The more than 500 feet you gain in elevation is spread out evenly enough to make this hike enjoyable. The trail doesn't join Smith Creek until you are almost in sight of the falls.

NEARBY ATTRACTIONS

Anna Ruby Falls

Dahlonega Gold Museum State Historic Site
Brasstown Bald
Moccasin Creek State Park
Vogel State Park
Appalachian National Scenic Trail

DIRECTIONS

Unicoi is located 2 miles northeast of Helen via GA 356.

FOR MORE INFORMATION

Unicoi State Park and Lodge, P.O. Box 849, Helen, GA 30545 (706-878-2201)

VICTORIA BRYANT STATE PARK
ROYSTON   406 ACRES

NE

Nestled in the rolling hills of the upper Piedmont, this park features a nine-hole golf course, camping, swimming and fishing. The park opened in 1952 when Paul E. Bryant of Royston

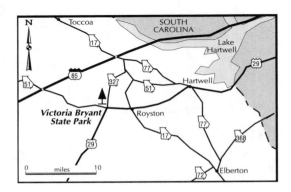

The Logue's mini-motorhome, Harry the Truck, wades through Rice Creek in Victoria Bryant State Park.

gave 45 acres of land to the state, dedicating it to his mother, Victoria Osborn Bryant. Since 1952, the park has grown to 406 acres.

The Cherokee and Creek Indians once inhabited these hills and valleys. Of particular beauty is Rice Creek, which flows through the center of the park and features a pretty cascade in the shoals area. Children will particularly enjoy the "upside-down bridge" where Rice Creek flows over the roadway.

Nearby Royston was the hometown of baseball star Ty Cobb.

GOLF

Victoria Bryant features one of the state parks system's five golf courses. It offers a nine-hole course and a driving range. Golf carts, clubs and pull carts may be rented. The pro shop has a variety of golf accessories and equipment for sale. Tee times are not required; play is on a first come, first-served basis. A monthly pass can be purchased for about $65 and is good only at Victoria Bryant. For more information, call 706-245-6770.

CAMPING

The park offers 19 campsites with water and electrical hookups, along with a comfort station with hot showers and a washer and dryer. A dump station is adjacent to the comfort station. There are also six improved campsites for tent campers, which are isolated from the RV sites for more privacy. Groups may camp in the pioneer campground, which is equipped with water and latrines. Reservations can be made up to 11 months in advance.

PICNICKING

There are 107 picnic tables and five shelters in the day-use area. The shelters may be reserved and are available on a first-come, first-served basis when not reserved.

FISHING

The park features two fishing ponds. One of them, located near the secondary entrance, is for campers' use only. The pond located at the main entrance is reserved for the use of the handicapped; those who wish to fish in this pond must register with a park ranger. Both ponds are fully stocked. There is no fee for fishing, although a valid Georgia license is required for those 16 years of age and older.

SWIMMING

During the spring and summer, the swimming pool and bathhouse are open to the public. The hours are 11 A.M. to 6 P.M. Tuesday through Friday and 11 A.M. to 7 P.M. Saturday and Sunday. The pool is closed on Mondays except for legal holidays. Qualified lifeguards are on duty, and a fee is charged for entrance except to registered campers.

HIKING

There are three trails in the park: The Nature Trail, an 0.5-mile trail that loops around Rice Creek; The Loop Trail, a 1.5-mile trail that forms a loop with both Perimeter and Nature Trails; and The Perimeter Trail, a 3.5-mile trail that forms a loop around the park. An interpretive guide to The Nature Trail is available in the park office.

OTHER FACILITIES

Three playgrounds are available. Two of them are in the day-use area. The one in the tent and RV area may be used by campers only.

ANNUAL EVENTS

The Junior-Senior Catfish Rodeo is scheduled for April or May. Snake programs are scheduled on request. Contact the park office for more information.

NEARBY ATTRACTIONS

Hart State Park
Lake Hartwell
Traveler's Rest State Historic Site

DIRECTIONS

Victoria Bryant is 2 miles north of Royston, 0.5 mile off U.S. 29 on GA 327.

FOR MORE INFORMATION

Victoria Bryant State Park, 1105 Bryant Park Road, Royston, GA 30662 (706-245-6270)

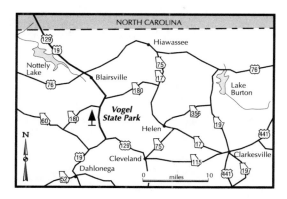

VOGEL STATE PARK

UNION COUNTY	280 ACRES

NE

At 2,500 feet in elevation and higher, Vogel is a popular camping spot during Georgia's hot summer months. It can fill up quickly. The park offers a variety of recreation as well—everything from trout fishing to hiking.

The park is named for August Vogel, who donated the land to the state in 1928. It is the second-oldest park in Georgia; Indian Springs State Park was established a year earlier.

Lake Trahlyta, created from the impoundment of Wolf Creek, which runs through the park, was named for a Cherokee princess who is buried in Stone Pile Gap, located at the junction of GA 60 and U.S. 19 some 9 miles north of Dahlonega.

Vogel is located 3 miles north of where the Appalachian Trail crosses U.S. 19 and U.S. 129 in Neel's Gap. It is here that the A.T. goes through a stone breezeway at the Walasi-Yi Cen-

ter—the only section of the 2,150-mile trail to go through a building.

CAMPING

The park features 95 tent and trailer sites with water and electrical hookups and 15 walk-in sites without amenities. There are three camping areas, each with a comfort station that includes hot showers and restrooms.

A pioneer camping area is available to organized groups by reservation. Additional shelters and privies are the only amenities.

COTTAGES

Vogel offers more cottages than any other park in the state, with 36 cottages scattered throughout the park. All of the one-, two- and three-bedroom cottages have fireplaces and HVAC and come with linens. The kitchens are equipped with cookware and utensils. No pets are allowed.

These cottages are particularly popular in the summer months. Reservations are accepted up to 11 months in advance.

HIKING

Vogel features four loop trails totaling more than 19 hiking miles.

The longest is Coosa Back-Country Trail at 12.7 miles, plus an extra mile if you want to hike to the top of Coosa Bald. Rated moderate to strenuous, it is more than a day-hike, and requires a permit for back-country camping. This trail begins at an elevation of 2,290 feet and climbs to 4,200 feet at its highest point.

The 4-mile Bear Hair Trail can be made into a 5-mile hike if you wish to make the side trip to an overlook. Like the other trails, it begins at 2,290 feet. It then climbs to 3,280 feet. If you make the trip to the overlook, you will be rewarded with a clear view down upon the park's Lake Trahlyta.

Byron Reece Nature Trail is an 0.6-mile loop that features interpretive signs about the natural features of the North Georgia forest. It is named for mountain farmer and poet Byron Reece, who once lived in the vicinity of the park.

Trahlyta Lake Trail, a 1-mile loop, offers an easy ramble around the shores of Lake Trahlyta. It features scenic wildlife, including Canada geese and other waterfowl.

PICNICKING

There are 65 picnic tables, four picnic shelters and one weatherized group shelter in the park. The picnic shelters may be reserved for a fee. They are available for free on a first-come, first-served basis when not reserved. The 75-person group shelter is heated. It offers an equipped kitchen, restrooms and a barbecue grill. It is available by reservation only.

TRAHLYTA LAKE

The lake is stocked with trout for bank fishing. No private boats are permitted on the 22-acre lake, but pedal boats may be rented.

The free swimming beach is open year-round.

No lifeguard is on duty, and swimming is at your own risk. The beach house is closed November through March.

OTHER FACILITIES

Vogel also offers a pavilion/theater, a miniature golf course and a playground.

ANNUAL EVENTS

A Wildflower Program in April and an Old Timers' Day in September are among Vogel's annual events. Mountain-music programs are offered at the pavilion. Check with the park office for a current schedule of events.

NEARBY ATTRACTIONS

Unicoi State Park
Dahlonega Gold Museum State Historic Site
Moccasin Creek State Park
Appalachian National Scenic Trail

DIRECTIONS

Vogel is located 11 miles south of Blairsville via U.S. 19/U.S. 129.

FOR MORE INFORMATION

Vogel State Park, 748 South Vogel State Park Road, Blairsville, GA 30152 (706-745-2628)

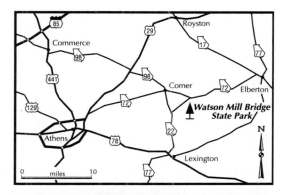

WATSON MILL BRIDGE STATE PARK

COMER   **785 ACRES**

NE CS

The activities at this park center around the picturesque bridge the park is named for. The 229-foot structure is the oldest remaining covered bridge in the state. Its four spans stretch across the South Fork River, one of the four main tributaries of the Broad River. The bridge's supporting structure, or truss, has lasted well over 100 years.

There are now fewer than 20 covered bridges remaining of the more than 200 that once dotted Georgia. This bridge was named after the old Watson gristmill, which was operated in the late 1800s by Gabriel Watson. The mill, which once housed a furniture shop on the bottom floor, has long since disappeared, but there is still evidence of the old hydroelectric plant fed by the river. The present dam and the raceway wall below the bridge were built in 1905 as part of the hydroelectric plant.

Watson Mill Bridge State Park features camping, swimming, picnicking, boating, hiking and horse trails.

CAMPING

The park has 21 tent and trailer sites with electrical and water hookups. The bathhouse in the camping area has hot showers, toilets, a washer and dryer and a soft-drink machine. There are also three pioneer camping areas for organized groups.

SWIMMING

The area near the mill bridge is a popular sunbathing and swimming spot in the summer. No lifeguards are on duty, however, so swimming is at your own risk.

BOATING AND FISHING

Rental canoes are available for use in the millpond. Private canoes are also permitted in the park. From spring through fall, the park offers guided canoe trips.

Fishing is permitted in the park's waters, but persons over 16 years of age must have a valid resident or nonresident fishing license.

OTHER FACILITIES

The park has 70 picnic tables and three picnic shelters. The shelters are available by reservation and on a first-come, first-served basis when not reserved. One of the shelters is screened-in and comes equipped with kitchen facilities and a barbecue pit; this shelter accommodates 90.

ANNUAL EVENT

A Candlelight Christmas Program is offered in December. Contact the park office for more information.

NEARBY ATTRACTION

Victoria Bryant State Park

DIRECTIONS

The park is 3 miles south of Comer off GA 22.

FOR MORE INFORMATION

Watson Mill Bridge State Park, Route 1, Box 190, Comer, GA 30629 (706-783-5349)

STATE HISTORIC SITES

This plain-style plantation house was built in 1847 by John Jarrell. Its front rooms once housed a general store, and for a few years, a post office.

T he thunder of the cannon's roar seems deafening. It commands the attention of everyone in earshot. Children, their fingers stuck in their ears to muffle the sound, smile and laugh. It's just another summer Saturday at Fort Morris on Georgia's "Colonial Coast."

Across the southern part of the state in Thomasville, a group quietly strolls through the Lapham-Patterson House with a guide, who points out its many odd angles and unique features.

Far to the north on the outskirts of Cartersville, a mother and daughter climb the more than 100 steps up the great temple mound and watch through the trees as the Etowah River drifts lazily by.

The 14 state historic sites offer a unique opportunity to explore Georgia's history. From Native American mounds, houses and towns through Georgia's Revolutionary and Civil War forts and battle sites to its plantations and farms, the historic sites interpret the state's rich history. The guides at the historic sites are very knowledgeable and often have interesting anecdotes to tell. This is especially true on the home tours, such as those of the Chief Vann House and Hofwyl-Broadfield Plantation.

School groups always take advantage of the audio-visual programs, and families will want to benefit from them, too. The slide shows or videos are usually 10- to 20-minute programs orienting visitors to the sites' history. They are good preparation for touring a museum or walking the grounds.

Many of the sites have living-history demonstrations and special educational programs. These are usually held in the summer months but sometimes coincide with a special season or date. The public information office of the Georgia Department of Natural Resources publishes a calendar of special events each March. Call 404-656-3530 to get the latest guide.

Sightseeing is the primary activity at historic sites, but several sites offer hiking trails as well. In fact, you won't see anything but the museum at Fort King George, Fort Morris, Hofwyl-Broadfield Plantation, Jarrell Plantation, the Little White House, New Echota, Pickett's Mill and Wormsloe unless you go for a walk. A hike of 0.2 mile to 1 mile is needed to see these sites. Most of the trails are handicapped-accessible. Picnicking is another popular activity at historic sites, with nine of the 14 sites and all of the state historic parks offering picnic tables.

All of the sites charge a fee for entry which is not covered by the Annual ParkPass offered for state parks. Fees vary from site to site. At the time this book went to press, the prices ranged from $1.50 to $4.00 for adults and from $.75 to

$2.00 for children five to 18 years of age. Children under the age of five are free. Special rates are available by reservation to organized groups of 15 or more people. An Annual Historic Site Pass is also available. In 1995, the pass cost $10 per adult and $8 per child, or $25 for a family of up to six people. This pass is valid for entry at the museums in A. H. Stephens, Fort McAllister and Kolomoki Mounds State Historic Parks. These historic sites within state parks should not be overlooked.

CHIEF VANN HOUSE STATE HISTORIC SITE
CHATSWORTH

Built of locally made brick in 1804, this home was known as "The Showplace of the Cherokee Nation." It was the residence of Chief James Vann, the son of Scotch trader Clement Vann and his wife, a Cherokee chieftain's daughter. Many of Vann's business ventures were in the vicinity of his Spring Place (now called

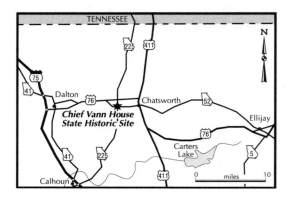

Chatsworth) home, as was much of the slave-tended land he owned. Vann was also the sponsor of Spring Place Mission.

A shrewd and amiable but violent man, Vann shot and killed his brother-in-law during a duel in 1808. In accordance with tribal law, Vann was in turn killed by the victim's relatives the following year. His son, Joseph, inherited the estate but was later expelled from Georgia. A charred floorboard on the landing is the lasting sign of a burning log thrown to smoke out "Rich Joe" Vann and a boarder, Spencer Riley, who tried to maintain their claim on the house.

Joseph Vann remade his fortune with a racehorse named Lucy Walker. He later wound up in Webber Falls, Oklahoma. Joseph built a replica of the Georgia home there, which was destroyed during the Civil War. He died while racing his steamboat, the *Lucy Walker*, on the Ohio River. The ship's boiler exploded near Louisville, Kentucky, in October 1844.

The Chief Vann House also experienced a turbulent history. After Joe Vann left, it went through 15 owners, but as it was often rental property, it had more than 50 tenants during the century after the Vanns were evicted. It finally fell into disrepair and was purchased by a group from Atlanta, Dalton and Chatsworth in 1952. The group deeded the historic home to the Georgia Historical Commission. In time, it was restored and was dedicated as a state historic site in 1958. It now serves as a monument to the Cherokee culture.

CHIEF VANN HOUSE TODAY

The entire house is included on the tour, from

The "Showplace of the Cherokee Nation" endured more than 50 residents in the century after the Vanns left, before it was restored to its former glory.

The dining room at the Chief Vann House. A large portrait of "Rich Joe" Vann hangs over the mantel.

the basement to the third-floor children's rooms. A showcase in the main hallway contains Joseph Vann's violin and other artifacts. There are prints of 19th-century American Indian leaders over the showcase. A small souvenir area in the hall offers T-shirts, postcards and other gifts.

On the grounds is a cabin, now used as an office, which was moved to this site in 1956.

There are handicapped-accessible restrooms near the parking lot.

The site is open Tuesday through Saturday from 9:00 A.M. to 5:00 P.M. and Sunday from 2:00 P.M. to 5:30 P.M. It is closed on Thanksgiving, Christmas and New Year's and on Mondays except for legal holidays. A small fee is charged.

NEARBY ATTRACTIONS

New Echota State Historic Site
Fort Mountain State Park
Chattahoochee National Forest

DIRECTIONS

The house is on the edge of Chatsworth at the intersection of GA 52 and GA 225.

FOR MORE INFORMATION

Chief Vann House State Historic Site, 82 GA 225 North, Chatsworth, GA 30705 (706-695-2598)

DAHLONEGA GOLD MUSEUM STATE HISTORIC SITE
DAHLONEGA

Gold was discovered in this area by Benjamin Parks in 1828, beginning the nation's first notable gold rush. At the time, the area was Cherokee territory, but gold quickly changed that. The nearby town of Nuckollsville became a boom

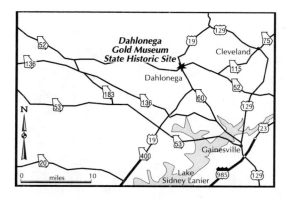

town and was soon renamed Auraria, meaning "gold," by Senator John C. Calhoun, who owned the Calhoun Mine. The county seat was moved to Dahlonega in December 1833. The town's name comes from the Cherokee word *Tahlonega,* or "golden."

Between 1829 and 1839, $20 million in gold was mined in the immediate vicinity. A United States branch mint was built here in 1838 and operated until 1861. During that time, it minted more than $6 million in gold coins.

The courthouse that the museum is housed in was built in 1836 to replace a log building used the previous four years. From the steps of the courthouse in 1849, Dr. M. F. Stephenson, assayer for the mint, gave a speech to convince miners not to leave for the California gold rush. His oration was not convincing enough to keep most of them on.

The 30-minute film *Gold Fever* is shown upstairs throughout the day. It does an excellent job of both giving the facts and figures about the gold rush and capturing the emotional side of being struck by "gold fever." The seats in the

theater were once seats for the courthouse, which met in the same room.

Photos and exhibits including gold nuggets weighing as much as five ounces help interpret the story of this gold-rush town. The museum is open year-round Monday to Saturday from 9 A.M. to 5 P.M. and Sunday from 10 A.M. to 5 P.M. except for Thanksgiving, Christmas and New Year's.

NEARBY ATTRACTIONS

Amicalola Falls State Park and Lodge
Chattahoochee National Forest
Unicoi State Park and Lodge
Vogel State Park

DIRECTIONS

The museum is located in the center of the public square in Dahlonega.

FOR MORE INFORMATION

Dahlonega Gold Museum State Historic Site, Public Square, Box 2042, Dahlonega, GA 30533 (706-864-2257)

ETOWAH INDIAN MOUNDS STATE HISTORIC SITE
CARTERSVILLE

In the year 1817, the Reverend Elias Cornelius was exploring the wilderness along the Etowah

The top of the temple mound steps lends a view of Mound B, a lower temple platform, with the Etowah River in the background.

River with eight Cherokee Indians when he nearly stumbled into a "ditch." Astounded that it was nearly 20 feet wide and 10 feet deep, the missionary was told that the ditch extended all the way to the river.

Cornelius noted in his journal that he did not have to wonder long where the dirt from the ditch had gone: "I had scarcely proceeded 200 yards when, through the thick forest trees, a stupendous pile met the eye, whose dimension were in full proportion to the entrenchment."

The flat-topped earthen mounds of the Etowah Indians offer a commanding view of the Etowah River Valley and the river as it winds its way to the north and west. Standing atop the great temple mound, already overgrown

when Cornelius discovered it 300 years after the last Indian left the village, it is easy to imagine the thriving Indian community that farmed the valley for more than 500 years. The land lying below and most of the mound have been cleared

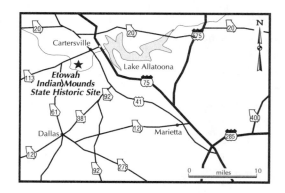

and appear much as they did from 1000 A.D. to 1500 A.D., when the Etowahs lived here.

Using a muscadine vine as a surveyor's chain, Cornelius measured the mound at not less than 75 feet in height and 1,114 feet in circumference. Close. Today, the official height is 63 feet. Some 4.3 million cubic feet of earth make up the great temple mound, better known as Mound A.

Etowah Indian Mounds is a well-restored Indian site made up of three large mounds, four small mounds, a plaza and a defensive moat. The moat—which Cornelius nearly stumbled into— once stretched from riverbank to riverbank in a half-moon that encased the village. Enclosing 52 acres of river bottom, the nine- to 10-foot- deep moat was the community's first line of defense. If an attacker made it across the moat, he then faced a 12-foot palisade complete with bastions that projected over the moat and allowed the Indians to repel their attackers with spears and arrows while firing from a safe distance.

Inside the palisade, the Indians' homes were scattered in order to protect against accidental fires and flaming arrows. The Etowahs carted red clay to the center of the compound to construct their ceremonial plaza, which was similar to a town square.

To the west were three large mounds.

The largest, more than six stories tall, was the temple mound, where the chief-priest presided over town ceremonies. This mound has never been excavated because other Mississippian sites have shown that temple mounds rarely have any significant burials or interior structures.

The second mound, a temple mound located at the edge of the plaza, was only partially excavated. The test pit turned up burials as well as trash pits, which included the remains of deer, turtles, plants and fish.

The third mound, to the west of the second mound and south of the great temple mound, was the Indians' burial mound. It was completely excavated and restored by archaeologists, who discovered 350 burials that taught much about burial practices, classes of people within the community, dress, diet, diseases, trade patterns and ceremonial practices. This mound was not only built up in layers but featured changes in the structure of its temples and fences and in its burial practices. The site's famous marble statues were discovered near the bottom of this mound. Most of the museum's artifacts were extracted from this mound as well. They include shell beads, copper ear ornaments and ceremonial objects made of stone, wood, seashells and copper.

At times when the river is low (when the Allatoona hydroelectric plant is not generating), you can see the restored fish trap and gravel shoals. Fish traps were built of piled stones, and woven baskets were used at the point of the V- shaped trap to catch gar, drum and catfish.

A walk along the river trail will show you the walnut, hickory and persimmon trees that provided sustenance for the Indians. The Etowah Indians used the river cane for arrow shafts, thatch roofs, baskets and mats for walls and floors. The privet, honeysuckle and mimosa here were introduced by Europeans.

Etowah and other similar Mississippian sites have taught archaeologists much about the history of the mound-building Indians, particularly the fact that their culture was largely based around warfare, up to and including their religion. The moat at Etowah was important because the village was nearly constantly at war with other Indian communities. The demise of the Mississippian culture, on the other hand, remains a mystery. A change in climate? A decline in power? Epidemics? Constant warfare? All these are possibilities. Archaeologists admit that the more they learn about the Mississippian culture, which flourished from 900 to 1540 A.D., the less they know and the more questions are raised.

Etowah Indian Mounds State Historic Site offers a fascinating look into the past. The museum offers a video program on the history of the site and very detailed exhibits about the site itself. The site is open year-round Tuesday to Saturday from 9:00 A.M. to 5:00 P.M. and Sunday from 2:00 P.M. to 5:30 P.M. except for Thanksgiving, Christmas and New Year's.

NEARBY ATTRACTIONS

Allatoona Lake
Red Top Mountain State Park and Lodge
Pickett's Mill Battlefield State Historic Site

DIRECTIONS

The mounds are 5 miles southwest of Exit 124 off I-75.

FOR MORE INFORMATION

Etowah Indian Mounds State Historic Site, 813 Indian Mounds Road S.W., Cartersville, GA 30120 (404-387-3747)

FORT KING GEORGE STATE HISTORIC SITE
DARIEN

This ill-fated fort once marked the southern end of the British Empire in the New World. Though attacks from the Spanish and the Indians were a constant threat, it was sickness that took two-thirds of the soldiers stationed at this lonely outpost on the English frontier.

Before the British took an interest in the New World, this site was a Guale Indian settlement. A Spanish mission was built here in the late 1500s, but both the Indians and the Spanish had abandoned the area by the end of the 17th century.

It was Colonel John "Tuscarora Jack" Barnwell who convinced the English Board of Trade to establish a fort at the mouth of the Altamaha

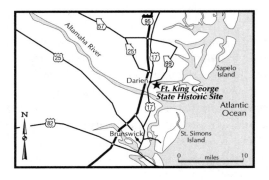

River. The fort's purpose was to establish British dominion in an area under threat from the Spanish to the south and the French and Indians to the west.

In 1721, a small European-style field fort was built to stand guard over the river. The triangular earthworks and cypress-planked blockhouse were surrounded by a moat and a log palisade. The fort was named in honor of King George I. Barnwell was placed in command of the troops from His Majesty's Independent Company, made up of battle-scarred veterans of England's other foreign conquests. He had to use a group of Provincial Scouts from South Carolina to cut the four-inch-thick boards and construct the fort.

With the fort built and the invalid regiment on guard, the fortification's real enemies—boredom and sickness—attacked in force. Alcoholism and disease took their toll, and one of the

Fort King George was rebuilt in 1988 from plans in the British Public Records Office of London.

A cannon looks out from a window in the reconstructed Fort King George.

oldest British military cemeteries in the Southeast began to grow alongside Fort King George. Though the Spanish demanded the fort be abandoned and the Indians constantly threatened full attack, neither threat was responsible for more than a few of the 140 burials alongside the marsh.

In 1726, the fort accidentally burned to the ground. A new fort with thin planks replaced the original barracks buildings, but the British moved the garrison to Port Royal to better protect the area's plantations from raids. For the next 10 years, Fort King George was manned by two soldiers, who served only as lookouts.

After Darien was founded by Scots in 1736, the fort was occupied by Highland Scots, who soon built Fort Darien on Altamaha Bluff. These Scots provided the main thrust for the assault that repelled the Spanish at the Battle of Bloody Marsh on St. Simons Island. The Highland Scots also brought golf to the colony, setting up Georgia's first golf course in Darien in the 1730s.

Sawmills later became Darien's prime business. The town was one of the largest timber-exporting ports in the Southeast. The remains of three sawmills can be seen at the historic site.

THE MUSEUM

The Guale, Spanish and British presence on the coast, the Highland Scots and Darien's sawmills are all interpreted in the Fort King George Museum. The video shown in a building adjoining the museum complements the museum's displays and explains the area's historical significance.

The museum and site are open Tuesday to Saturday from 9:00 A.M. to 5:00 P.M. and Sunday from 2:00 P.M. to 5:30 P.M. They are closed Mondays (except for some legal holidays), Thanksgiving, Christmas and New Year's.

THE FORT

In 1988, the state of Georgia used the original plans found in the British Public Records Office to reconstruct the cypress blockhouse to its original specifications using precolonial construction methods. The ground floor was used to store powder and ammunition, the second floor was a gun room with cannon ports and the third floor was used by lookouts to keep an eye on the river. Though no longer in existence, an enlisted man's barracks and an officer's house were located inside the compound.

Living-history programs presented throughout the year give insight into 18th-century clothing, equipment and life. Cannon firings are presented on the second and fourth Saturdays of the month, weather and crew permitting.

WALKING TOUR

A brochure available in the museum interprets the self-guided walking tour of the fort area. Among the seven sites on the tour are the tabby ruins of an antebellum house, a Spanish mission, Indian village sites, a British cemetery and the millpond. The alligator in the millpond, named Wally by the staff, is wild. Do not feed the alligator or walk close to him.

Not on the tour is a nature trail that circles from the fort through the marsh and back to the museum. It can be combined with the trail to the fort for a loop hike.

ANNUAL EVENTS

Two reenactments, nature programs and the Fort King George Christmas celebration are among the site's annual events. Contact the site office for information on historical reenactments and other events.

NEARBY ATTRACTIONS

Hofwyl-Broadfield Plantation State Historic Site
Harris Neck National Wildlife Refuge
Jekyll Island
Fort Frederica National Monument

DIRECTIONS

The site is on Fort King George Drive in Darien, 3 miles east of Exit 10 off I-95.

FOR MORE INFORMATION

Fort King George State Historic Site, P.O. Box 711, Darien, GA 31305 (912-437-4770)

FORT MORRIS STATE HISTORIC SITE
SUNBURY

This earthwork fortification was given three different names by the English and the colonists

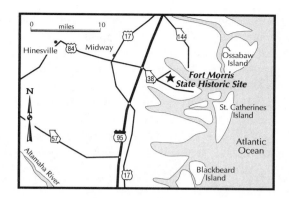

who fought for control of Georgia during the Revolutionary War and the War of 1812. But this site was of historical significance before the fort was first built. When the Spanish arrived in the 1600s, a Guale Indian settlement was located here. The Spanish built a mission on nearby St. Catherines Island. But both the Spanish and the Guale Indians were just a memory when General James Oglethorpe held the first Masonic meeting in the colony of Georgia here on February 21, 1734.

In 1757, a small battery was built on the fort site. A year later, the town of Sunbury was founded on the north side. The town soon became a thriving port, due in part to the deep natural channel on the Medway River, which flowed past the town. In 1760, a log fort was built at this site to protect residents from Indian attack.

Sunbury became home to Lyman Hall, a signer of the Declaration of Independence and a governor of Georgia. Hall was present in 1776 when the Continental Congress voted to create a fortification at Sunbury to protect the port from British attack.

Fort Morris, named for Captain Morris, who commanded an artillery company at the fort, was built on high ground along the river. From here, artillery could sweep a ship with cannon fire before it came broadside of the fort. Like most pre-19th-century fortifications in the United States, it was an earthwork structure.

When the fort fell to the British during the Revolution, it was renamed Fort George. During the War of 1812, Fort Defiance was built on the remains of the earlier fort. Though this historic site is named Fort Morris, the earthworks you see today are what is left of Fort Defiance.

No fortifications were built here during the Civil War. The trees on the site have grown up in the years since the fort was last manned.

MUSEUM

Both the town of Sunbury and the fort itself are interpreted in the museum. An audio-visual presentation explains Georgia's role in the Revolutionary War. The museum is open Tuesday through Saturday from 9:00 A.M. to 5:00 P.M. and Sunday from 9:30 A.M. to 5:30 P.M. The museum is closed Mondays (except for some legal holidays), Thanksgiving, Christmas and New Year's.

BLACKSMITH SHOP

In 1994 and early 1995, the Friends of Fort Morris built a blacksmith shop to use in presenting living-history demonstrations. Two blacksmiths have volunteered to present the demonstrations using authentic tools and techniques. This new area operates in addition to the regular schedule of cannon firings and Revolutionary War–era living-history demonstrations at Fort Morris. Contact the site office for more information on these programs.

CAMPING

A primitive camping area with a fine view of St. Catherines Sound is available to organized groups for a small fee. Pit toilets and a spigot with drinking water were the only amenities at the time of this writing, but a three-sided Adirondack-style shelter was planned to be built during 1995.

ANNUAL EVENTS

Revolutionary War reenactments in October and the Christmas 1776 celebration, held in December, are among the historic site's regularly scheduled events.

NEARBY ATTRACTIONS

Fort McAllister State Historic Park
Fort King George State Historic Site
Harris Neck National Wildlife Refuge
Skidaway Island State Park

DIRECTIONS

Fort Morris is 7 miles east of Exit 13 off I-95 via GA 38.

Fort Morris State Historic Site, Route 1, Box 236, Midway, GA 31320 (912-884-5999)

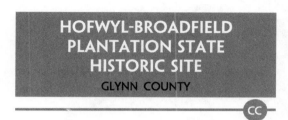

HOFWYL-BROADFIELD PLANTATION STATE HISTORIC SITE
GLYNN COUNTY

Five generations of Brailsfords, Troups and Dents farmed this Altamaha plantation until it was turned over to the Nature Conservancy at the death of the last surviving family member in 1973.

Broadface was purchased by William Brailsford of Charleston, South Carolina, in 1807 and was soon renamed Broadfield. Before cotton was king, Brailsford and his contemporaries farmed the coastal Georgia and South Carolina lowlands, growing rice in the richly silted soil. The virgin cypress swamps were per-

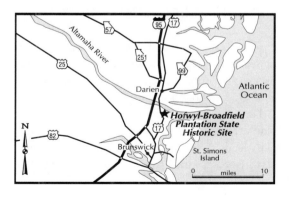

fect for rice but deadly for those who worked the land. The owners, transplanted Europeans, were forced to leave the lowlands from April through September, relying on slave labor to see that the process of growing rice continued.

Brailsford's son-in-law, James M. Troup, acquired additional land along the Altamaha River. By the time of his death, Broadfield Plantation consisted of 7,300 acres of land, 357 slaves and several homes.

The family fled to a refugee camp near Waycross to wait out the Civil War. In the aftermath of the war, the plantation began to fail. Not only did labor have to be paid for, but many of the freed slaves were no longer interested in toiling under the grueling heat of the Georgia sun for any price. Rice plantations from Charleston southward began to fail. The only positive aspect of the Civil War was that somehow Federal troops missed the simple plantation house and the accumulated treasure—at the time, mostly of sentimental value—that filled its airy rooms.

Today, the 1790s Charleston Rice Bed is one of only a few remaining.

Although the former Broadfield slaves were generally loyal to the homeowners here, there was just too much to be done. The plantation struggled on for another 50 years, but by the time Miriam and Ophelia Dent took over in 1915, the growing of rice was no longer even close to profitable. It was at this time that Miriam and Ophelia, with the help of Gratz Dent, converted Hofwyl-Broadfield Plantation into Hofwyl Dairy, the estate having picked up the name at an earlier date in honor of a school in Switzerland.

An immense live oak dominates the pasture at Hofwyl-Broadfield Plantation State Historic Site.

For the next 30 years, the dairy was operated by Miriam and Ophelia, neither of whom ever married. Gratz, who did marry, moved to Savannah and died at the age of 50 without an heir. Ownership of his portion of the estate reverted to his sisters. It was Hofwyl Dairy that supplied milk to the Millionaires' Club on Jekyll Island, and the sisters often entertained the club's members at Hofwyl-Broadfield. Bird hunting was popular, and the sisters were comfortable taking aim alongside DuPonts, Rockefellers, Morgans and Astors. Author Margaret Mitchell also spent many an hour in the company of Ophelia and Miriam.

The dairy closed in 1942, with the plantation once again solvent. Following the death of her sister, Ophelia lived out her remaining years at Hofwyl-Broadfield. Upon her death in 1973, the estate was turned over to the Nature Conservancy, which in turn granted it to the state of Georgia.

HOFWYL-BROADFIELD TODAY

The visitor center at the plantation offers a museum and a 1994 film that provides wonderful background information on Hofwyl-Broadfield, as well as firsthand accounts of plantation life.

There is a 1-mile loop trail that passes the plantation house. From the visitor center, the path leads through a pasture where cows graze and live oaks with Spanish moss add to the bucolic atmosphere. On the way to the house, visitors pass the bottling house, the dairy barn, the commissary, the pay shed and the servant quarters. Visitors can pay a fee for a guided tour to get a firsthand look at what it was to reside in a plantation house. Five generations of Troup and Dents lived in this home, built in 1851. Although the house has seen minor renovations throughout the years, very little has changed since it was built. Even the furniture is much as it looked when Federal troops sailed past the silent estate more than a century ago.

From the house, you can see the former rice fields, now a freshwater marsh, extending toward tree-lined Dent Creek and the Altamaha River beyond. Behind the house is a breezeway that connects to the kitchen and butler's pantry; heat and the possibility of fire necessitated detached kitchens in Southern plantation homes. Adjacent to the house are a laundry room, a doghouse, an icehouse, a laundry yard and a garage.

The trail continues through the pasture toward the marsh. Note the bat boxes hanging from some trees. These wonderful creatures help wage war against the ever-present insects. The nature trail takes you past the ruins of the rice mill and along an old rice dike to an observation deck. From here, you can see the old rice-boat canal at high tide.

ANNUAL EVENTS

The plantation features events centered around Black History Month in February and the Plantation Christmas celebration in December. Contact the site office for more information.

The kitchen at Hofwyl-Broadfield Plantation is well stocked with vintage cookware.

NEARBY ATTRACTIONS

St. Simon's Island
Fort King George State Historic Site
Fort Frederica National Monument
Cumberland Island National Seashore

DIRECTIONS

From Exit 9 off I-95, go 1 mile east on GA 99, then turn right on U.S. 17. The plantation is 200 yards south, on the left.

FOR MORE INFORMATION

Hofwyl-Broadfield Plantation State Historic Site, 5556 U.S. 17N, Brunswick, GA 31525 (912-264-7333)

JARRELL PLANTATION STATE HISTORIC SITE
JONES COUNTY

HH

A desk inside John Jarrell's 1847 home. Part of the residence would later be run by his daughter Mattie as a general store and, for a few years, a post office.

This homestead was founded in 1847 by John Jarrell, who built the simple plantation home on the property. By the start of the Civil War, he had built up the cotton plantation to 600 acres, worked by 39 slaves. The original home was lived in until 1957, when John's daughter Mattie died. Almost all of the many pieces in the house are original. One room was used for many years as a general store, run by Mattie.

She also operated a post office out of the house for three years.

John Jarrell's son B. R. "Dick" Jarrell diversified the plantation with a gristmill, a sawmill and other enterprises. By the time the boll weevil and the Depression dealt a death blow to cotton as king of the crops, it didn't hurt the Jarrells as severely as other farmers.

A second home on the property was built by Dick Jarrell in 1895. The two front rooms were a family room and a sleeping area for Dick, his wife, Mamie, and their 12 children (nine of whom lived to adulthood). The back wing was used for cooking and eating. Like the first Jarrell home, it contains numerous furnishings and belongings original to the house.

The third Jarrell residence, built in 1920 by Dick Jarrell, is not within the historic site. This 10-room home is still owned by a Jarrell descendent. Although not open to the public, it can be seen from the tour.

In addition to the Jarrell homes, there are 18 barns, sheds and outbuildings on the site. With all their equipment and furnishings, these buildings give a unique glimpse into a self-sufficient farm. Here, family members operated a steam-powered gristmill, a sawmill, a cotton gin, a syrup mill and a planer. The family's spinning wheels, looms and cobbler's bench attest to the history of making clothes and shoes on the farm. This heritage is highlighted during the 100 Years of Jarrell Clothing Display, held for a month each year. The display of homemade clothes culminates with a sheepshearing, spinning and weaving demonstration.

Other buildings on the plantation include a

A chicken peers through a piece of fence at Jarrell Plantation State Historic Site, which houses a unique collection of original furnishings, clothing, and farm equipment.

three-story barn and a chicken house, both built in 1912. The "smokehouse," built in 1909, was actually used to salt meat, using salt the family boiled out of seawater.

Some of the Jarrells' 600 acres were bought for part of the adjoining Piedmont National Wildlife Refuge. The plantation was a working farm until 1965. The Jarrell family donated the 50-acre site to the state in 1974.

JARRELL PLANTATION TODAY

The visitor center, built in 1989, offers a seven-minute slide show and displays to orient visitors to the site. A brochure is available for a self-guided tour of the plantation's many buildings. If you would like additional information, there are several three-ring binders with a more detailed tour inside. These binders must be returned after being used for the tour.

Along the 0.5-mile self-guided tour, you can see inside the family's first two residences and pass by the third house. Almost all of the other buildings can be toured as well. Fortunately, the state has kept the farm much as it was when the Jarrells worked it. But because of this, there are many areas with steep steps and slippery slopes.

The site is open Tuesday through Saturday from 9:00 A.M. to 5:00 P.M. and Sunday from 2:00 P.M. to 5:30 P.M. It is open Mondays for some legal holidays but is closed on Tuesday when open on Monday. The site is also closed on Thanksgiving, Christmas and New Year's. A small admission fee is charged. Group rates are available with advance notice.

ANNUAL EVENTS

The 100 Years of Jarrell Clothing Display in March, the Fourth of July Celebration, Family Farm Day and Christmas Candlelight Tours are among the site's annual events.

NEARBY ATTRACTIONS

Piedmont National Wildlife Refuge
High Falls State Park
Indian Springs State Park

DIRECTIONS

From Exit 60 off I-75, it is 18 miles on GA 18 to the historic site. If you are coming by way of Macon, take Exit 55 off I-75; from Exit 55, follow the signs 18 miles to the site.

FOR MORE INFORMATION

Jarrell Plantation State Historic Site, Route 2, Box 220, Juliette, GA 31046-9623 (912-986-5172)

LAPHAM-PATTERSON HOUSE STATE HISTORIC SITE
THOMASVILLE

"Half a bubble off plumb" is an expression used to describe someone who isn't quite right. That description also fits the Lapham-Patterson House. It's not that the Queen Anne–style "cot-

There are no right angles in the Lapham-Patterson House in Thomasville, Georgia.

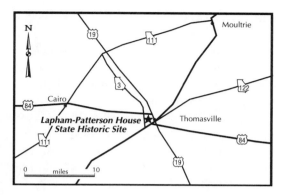

tage" isn't beautiful or well built. It's just that there aren't any right angles anywhere in this extraordinary house.

To understand why, you need to know about C. W. Lapham, the Chicago shoe merchant who had this house built in 1884 and 1885. Lapham was a survivor of the Great Chicago Fire, which left his lungs damaged. Later in life, his doctor suggested that wintering in the South could improve his health. Due to its convenient loca-

tion at the end of a rail line, Thomasville was a popular resort town at the turn of the century, with Northerners seeking mild weather and the supposed therapeutic benefits of the pine air. (For more information on the history of the area, visit the Thomas County Historical Society Museum, located a half-block from the historic site.)

Queen Anne houses, popular at the time, often featured asymmetrical elements, but Lapham carried it to an extreme. The belief commonly held was that right angles were unnatural. Asymmetrical angles and corners were supposed to be better for air circulation—and consequently for your health. Note, for example, that no two sides of the hexagonal dining room of the Lapham-Patterson House are equal in length.

The cottage also bears clear marks of having been designed by a fire survivor. Each room has a door to the outside. There were also fire extinguishers in every room. The unique double-flue chimney with a walk-thru stairway and cantilevered balcony is safer in a chimney fire than a single-flue chimney. The house was ahead of its time in other ways as well. It was built with gas lighting, hot and cold running water, indoor toilets upstairs and downstairs and closets in the bedrooms. Unlike many homes of the time, the kitchen was attached to the house; during winter, the heat from the kitchen was beneficial to the cottage.

After just nine years, Lapham sold the house in 1894 to a family who never used it. It was bought in 1905 by James G. Patterson. The house remained in the Patterson family until it was sold to the city of Thomasville in 1970 for $18,000. The city gave the house to the state for use as a historic site. It was named a National Historic Landmark in 1975.

Today, the house is decorated with furniture from the 1880s to the 1920s. A number of pieces are original to the house.

ANNUAL EVENTS

The Rose Show in April and the Victorian Christmas celebration each December are among the site's annual events. There is also the annual Quilt Show and the popular Evening of Edgar Allan Poe.

HOURS

The site is open year-round Tuesday to Saturday from 9:00 A.M. to 5:00 P.M. and Sunday from 2:00 P.M. to 5:30 P.M. It is closed Mondays (except some legal holidays), Thanksgiving, Christmas and New Year's. Tours are given on the hour from 9:00 A.M. to 4:00 P.M. and last approximately 45 minutes.

NEARBY ATTRACTION

Seminole State Park

DIRECTIONS

The Lapham-Patterson House is located at 636 North Dawson Street in Thomasville.

FOR MORE INFORMATION

Lapham-Patterson House State Historic Site, 626 North Dawson Street, Thomasville, GA 31792 (912-225-4004)

LITTLE WHITE HOUSE STATE HISTORIC SITE
WARM SPRINGS

In 1924, Franklin Delano Roosevelt made his first trip to Warm Springs seeking relief from the polio that had struck him three years ear-

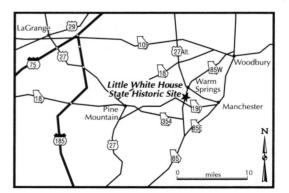

lier. Over the next 21 years, Roosevelt made 41 visits to the community of 500. In 1932, he built the Little White House as a refuge from the pressures of Washington. The house has been preserved as he left it when he died here of a stroke in 1945. The *Unfinished Portrait*, which was being painted when he died, still sits in the living room near the chair the president was posing in.

The adjoining guesthouse and garage/servant quarters are also open for tours. In the garage is Roosevelt's 1938 Ford convertible roadster, equipped with hand controls. The president used the car to visit neighboring Meriwether County farms and towns.

MUSEUM

The Walk of the States is lined with flags and native stones from each of the 50 states and the District of Columbia. It leads up to a museum. Inside are numerous photographs and mementos from FDR's presidency. A 12-minute film, *A Warm Springs Memoir of Franklin Delano Roosevelt*, uses newsreel footage and rare home movies to tell the story of the president's visits to the area.

ANNUAL EVENTS

FDR's birthday on January 30, his wedding anniversary on March 17, the commemoration of his death on April 12, and a Warm Springs Thanksgiving are among the annual events. Contact the historic site for more information.

HOURS

The site and the museum are open from 9:00 A.M. to 5:00 P.M. daily, with the last full tour beginning at 4:15 P.M. The park is open year-round except for Thanksgiving and Christmas.

NEARBY ATTRACTIONS

Franklin Delano Roosevelt State Park
Callaway Gardens

DIRECTIONS

The Little White House is 0.25 mile south of Warm Springs on GA 85W.

FOR MORE INFORMATION

Little White House State Historic Site, Route 1, Box 10, Warm Springs, GA 31830 (706-655-5870)

NEW ECHOTA STATE HISTORIC SITE
CALHOUN

Established as the capital of the Cherokee nation on November 12, 1825, New Echota became the headquarters for the small, independent Indian nation that once spread across northern Georgia into western North Carolina, eastern Tennessee and northeastern Alabama.

The printing press and other newspaper gear are on display in the reconstructed office of the *Cherokee Phoenix*. It is among several buildings to see at New Echota, the former captial of the Cherokee Nation.

By the time New Echota was established, the Cherokees had already patterned their government after that of the United States. The principal meeting place of their legislative branch from 1819 on was the council house at New Town, which became New Echota.

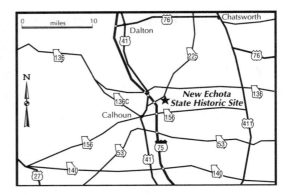

It was at New Echota that Sequoyah's Cherokee alphabet, with syllables represented by symbols, was first put to use. Sequoyah was born George Guest (or Gist). As an honor, his Cherokee name was given to the redwood tree. The first issue of the *Cherokee Phoenix*, a newspaper in English and Cherokee, was printed on February 21, 1828, in the print shop at New Echota. The paper was published until 1834.

By 1828, New Echota boasted a national newspaper and printing office, a legislative hall, a supreme courthouse serving the entire Cherokee nation, a mission station and several dwellings and commercial establishments. Following the westward removal of the Cherokees along the Trail of Tears in 1838–39, the capital, which had served as a center for the removal activity, fell into disuse. The buildings were torn down and the land was parceled off for farming. The actual site of the capital was eventually lost from knowledge. The missionary's home became known as the Boudinot House, after the editor of the *Cherokee Phoenix*.

In the early 1950s, some residents of Calhoun initiated the events that led to the restoration of New Echota. The site was located and 200 acres donated to the state of Georgia. Excavations and research led to the rebuilding and restoration of the capital's buildings. Today, you can tour the courthouse, the council house, the print shop, the Boudinot House site, the Worcester House and more.

In the vicinity of the New Echota site is the New Echota Cemetery, which includes the marked graves of Pathkiller and Harriet Gold Boudinot. Pathkiller was the principal chief of the Cherokee nation until his death in 1827. He was also a colonel during the War of 1812. Mrs. Boudinot was the wife of Elias Boudinot, the editor of New Echota's *Cherokee Phoenix*. The cemetery also contains the grave of Jerusha Worcester, the infant daughter of Samuel and Ann Worcester, missionaries at New Echota.

New Echota is on Chieftains Trail, a 150-mile-long loop drive that connects seven primary attractions that tell the story of the Native Americans who once lived in northwest Georgia. Inquire at the information desk for more information.

HIKING

A 30- to 45-minute self-guided tour leads through the many buildings at the site, including the *Cherokee Phoenix* office and the legislative hall. There is also a 1-mile nature trail near the Worcester House.

MUSEUM

The museum features interpretive displays on the history of New Echota, the Trail of Tears and the Cherokee nation. There is also a short film on these subjects. Guided tours are available on Saturday and Sunday.

The site and the museum are open from 9:00 A.M. to 5:00 P.M. Tuesday through Saturday and from 2:00 P.M. to 5:30 P.M. Sunday. The site and the museum are closed on Mondays, Thanksgiving and Christmas.

NEARBY ATTRACTIONS

Chief Vann House State Historic Site
Fort Mountain State Park
Chattahoochee National Forest

DIRECTIONS

New Echota is located on GA 225 approximately 1 mile east of I-75 near Calhoun. Take Exit 131.

FOR MORE INFORMATION

New Echota State Historic Site, 1211 Chatsworth Highway, Calhoun, GA 30701 (706-629-8151)

PICKETT'S MILL BATTLEFIELD STATE HISTORIC SITE
DALLAS

If General Sherman could have controlled history, the battle of Pickett's Mill would have been forgotten. Though 1,600 Union men died in intense fighting in the cornfield and the thick woods near the mill, the general mentioned the fight in neither his official reports nor his memoirs. The loss was an embarrassment to the Union army that the general chose to ignore.

On May 25, 1864, the Union army's march to Atlanta was interrupted by the Battle of New Hope Church. Two days later, General O. O. Howard was sent with 14,000 men to outflank the Confederates. After a grueling five-hour march, they found the Confederate flank near Pickett's Mill. The weary Federals attacked the well-rested 10,000 men under General Patrick Cleburne, and a fierce battle ensued. Due to poor communication, the Union army's two

brigades left in reserve did not make it into battle when they were sorely needed.

Darkness fell with the armies still too close for comfort. The Confederates launched a night assault that successfully pushed the Union troops back. The next morning dawned on 1,600 Union and 500 Confederate soldiers lying dead in the fields and woods, while spring wildflowers bloomed oblivious to the carnage.

VISITOR CENTER

This new historic site benefits from current technology. There is a large-screen 17-minute laser-disk presentation orienting visitors to the site. The museum has a number of displays depicting people and events at the site. An innovative multimedia game called "Take Command" uses a touch screen to allow visitors to command Union forces at Pickett's Mill. Visitors can keep brigades in reserve, plan their attack and change tactics based on reconnaissance. At the end of the day's action, they are ranked according to their success. As is fitting for a war game, the outcome is not always the same, as the program uses random variables to determine success or failure.

A variety of educational talks, walks and demonstrations is offered at this site. There is a living-history program on the first and third weekends of each month. Call the office for a current list of events.

The site is open Tuesday to Saturday from 9:00 A.M. to 5:00 P.M. and Sunday from 2:00 P.M. to 5:30 P.M. It is closed Thanksgiving, Christmas, New Year's and Mondays (except for some

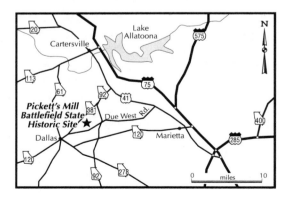

legal holidays). A small admission fee is charged. A group rate is available to organized groups by reservation only.

HIKING

There are three loop trails you may use to tour the battlefield and see the remains of the mill. The loops are 1.1, 1.5 and 1.7 miles long. Brochures available at the visitor center interpret the hikes with natural and historic information. The brochures must be turned back in after your hike, as a limited number are available. Groups may arrange guided tours of the site by calling at least two weeks in advance for a reservation.

GROUP SHELTER

The screened shelter has plexiglass panels to allow heating for year-round use. The shelter accommodates up to 175 people. It is equipped with a small kitchen, restrooms, a fireplace and a barbecue pit. The shelter is available by reservation only; a fee is charged.

ANNUAL EVENT

The Battle of Pickett's Mill Commemoration, held in May, is the site's main annual event.

NEARBY ATTRACTIONS

Kennesaw Mountain National Battlefield Park
Red Top Mountain State Park and Lodge
Allatoona Lake
Etowah Indian Mounds State Historic Site

DIRECTIONS

The site is 5 miles northeast of Dallas off GA 381 on Mount Tabor Road.

FOR MORE INFORMATION

Pickett's Mill Battlefield State Historic Site, 2640 Mount Tabor Road, Dallas, GA 30132 (404-443-7850)

ROBERT TOOMBS HOUSE STATE HISTORIC SITE
WASHINGTON

CS

Erected between 1794 and 1801, this home was purchased and remodeled by Robert Toombs in 1837. It features two-story Doric columns adorning the veranda and French windows that lead into high-ceilinged rooms. This home was in the Toombs family for more than a century and is now owned by the state. A museum downstairs includes historical exhibits; a film

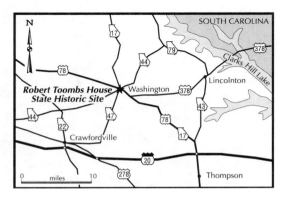

featuring an actor portraying Toombs can also be viewed during the tour. Renovations are taking place that will eventually restore the home to its former glory. The second floor has already been completed and furnished in the style of Robert Toombs's time.

Robert Augustus Toombs was born in Wilkes County in 1810 and later moved to the county seat of Washington, Georgia. After graduating from Union College in Schenectady, New York, Toombs established a law practice that was interrupted by half a dozen terms in the Georgia legislature. He was elected to the United States House of Representatives in 1844 and was influential in passing the compromise acts of 1850, which helped to ease the unrest in the South caused by the Wilmot Proviso. He became a United States senator in 1853 and later advocated secession.

He was appointed secretary of state for the Confederacy but resigned in 1861 to become commander of a Georgia brigade in Virginia. It was during this time that he distinguished himself for bravery at the Battle of Antietam. When the war ended, Toombs refused to swear allegiance to the Union and was chased from his home in Washington, Georgia, ending up first in New Orleans and later in London.

When he returned home in 1867, he reestablished his law practice and fought for the maintenance of popular rights. Dominating the Georgia legislative conference of 1877, he helped repudiate the carpetbag rule and revise the state constitution.

Extensive renovations have brought the Robert Toombs House back to its former glory.

A brilliant orator, Toombs was known for his easy laughter and extraordinary personality. Until his death in 1885, he insisted that respectable visitors to Washington, Georgia, stay in his home. Toombs scorned the thought of a political pardon and in 1880 boasted, "I am not loyal to the existing government of the United States and do not wish to be suspected of loyalty."

NEARBY ATTRACTIONS

A. H. Stephens State Historic Park
Mistletoe State Park

DIRECTIONS

The site is at 216 East Robert Toombs Avenue at the Washington, Georgia, city limits.

FOR MORE INFORMATION

Robert Toombs House State Historic Site, P.O. Box 605, Washington, GA 30673 (706-678-2226)

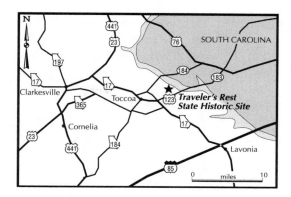

TRAVELER'S REST STATE HISTORIC SITE
TOCCOA

NE

In the early 1800s, the Tugaloo Valley in northeast Georgia lay at the intersection of two important roads—the Federal Road from New England to Florida and the Unicoi Turnpike, completed in 1816, which connected eastern Tennessee to the Federal Road at Traveler's Rest. It was here in 1815 that James Wyly built Traveler's Rest as an inn for stagecoach passengers.

When Devereaux Jarrett bought the house and land in 1833, he doubled the size of the house to its present dimensions of 91 feet by 39 feet. Jarrett was the richest man in the area. In the mid-1800s, he owned not only the inn and 14,000 acres of land, but 100 slaves, a sawmill, a gristmill, a tanyard, a smokehouse, a cotton gin, a store, a tavern, a toll bridge and a post office. In the days before rural free delivery, the post office on the premises would sell your mail to you, as stamps were not yet available.

The private room rented for $1 per night. It was here that Joseph E. Brown spent his honeymoon. Brown later served as governor of Georgia during the Civil War. The central common room had four beds, with each bed space rented for $.25 for each of the two or three men to a bed. That price included a breakfast described by travelers of the time as excellent. There was also an unheated area where late-arriving or unruly travelers—there was a tavern on the river about 0.25 mile away—would stay; the price charged for bed space there has been lost to time. Other than the Joe Brown Room, there were no accommodations for women travelers, who lodged in houses nearby.

In the 1836 book *Canoe Trip up the Minray Sotor*, George Featherstonhaugh wrote, "What a charming country this would be to travel if one was sure of meeting with such nice clean quarters once a day." Featherstonhaugh remembered the landlord as a "quiet, intelligent, and well-behaved man."

Like many plantation owners in the area, the Jarrett family was hit hard by the Civil War.

Though only a few outbuildings were destroyed, the family never fully recovered from the toll the war took. By 1873, when the railroad came through, the inn was already past its prime. The house remained in the family, and boarders were taken in to make extra money.

Devereaux Jarrett's granddaughter, Mary Jarrett White, named the house Jarrett Manor in 1915. She continued to entertain in grand style, with dinners prepared in the first-floor kitchen and served in the formal dining room. She was the first woman in the state to vote and was named Georgia Woman of the Year in 1920. With no heirs to pass the house down to, she sold the manor to the state in 1955. In 1966,

The 90-foot-long front porch is one of the memorable architectural features of Traveler's Rest, an old stagecoach inn near Toccoa in Northeast Georgia.

Traveler's Rest was listed as a National Historic Landmark for its historic value and architectural features, like its 20-inch paneling and 90-foot-long porch across the front.

On a tour of the inn, you can see a number of fine antiques made by local craftsmen, items used by the Jarrett family and the weaving room with its two working looms.

The site is open Monday to Saturday from 9 A.M. to 5 P.M. and Sunday from 2 P.M. to 5 P.M. It is closed Mondays. The entry fee is $2 for adults and $1 for children, with group rates available.

ANNUAL EVENT

In December, the inn is decorated for Christmas and Jarrett descendants return to the house to tell stories of bygone days.

NEARBY ATTRACTIONS

Black Rock Mountain State Park
Tallulah Gorge State Park

DIRECTIONS

Traveler's Rest is 6 miles east of Toccoa, 0.25 mile off U.S. 123.

FOR MORE INFORMATION

Traveler's Rest State Historic Site, Route 3, Toccoa, GA 30577 (404-886-2256)

WORMSLOE STATE HISTORIC SITE
SAVANNAH

Live oaks draped in Spanish moss line the 1.5-mile drive that leads to the site of Wormsloe. The fortified home of Noble Jones once guarded the strategic channel called Jones Narrows. Today, only tabby ruins overlook the marshland.

Noble Jones was among the 114 persons chosen to make the voyage to Georgia with James Oglethorpe. A physician and carpenter from Surrey, England, Jones arrived in Georgia in 1733 and soon found himself serving as a constable, rum agent, surveyor and member (for 18 years) of the Royal Council.

One of only a few of the original settlers to survive hunger, plague, Indians, Spaniards and the environment, Jones was granted 500 acres on the Isle of Hope in 1736. After building the home he called Wormslow, Jones set about fortifying it. He built eight-foot tabby walls around

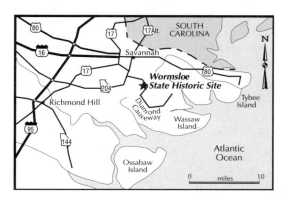

the house and constructed bastions on each corner so that muskets could be fired from gunports covering all approaches. There was a well inside the compound, as well as a cellar. During its heyday, Wormslow was considered a "most agreeable" spot.

But upon Jones's death in 1775, the home was left to his daughter, Mary Jones Bulloch, who seldom used the estate, preferring to live in Savannah. When she died 20 years later, possession of Wormslow went to her brother Noble Wimberly Jones. Because Noble Jones's son also visited Wormslow only occasionally, the structure soon fell into disrepair. When Noble Jones's grandson returned to Wormslow in 1828, he abandoned the tabby home and built another house 0.5 mile up the waterfront. It was Noble Jones's great-grandson G. W. Jones who changed the spelling from Wormslow to Wormsloe in the mid-1850s. He also changed his last name to DeRenne to avoid confusion among the many Joneses.

WORMSLOE TODAY

On a walking tour of the site, you will see not only the ruins of Wormsloe, but also the grave site that once contained Noble Jones and still contains his wife, Sarah, and their youngest son, Inigo. The monument was placed at the site by George Wymberley Jones DeRenne.

Continuing on the tour, you will reach the Colonial Life Area, where living-history demonstrations are occasionally performed. Costumed staff demonstrate the skills and crafts necessary to Georgia's early settlers. This is the area where Noble Jones housed his marine boatmen, who helped guard the estate, his indentured servants and the slaves he purchased once slavery became legal in 1750. These people lived in small wattle-and-daub huts that, although cramped, provided relief from heat in the summer and cold in the winter, thanks to the warmth from their fireplaces. One of these huts has been rebuilt. There were also covered shelters for livestock and storage of tools and a garden surrounded by a split-rail fence, where the land was cultivated for the estate's food. Both servants and family worked this garden. The Joneses also grew mulberry trees for the production of silk, as well as indigo and cotton.

The remainder of the tour involves a nature walk complete with wildlife prints drawn by naturalist Mark Catesby, displayed in laminated interpretive signs along the trail. Catesby toured this region in 1723, illustrating the many new animals unfamiliar to Europeans. Both the Carolina parakeet and the ivory-billed woodpecker have since become extinct.

The interpretive trail leads back to the museum and the visitor center, where you can view artifacts excavated at Wormsloe and learn about the colonial history of the area. There is also an audio-visual show about the founding of Georgia. Guided tours and living-history demonstrations can be arranged in advance. As with all Georgia historic sites, a small fee is charged to enter the museum. There are several picnic areas adjacent to the parking area for those interested in combining a tour with a picnic lunch.

ANNUAL EVENTS

Colonial Living demonstrations (Memorial Day and Labor Day), Georgia Week (February) and the Colonial Christmas celebration (December) are among the park's annual events.

NEARBY ATTRACTIONS

Skidaway Island State Park
Fort McAllister State Historic Park
Fort Pulaski National Monument

DIRECTIONS

Wormsloe is 10 miles south of historic downtown Savannah on Skidaway Road.

FOR MORE INFORMATION

Wormsloe State Historic Site, 7601 Skidaway Road, Savannah, GA 31406 (912-353-3023)

NATIONAL FORESTS

Near Warwoman Dell Picnic Area a 0.35-mile hike leads to Dick's Creek Falls, a 60-foot cascade pouring into the Chattooga River.

T he United States Forest Service (USFS) administers the nation's timberlands in a constant balancing act. The USFS is part of the Department of Agriculture and manages its land accordingly—as a working forest—while its governing multiuse concept calls for recreational opportunities and wilderness protection as well. The USFS's timber sales and clear-cutting have been under near-constant attack from environmental groups around the country in recent years. Changes within the agency have shown that it responds to public pressure.

Some 863,000 of the USFS's 191,000,000 acres are in Georgia. Both forests are managed by the Forest Supervisor's Office in Gainesville.

CAMPING

Primitive camping is allowed anywhere in national forests unless otherwise posted. Camping is prohibited in day-use areas, including picnic areas, swimming beaches and scenic spots. RVs and trailers are permitted in developed campgrounds and the general forest area. Only Rabun Beach in Chattahoochee National Forest has electrical and water hookups. Lake Russell, Lake Sinclair and Rabun Beach are the only camping areas in either of the national forests that provide dump stations. Camping is limited to 14 consecutive days or as posted.

You do not need a permit to light a campfire, but you are legally responsible for any damage your campfire creates. In developed camping areas, fires are limited to stoves, grills, fire rings and fireplaces provided. Only dead, downed wood may be used to build a fire. Make sure your fire is completely extinguished before going to sleep at night and before breaking camp.

HUNTING AND FISHING

Legal hunting and fishing are permitted year-round in both of Georgia's national forests. Persons over 16 must have a valid Georgia hunting or fishing license, as well as any special permits such as a trout stamp or a big-game license. For more information on where to hunt, see the section in this book on Wildlife Management Areas. Complete hunting and fishing regulations are published annually by the state and are available free of charge from the Georgia Department of Natural Resources Game and Fish Division (404-656-3522) or wherever hunting or fishing licenses are sold.

OFF-ROAD VEHICLES

Licensed ORVs are permitted on any road in the national forests that is open to public use. ORVs must be driven by a licensed driver in conformance with all state laws. Unlicensed ORVs are permitted only on designated ORV trails. To prevent forest fires, your ORV must be equipped with a working spark-arresting device. Stay on the trails at all times, and don't operate from a half-hour after sunset to a half-hour before sunrise unless your ORV is equipped with working headlights and taillights. ORV areas are closed periodically to allow them to recover from overuse. Contact the district ranger's office at the time of your trip to find out which areas are open.

HORSEBACK RIDING

Horses are allowed on any trails specifically designated for horses and on some foot trails which are designated multiuse. However, horses are prohibited on the Appalachian Trail and many other trails. Contact the district ranger's office before bringing your horses to a trail.

USAGE FEES

A pay-as-you-go fee system for federal recreation areas was authorized in the Land and Water Conservation Fund Act of 1965. Only recreation areas that have facilities or services provided at federal expense—which includes about two-thirds of the recreation areas in Georgia—can charge a usage fee. There are no usage fees for activities in the general forest area, including hiking, biking and horseback-riding the trails with trailheads outside of developed areas.

Golden Age and Golden Access Passports provide free entrance to any federally administered recreation area, including both national forests and national parks. Passport holders also receive a 50-percent discount on usage fees for camping, swimming and more. Golden Age Passports, for persons over 62 years of age, can be obtained at any national forest office or national park office. Golden Access Passports are available to persons medically determined to be permanently blind or disabled and who are eligible to receive benefits under law. To obtain a Golden Access Passport, you must bring proof of disability to any national forest office or national park office. The discounts from the passport program do not extend to fees charged by private concessionaires.

FOR MORE INFORMATION

Forest Supervisor, United States Forest Service, 508 Oak Street N.W., Gainesville, GA 30501 (404-536-0541)

Sprawling across North Georgia, staining maps green, Chattahoochee National Forest offers recreational opportunities at every turn. The forest has more than 500 campsites, 400 miles of trails, 200 picnic tables, hundreds of miles of streams and thousands of acres of lakes to fish and much more.

The forest's name comes from the Chattahoochee River, which begins in the forest as a spring at Chattahoochee Gap, along the Appalachian Trail. The river is believed to be named after an early Indian settlement. The name's meaning is not certain. It could have de-

rived from *Chatta Ochee*, which means "Sparkling Rocks" or "Flowered Rocks." The Yuchi Indians called the river *Tiah*, a word whose meaning has been forgotten over time.

Only nine of the 23 developed recreation areas are open year-round. Unless noted as year-round facilities, they are only open from spring to early fall.

A map of Chattahoochee National Forest is available at any district office and at many outdoor stores. It is particularly useful for navigating your way through the forest on USFS roads.

HIKING

The hundreds of miles of trails range from an easy leg-stretcher hike to a waterfall to the 70-plus-mile Benton MacKaye and Appalachian Trails. The best guide to hiking in Chattahoochee National Forest is Tim Homan's book *The Hiking Trails of North Georgia*, published by Peachtree Publishers.

When hiking to any of the numerous waterfalls, you should not climb on the rocks in and around the falls. Many deaths have resulted from hikers "carefully" climbing on the slippery rocks.

FISHING

Trout fishing is very popular in Chattahoochee National Forest. Coleman River, Dukes Creek, Waters Creek and Warwoman Creek are among the many popular streams. Get a current copy of Georgia's fishing regulations wherever you buy your license for a complete listing of streams and special regulations.

FOR MORE INFORMATION

To find out more about Chattahoochee National Forest, you can contact either the Forest Supervisor's Office, United States Forest Service, 508 Oak Street N.W., Gainesville, GA 30501 (404-536-0541) or the district ranger's office for the area you wish to visit at the addresses below:

Armuchee Ranger District
806 East Villanow Street
P.O. Box 465
LaFayette, GA 30728
706-638-1085

Brasstown Ranger District
1881 GA 515
P.O. Box 9
Blairsville, GA 30512
706-745-6928

Chattooga Ranger District
P.O. Box 196, Burton Road
Clarkesville, GA 30523
706-754-6221

Chestatee Ranger District
1015 Tipton Drive
Dahlonega, GA 30533
706-864-6173

Cohutta Ranger District
401 Old Ellijay Road
Chatsworth, GA 30705
706-695-6736

Tallulah Ranger District
825 U.S. 441 South
P.O. Box 438
Clayton, GA 30525
706-782-3320

Toccoa Ranger District
East Main Street, Box 1839
Blue Ridge, GA 30513
706-632-5243

ANDREWS COVE RECREATION AREA
CHATTOOGA RANGER DISTRICT

Camping, hiking and fishing are featured at this recreation area, located along a beautiful mountain stream. Andrews Cove has 10 campsites, flush toilets and drinking water. A fee is charged for use.

HIKING

Beginning at Andrews Cove Recreation Area, the 2-mile Andrews Cove Trail follows an old logging road up Andrews Cove to the Appalachian Trail (A.T.) and F.R. 283 at Indian Grave Gap. North on the A.T., it is 2.5 miles to Tray Mountain; south on the A.T., it is 2.7 miles to GA 75 at Unicoi Gap.

NEARBY ATTRACTIONS

Unicoi State Park and Lodge
Appalachian National Scenic Trail

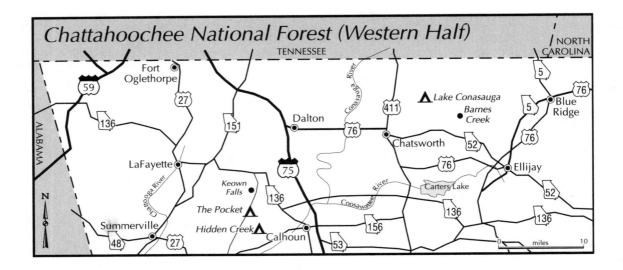

Chattahoochee National Forest (Western Half)

Anna Ruby Falls Recreation Area
High Shoals Falls Scenic Area

DIRECTIONS

Follow GA 75 about 5 miles north of Helen and turn right into Andrews Cove Recreation Area.

ANNA RUBY FALLS RECREATION AREA
CHATTOOGA RANGER DISTRICT

Curtis and York Creeks join to form Smith Creek in the middle of this spectacular double waterfall on the side of Tray Mountain. Curtis Creek drops 153 feet down the exposed rock and is joined by York Creek for 50 feet of the falls.

At the base of the falls, Smith Creek flows down to Unicoi Lake and ultimately to the Chattahoochee River.

The waterfall was named for Anna Ruby Nichols by her father, Colonel John H. Nichols, who purchased the falls and surrounding land after the Civil War. Anna Ruby and her father spent many days horseback riding in the woods around the falls. The Victorian mansion at the junction of GA 17 and GA 75 is the house the two lived in (Anna Ruby's mother and two infant brothers died early in her life). The gazebo on the Indian mound near that junction was also built by her father.

The land around the falls was purchased by the Byrd-Mathews Lumber Company at the turn of the century. The land was purchased to become part of Chattahoochee National Forest in 1925.

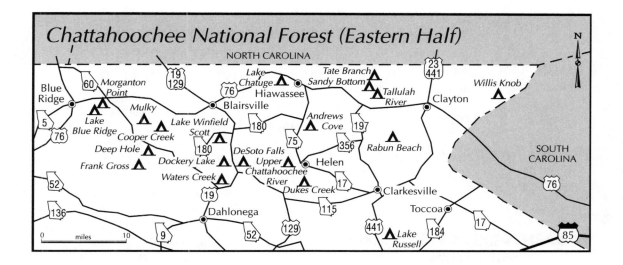

Chattahoochee National Forest (Eastern Half)

In early spring, the trail and the falls are surrounded by many wildflowers, including trilliums and bird's-foot violets. Ferns and mosses also thrive in the area. Mountain laurel blooms in late May and rhododendron in June. This recreation area is open year-round. A fee is charged.

HIKING

An 0.4-mile paved footpath leads to the falls from the parking area. For hikers interested in a more challenging day hike, the 4.6-mile Smith Creek Trail starts at the base of the falls at Smith Creek and passes over a mountain before descending to Unicoi State Park.

STORE

The Chattahoochee-Oconee Heritage Association is a volunteer group that runs a retail store at Anna Ruby Falls, along with another store on Brasstown Bald. The stores specialize in fine arts and crafts, with an emphasis on work by local artisans. Proceeds support interpretive and preservation projects in Georgia's national forests.

OTHER FACILITIES

There are flush toilets and 13 picnic tables at this area.

Andrews Cove Recreation Area
Moccasin Creek State Park
Unicoi State Park and Lodge

DIRECTIONS

Anna Ruby Falls is 3.6 miles north of GA 356 and 1.5 miles east of GA 75 in the community of Robertstown.

BARNES CREEK PICNIC AREA
COHUTTA RANGER DISTRICT

Picnicking is the main attraction at Barnes Creek. The entrance to the picnic area is along backwoods roads through an especially scenic area. Picnicking is on the bank of a stream that has a small waterfall. Barnes Creek has two picnic sites and is open year-round.

NEARBY ATTRACTIONS

Fort Mountain State Park
Cohutta Wilderness Area

DIRECTIONS

Follow U.S. 411 north from Chatsworth for 4 miles and turn right (east) at the traffic light in Eton. From here, follow F.R. 18 east for 10 miles before turning left (northeast) on F.R. 68 for 4 miles.

BRASSTOWN BALD RECREATION AREA
BRASSTOWN RANGER DISTRICT

With its commanding, panoramic view from the highest point in the state (elevation 4,784 feet), the visitor center on top of Brasstown Bald makes a worthwhile side trip. The United States Forest Service operates the visitor center at the "roof" of Georgia daily from late May through October. There are exhibits, a video and an observation deck at the center, which is reached by an 0.5-mile paved path or a shuttle service run by a concessionaire. The Chattahoochee-Oconee Heritage Association operates a bookstore and gift shop at the parking lot. A parking fee is charged.

The name Brasstown comes from a misunderstood Cherokee word used in naming the nearby town. The Cherokees called the area *Itse' yi*, which translates to "Town of the Green Valley," but it was heard by early settlers as *Untsai' yi*, which means "Brass." To the Cherokees, this mountain was *Enotah*.

HIKING

In addition to the paved path to the summit, there are three other trails at Brasstown Bald.

Arkaquah Trail descends 5.5 miles from the parking area to Track Rock Road.

The 4.5-mile Jack's Knob Trail connects the parking lot at Brasstown Bald to the Appalachian Trail at Chattahoochee Gap. It is in Chattahoochee Gap that the river this national forest is named for is born as a mountain spring. The spring is just downhill from the gap. This trail passes through the Mark Trail Wilderness after crossing GA 180.

The third trail is the 7-mile Wagon Train Trail.

All three of these trails are described in the section on the Brasstown Wilderness.

NEARBY ATTRACTIONS

Andrews Cove Recreation Area
Anna Ruby Falls Recreation Area
Unicoi State Park
Vogel State Park

DIRECTIONS

From Blairsville, go south on U.S. 19/U.S. 129 for 8 miles. Turn left on GA 180 and drive 9 miles, then turn left again on GA 180 Spur. The spur road leads 3 miles to the parking area for Brasstown Bald.

BRASSTOWN WILDERNESS
BRASSTOWN RANGER DISTRICT

In 1986, some 11,405 acres within Chattahoochee National Forest were designated by Congress as the Brasstown Wilderness. Approximately 1,200 more acres were added to this wilderness area by Congress in 1991.

Surrounding Brasstown Bald is a narrow ring of ultrabasic rocks—soapstone, dunite and olivine. This is the southernmost habitat for a number of Northern plant and animal species. Among the animals you will find here are the red-back vole and the raven. A huge old-birch forest covers the north face of the mountain. This is called a "cloud" forest because it is often covered in clouds and the trees constantly drip with moisture. The yellow birch trees in this type of forest are draped with a lichen called old-man's-beard.

HIKING

There are three trails through the wilderness that begin atop Brasstown Bald.

Jack's Knob Trail, built by the CCC in the 1930s, travels 4.5 miles southward along a ridge, following the boundary of Towns and Union Counties. It crosses GA 180 in Jack's Gap at an elevation of 3,000 feet before ascending Hiawassee Ridge to Jack's Knob at an elevation of 3,805 feet. Jack's Knob Trail joins the Appalachian Trail in Chattahoochee Gap, home to the source of the Chattahoochee River, which flows southward to Florida.

Arkaquah Trail travels 5.5 miles westward along a ridge top to Track Rock Gap Archaeological Area (listed separately in this section of the book). Rated as moderate to strenuous, it is not a beginner's trail. It passes Blue Bluff Overlook and Chimney Top Mountain, with its views of Rocky Knob to the south.

Wagon Train Trail is an easy 7-mile walk along what was once to be GA 66. Only 5.5 miles of the trail are in the national forest; the last 1.5 miles are on a roadbed through private property. This trail features fine views and passes outstanding cliffs and boulder fields in which rock tripe, lichens, reindeer moss, old-man's-beard and club moss all flourish. Wildflowers are abundant along the trail during the spring. The trail ends behind the women's dormitory on the Young Harris College campus.

CHATTOOGA NATIONAL WILD AND SCENIC RIVER
TALLULAH RANGER DISTRICT

The Chattooga River is one of the most primitive free-flowing rivers in the Southeast. The river is extremely popular with kayakers and rafters, who flock to the Chattooga to enjoy paddling through rapids such as Sockem Dog, Corkscrew and Seven-Foot Falls. The river gained national attention when the 1970s movie *Deliverance* used the Chattooga to depict the fierce rapids on an ill-fated trip down the fictional Cahulawassee River in an adaptation of James Dickey's book. The river can be enjoyed by novices on a properly equipped, guided raft trip with a commercial rafting outfitter. Only expert paddlers should attempt the Chattooga in a kayak or canoe. Maps of the river are available from the USFS.

The river was named for the Cherokee town *Cha tu' gi*, which was on the South Carolina side of the river near the present-day town of Clayton, Georgia. The meaning is in doubt, but it could have derived from the Cherokee word *Tsatu' gi*, or "He drank by sips."

Hiking, trout fishing and whitewater paddling are all popular along the Chattooga National Wild and Scenic River on the South Carolina state line.

HIKING

The 10.7-mile Chattooga River Trail follows the Georgia side of the river upstream from U.S. 76 to meet Bartram Trail near Sandy Ford Road. Much of the hike is within the corridor protected by Wild and Scenic River status.

FISHING

The Chattooga River and many of its tributaries are productive trout streams.

NEARBY ATTRACTIONS

Tallulah Gorge State Park
Black Rock Mountain State Park
Warwoman Dell Picnic Area

DIRECTIONS

The easiest access to the river is via U.S. 76 at the South Carolina line, 9 miles west of Clayton.

CHESTATEE OVERLOOK RECREATION AREA
CHESTATEE RANGER DISTRICT

This overlook on GA 60 features three picnic tables and a scenic view of Blood Mountain Cove. It is open year-round.

NEARBY ATTRACTIONS

Woody Gap Recreation Area

Dockery Lake Campground
Dahlonega Gold Museum State Historic Site

DIRECTIONS

Follow GA 60 north from Dahlonega for 12 miles.

COHUTTA WILDERNESS AREA
COHUTTA RANGER DISTRICT
37,042 ACRES

The Cohutta Wilderness Area received its designation from Congress in January 1975. Though once nearly logged out, the Cohuttas have come back to a wild, if not pristine, state that makes this a popular area to hike and camp. This mountain range in northwest Georgia forms the end of the western branch of the Blue Ridge Mountains. The wilderness area is home to black bear, bobcats, deer, wild turkeys and other wildlife. Cohutta comes from the Cherokee word for frog.

Across the Tennessee line, the Cohutta Wilderness Area is bordered by Cherokee National Forest's Big Frog Wilderness. A small portion of the Cohutta Wilderness Area extends into Tennessee as well.

A map of the Cohutta Wilderness Area is sold by the USFS and is available in many outdoors stores in Georgia as well.

HIKING

There are 16 trails through the Cohuttas

Victoria Logue hikes on the Benton MacKaye Trail in the Cohutta Wilderness Area in the Chattahoochee National Forest.

totaling more than 90 miles. All of the trails are covered in detail in *The Hiking Trails of North Georgia*, by Tim Homan.

The two most heavily used trails are Jacks River and Conasauga River Trails. Both of these trails have frequent fords (78 river crossings between them) that make for very wet hiking. Hiking these trails after heavy rains is ill-advised at best and dangerous at worst. You may become trapped as the creek-fed rivers rise. Always wear boots, tennis shoes or river sandals when fording the streams, as bare feet slip easier on the wet rocks. Conasauga River Trail extends 13.2 miles from F.R. 17B upstream to Betty Gap. The 16.7-mile Jacks River Trail goes upstream

from Alaculsy Valley to Dally Gap. The many other trails in the Cohuttas all interconnect with these two main trails.

The third main trail in the Cohuttas is Benton MacKaye Trail. This 70-plus-mile trail is still growing. The trail is named for Benton MacKaye (rhymes with sky), who proposed the idea for the Appalachian Trail in the 1920s. The original route planned for the A.T. went through the Cohuttas. Benton MacKaye Trail begins with the Appalachian Trail on Springer Mountain and passes through the Cohuttas on its way to the Tennessee line. When completed, the trail will end at Davenport Gap in Great Smoky Mountains National Park, forming a big loop with the Appalachian Trail. For more information, contact the Benton MacKaye Trail Association at P.O. Box 53271, Atlanta, GA 30305.

FISHING

The Jacks and Conasauga Rivers offer good trout fishing. Because this isn't exactly a secret, the rivers can be crowded at times.

NEARBY ATTRACTIONS

Carters Lake
Chief Vann House State Historic Site
Fort Mountain State Park

DIRECTIONS

The Cohutta Wilderness Area is located between U.S. 411 north of Chatsworth and U.S. 76 north of Ellijay.

COLEMAN RIVER SCENIC AREA
TALLULAH RANGER DISTRICT

There are no facilities in this scenic area, which is traversed by Coleman River Trail. The trail begins about 150 yards north of the Tallulah River Recreation Area at the Coleman River Bridge and cuts through an old-growth forest. Nearly a mile long, the trail follows the right bank of the Coleman River upstream. This trail boasts one of the largest white pines in North Georgia. It is more than 150 feet tall and about 10 feet in circumference.

FISHING

Trout may be taken with artificial lures on the Coleman River only between its junction with the Tallulah River and the bridge on F.R. 54.

The 2,150-mile Appalachian Trail's southern terminus on Springer Mountain in the Chattahoochee National Forest is marked by this plaque from the Georgia Appalachian Trail Club.

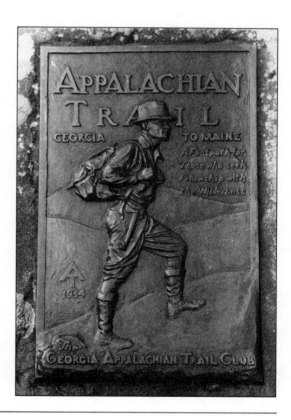

Sandy Bottom Campground
Tallulah River Campground
Tate Branch Campground

DIRECTIONS

From Clayton, go west on U.S. 76 for 8 miles. Turn right on an unnumbered county road and drive 4 miles, then turn left on F.R. 70 and drive 1.25 miles.

COOPER CREEK CAMPGROUND
TOCCOA AND CHESTATEE RANGER DISTRICTS

This recreation area offers camping, picnicking, hiking and fishing along the banks of Cooper Creek, a sparkling mountain stream stocked with fish. Cooper Creek has 17 campsites, flush toilets and drinking water. A fee is charged.

The creek is named for William and Joseph Cooper, who traded in this area in the late 1600s.

HIKING

Cooper Creek Trail, 0.4 mile in length, is really a connector between Mill Shoals Trail and Yellow Mountain Trail. Cooper Creek Trail follows an old logging road. It can be reached via a 0.6-mile hike on Mill Shoals Trail or a 1-mile hike on Yellow Mountain Trail.

The 2.4-mile Mill Shoals Trail begins just north of the Cooper Creek Recreation Area. It, too, follows an old logging road until it crosses Mill Shoal Creek. From there, it travels along Duncan Ridge Road before ending at Spencer Ridge.

Yellow Mountain Trail is a 3.1-mile or 2.1-mile trail that begins at Cooper Creek Recreation Area. It follows an old logging road through forests of hemlock, pine and hardwoods. At 1.3 miles, you will reach a fork in the trail. The left fork heads 0.5 mile north along a ridge top to Shope Gap, where it crosses a small creek before ending at Spencer Ridge. The right fork heads 1.5 miles to Addie Gap.

Eyes on Wildlife Trail is a 2-mile footpath that passes through diverse natural and managed habitats.

SCENIC AREA

The 1,240-acre Cooper Creek Scenic Area features beautiful Cooper Creek and its tributaries, which are stocked with trout. This is also a popular whitewater creek for canoes and kayaks.

NEARBY ATTRACTIONS

Amicalola Falls State Park and Lodge
Appalachian National Scenic Trail
Brasstown Bald Recreation Area

DIRECTIONS

Follow GA 60 north from Dahlonega for 26 miles; turn right on F.R. 4 and follow it for 6 miles. You can also take GA 60 south from Morganton for 16 miles, turn left on F.R. 4 and drive 6 miles.

DE SOTO FALLS CAMPGROUND
CHESTATEE RANGER DISTRICT

Camping, hiking, fishing and picnicking are popular activities at this recreation area and the adjoining De Soto Falls Scenic Area.

The five waterfalls on a 2.5-mile section of trail are the area's main attraction. The falls get their name from Hernando De Soto. A piece of armor was once found near the falls, which tradition states was left by someone in the Spanish explorer's 16th-century expedition through North Georgia.

Legal fishing is permitted year-round. The recreation area is closed in the winter, when no camping is allowed, but the falls are accessible by foot year-round.

WATERFALLS

As you hike up De Soto Falls Trail, you will see the waterfalls in ascending order. In 0.25 mile, you will come to the lower falls—a 30-foot cascade that can be viewed from a large observation deck. The middle falls is 0.8 mile beyond the lower cascade. It is really a set of drops that totals more than 80 feet; there is also an observation deck at this waterfall. The trail gets rougher after the middle falls. It is 1.5 miles to the upper falls, a 200-foot cascade of water plummeting over granite.

Not up to the hike, but still want to see the falls? They are visible from U.S. 129, which runs alongside the scenic area. If you plan to hike in the summer, it is a good idea to scout the falls from U.S. 129, as water volume can be low in periods of little rain.

CAMPING

There are 24 campsites near De Soto Falls. A fee is charged for using the camping area, which has bathhouses with flush toilets and showers.

NEARBY ATTRACTIONS

Dahlonega Gold Museum State Historic Site
Dockery Lake Campground
Unicoi State Park and Lodge
Vogel State Park
Woody Gap Recreation Area

DIRECTIONS

De Soto Falls is 15 miles north of Cleveland on U.S. 129 and 18 miles north of Dahlonega on U.S. 19.

DEEP HOLE CAMPGROUND
TOCCOA RANGER DISTRICT

Located on the Toccoa River, Deep Hole features camping and fishing in its beautiful mountain setting. The river here is stocked with trout.

CAMPING

There are eight campsites, flush toilets and drinking water. A fee is charged.

Deep Hole Recreation Area is on GA 60 some 27 miles north of Dahlonega and 16 miles south of Morganton.

DOCKERY LAKE CAMPGROUND
CHESTATEE RANGER DISTRICT

At 2,388 feet, Dockery Lake is a true mountain lake—cold, clear and good for trout fishing. Picnicking, camping, fishing and hiking are among the recreational opportunities here. The lake has six picnic sites, 11 campsites, flush toilets and drinking water. A fee is charged. The area is closed in the winter.

HIKING

There are two trails at Dockery Lake, as well as access to the Appalachian Trail.

Beginning behind the trailhead signs at the back of the picnic-area parking lot, the 3.4-mile Dockery Lake Trail gently descends before climbing to Miller Gap at the Appalachian Trail; the elevation at the trailhead is 2,420 feet. The trail follows the ridge briefly before descending along tributaries of Waters Creek to 2,040 feet. From here, it is a strenuous 0.5-mile climb toward Miller Gap before the grade becomes more moderate. A small cascade can be seen after 2 miles. To the right is a good view (particularly in the winter) of the Waters Creek watershed. From here, the trail continues to climb to a gap before turning onto an old road-bed before reaching Miller Gap at 2,980 feet. At this point on the A.T., it is 2.9 miles west to Woody Gap at GA 60 and 8.6 miles to Neels Gap at U.S. 19/U.S. 129.

Lakeshore Trail, an 0.5-mile loop trail, is an easy ramble around the six-acre Dockery Lake. This is an especially good hike for children, who will enjoy the view from the numerous platforms along the water's edge.

NEARBY ATTRACTIONS

Chestatee Overlook Recreation Area
Appalachian National Scenic Trail
Dahlonega Gold Museum State Historic Site
Vogel State Park
Woody Gap Recreation Area

DIRECTIONS

Follow GA 60 north from Dahlonega for 12 miles. Turn right (east) on F.R. 654 and follow it east for 1 mile.

DUKES CREEK FALLS RECREATION AREA
CHATTOOGA RANGER DISTRICT

The main attraction here is the 250-foot Dukes Creek Falls, which plummets into a scenic gorge. Along with a 1.1-mile trail to the falls, Dukes Creek offers fishing and a crafts shop, along with flush toilets. A usage fee is charged. If you are interested in panning for gold, this area offers excellent opportunities. A new observation deck in the parking area offers great views of the falls for those unable to, or disinclined to, take the trail.

DUKES CREEK FALLS AND TRAIL

The 1.1-mile trail leads to the convergence of Davis and Dukes Creeks, where the falls spill nearly 250 feet down a sheer granite canyon before plunging into Dukes Creek. The inappropriately named waterfall is actually on Davis Creek.

The well-designed trail—graded, covered with gravel and offering benches for the tired and steps to smooth out the steep spots—winds its way gently down the mountain. If you tour the falls during the wet season, you will hear its roar well before you reach it. Keep an eye out as you hike. There are several excellent long-range views of the falls.

There is also a slippery-rock water slide near the base of the falls.

FISHING

Dukes Creek is an excellent trout stream that is being managed as a native trout stream by the Georgia Department of Natural Resources.

NEARBY ATTRACTIONS

Raven Cliffs Wilderness Area
Unicoi State Park and Lodge

DIRECTIONS

Follow GA 75 north from Helen for 1.5 miles.

Turn left on GA 356 (GA 75 Alternate) and travel 2.3 miles to the Richard Russell Scenic Highway. Turn right and travel 2 miles to the Dukes Creek Falls Recreation Area.

ELLICOTT ROCK WILDERNESS AREA
TALLULAH RANGER DISTRICT

This 9,012-acre tract of land is split nearly equally among three states—Georgia, North Carolina and South Carolina. In 1975, it came under the full protection of the 1960 Wilderness Protection Act; the tract was expanded in 1985. These unspoiled mountains and primitive lands are both isolated and well protected. The Chattooga River, a National Wild and Scenic River, flows through this wilderness area, cascading from 2,381 feet to 2,100 feet within its boundaries. The second-highest point in South Carolina, Fork Mountain (elevation 3,294 feet), also lies within the wilderness area.

The most important aspect of Ellicott Rock Wilderness Area is the number of unique plant communities it protects, including several rare and endangered plants growing along the trails, evergreen forests with their dense understory of mountain laurel, stream-side rhododendron colonies and a varied population of animal life, including the eastern brook trout.

The only access to this wilderness area is by hiking the trails. Camping is allowed but must be done more than 0.25 mile from an approach road and 50 feet from a stream or maintained trail.

Ellicott Rock is named for Major Andrew Ellicott of Lancaster, Pennsylvania, who established this mark to designate the location of the 35th parallel, a boundary North Carolina and Georgia had been arguing about for years.

HIKING

The only trail in Georgia is Ellicott Rock Trail, but Chattooga River Trail follows the South Carolina side of the river downstream, as does part of Foothills Trail.

Ellicott Rock Trail begins near Highlands, North Carolina, and runs 3.75 miles to the surveyor's rock marking the intersection of the three states. It follows an old roadbed for more than 2 miles before making a left turn at a fork and descending into the wilderness area and the Chattooga River corridor.

DIRECTIONS

From the junction of U.S. 64 and N.C. 28 in Highlands, North Carolina, drive southeast on Main Street, which becomes Horse Cove Road (S.R. 1603). It is 4.6 miles down the mountain to the end of the pavement and the junction with Bullpen Road (S.R. 1178). Turn right on Bullpen Road and travel 1.7 miles, then turn right onto a parking spur with a trail sign. From here, you must hike 2 miles along an old road to the wilderness area.

FERN SPRINGS GROUP AREA
CHATTOOGA RANGER DISTRICT

The wooded area by Fern Springs has four picnic shelters that are reserved for use by organized groups only. Pit toilets and drinking water are the only amenities provided. A usage fee is charged. Call the Chattooga Ranger District Office (706-754-6221) for more information or to reserve a shelter.

NEARBY ATTRACTIONS

Lake Richard B. Russell
Tallulah Gorge State Park

DIRECTIONS

Go north from Gainesville on GA 365 to the exit for GA 197 (the Clarkesville exit). Turn right on Old GA 197 at the second stop sign. Turn left on Dicks Hill Parkway and drive 3.2 miles to the group area.

FRANK GROSS CAMPGROUND
TOCCOA RANGER DISTRICT

Situated along beautiful Rock Creek, Frank Gross Campground offers both camping and fishing. There are 11 campsites, flush toilets and drinking water. A usage fee is charged.

NEARBY ATTRACTIONS

Deep Hole Campground
Appalachian National Scenic Trail

DIRECTIONS

Follow GA 60 north from Dahlonega for 27 miles, then turn left (south) on F.R. 69 and drive 5 miles to Frank Gross. You can also follow GA 60 south from Morganton for 15 miles before turning right on F.R. 69.

HIDDEN CREEK
RECREATION AREA
ARMUCHEE RANGER DISTRICT

Hidden Creek received its name because it appears, runs clear and cool for a day or so and then disappears again. This underground creek may appear occasionally for no other reason than the random movement of rocks in its underground bed, which changes the flow of water. Camping, hiking and picnicking are all offered here. The 16 campsites share latrines. Drinking water is also available.

NEARBY ATTRACTIONS

The Pocket Recreation Area
James H. "Sloppy" Floyd State Park

DIRECTIONS

Follow GA 156 southwest from Calhoun for 7.5 miles, then turn left on Everett Springs Road. Travel 2 miles to Rock House Road S.W., turn right and travel another 3 miles to F.R. 955. Turn right and travel 1.3 miles to the entrance to Hidden Creek.

HIGH SHOALS FALLS
SCENIC AREA
BRASSTOWN RANGER DISTRICT

This 170-acre scenic area features two waterfalls along High Shoals Creek. The 25-foot Blue Hole, with its deep reflecting pool, and the 100-foot High Shoals Falls are the big attractions. Both are reached by the 1.2-mile High Shoals Trail. The cascades have observation decks reached by side trails off the main trail. The trail is not a loop, so reaching both the falls requires a 2.4-mile round-trip hike.

NEARBY ATTRACTIONS

Andrews Cove Recreation Area
Anna Ruby Falls Recreation Area
Brasstown Bald Recreation Area
Unicoi State Park and Lodge

DIRECTIONS

From Cleveland, go north on GA 75 for 22 miles. Turn right on F.R. 238. You will reach the trailhead after 1 mile. F.R. 238 is a gravel road, and you must drive through a creek.

KEOWN FALLS RECREATION AREA
ARMUCHEE RANGER DISTRICT

This often-dry falls can be viewed at the end of a short hike. Fourteen picnic tables are available, as are flush toilets and drinking water. A small shelter provides protection from the elements.

HIKING

Keown Falls Trail, a 1.8-mile loop trail, is part of the only scenic area in the Armuchee District of Chattahoochee National Forest. Beginning at Keown Falls Recreation Area, the trail soon enters the scenic area and approaches a small stream that will let you know whether or not the falls are dry; the lower the water in the stream, the less the chance of water spilling over the falls. There is also a sign at the trailhead that will let you know whether the trail is dry. From an observation deck, you can view the falls as it splits in two and sails about 50 feet to the rocks below. A second falls is located farther along the cliffs as the trail makes a loop back down the mountain. This second falls is about half the height of the first and more often than not is nothing but a mossy slide.

Johns Mountain Trail is a 3.5-mile loop trail that begins at an observation deck atop Johns Mountain. The trail follows the ridge for just over a mile before turning left and descending along a parallel line of bluffs. Johns Mountain Trail shares an observation deck with Keown Falls Trail; the observation deck offers a view of the 50-foot falls. The trail then continues upward to the first observation deck.

NEARBY ATTRACTIONS

The Pocket Recreation Area
James H. "Sloppy" Floyd State Park
Hidden Creek Recreation Area

DIRECTIONS

Follow GA 136 east from LaFayette for 13.5 miles. Just past Villanow, turn right (south) on Pocket Road (a county road) and drive about 5 miles to the entrance, on your right.

If you want to get to Johns Mountain Trail, follow GA 136 east from LaFayette for 13.5 miles. Turn right on Pocket Road and travel about 4 miles. Turn right on F.R. 208 and follow it to the observation deck and the Johns Mountain Overlook sign.

LAKE BLUE RIDGE CAMPGROUND
TOCCOA RANGER DISTRICT

This 3,290-acre lake's scenic setting makes it a popular spot for boating and camping. The lake is named for the nearby town of Blue Ridge. It is best visited from spring to midsummer, as the TVA uses it for flood control and lowers the level during the remainder of the year.

CAMPING

With 55 campsites, this is the second-largest camping area in Chattahoochee National Forest (Rabun Beach Recreation Area has 80 sites). This area is equipped with flush toilets and showers. A usage fee is charged.

HIKING

The 0.6-mile Lake Blue Ridge Loop Trail wanders along the side of the lake before looping back to the trailhead at the picnic area. This easy trail is a nice walk for children as well as adults.

NEARBY ATTRACTION

Morganton Point Campground

DIRECTIONS

From GA 515 in Blue Ridge, go east on Old U.S. 76 for 1.5 miles to Dry Branch Road. Turn right and go 3 miles to the entrance sign for the campground.

LAKE CHATUGE RECREATION AREA
BRASSTOWN RANGER DISTRICT

This recreation area is on a peninsula jutting into the TVA's 7,000-acre lake. Boating and fishing are its big attractions. A large camping area and a 1.2-mile nature trail help visitors make the most of the lake.

BOATING AND FISHING

Legal fishing is permitted year-round. All persons over 16 must have a valid Georgia fishing permit. There is a boat ramp in the recreation area.

CAMPING

There are 30 campsites in the camping area, which is equipped with flush toilets and showers. A usage fee is charged.

HIKING

The 1.2-mile Lake Chatuge Loop Trail encircles the peninsula the recreation area is located on and remains in sight of the lake for most of its length. The trailhead is at the parking area for the boat ramp.

NEARBY ATTRACTIONS

Brasstown Bald Recreation Area
Moccasin Creek State Park

DIRECTIONS

From Hiawassee, go west on GA 76 for 2 miles. Turn left on GA 288. You will reach the recreation area after 1 mile.

LAKE CONASAUGA RECREATION AREA
COHUTTA RANGER DISTRICT

This 19-acre lake is the highest lake in the state, at 3,100 feet above sea level. To help make the most of the secluded lake, there are 17 picnic sites, picnic shelters for groups and a swimming beach. Boating in the lake is limited to boats with electric motors only. Legal fishing is allowed, but persons over 16 must have a valid Georgia fishing permit.

The lake and river get their name from the Cherokee word *Kahnasagah*, or "grass."

CAMPING

There are 35 campsites near the lake. Flush toilets are provided. A usage fee is charged.

HIKING

There are three trails at the recreation area, for nearly 4 miles of hiking near the scenic lake. The 2-mile Grassy Mountain Tower Trail leads from the dam up to the old fire tower on Grassy Mountain. The fire tower is kept locked, but the impressive views of the Cohutta Mountains from the stairs leading up the tower make the 4-mile round trip worthwhile. Conasauga Loop Trail is a 1.2-mile trail around the lake that is often used by bank fishermen. The 1.7-mile Songbird Trail goes through an area of maintained openings whose vegetation offers food to numerous songbirds.

MOUNTAIN BIKING

Although not in the recreation area itself, the 5-mile Windy Gap Cycle Trail has its northern trailhead on F.R. 49 between the lake and Grassy Mountain. The southern trailhead is on F.R. 218, which is locally marked as Muskrat Road; to get to this trailhead, go east on U.S. 411 for 5 miles from Eton, turn left on Muskrat Road and go 3 miles to the trailhead.

ORV TRAILS

Two other trails near Lake Conasauga are designated for off-road vehicles. The 4-mile Milma Creek ORV Trail and the 5-mile Tibbs ORV Trail are accessed via Windy Gap Cycle Trail. These trails are suitable for all-terrain vehicles. Tibbs ORV Trail is closed by gates at each end.

NEARBY ATTRACTIONS

Barnes Creek Picnic Area
Chief Vann House State Historic Site
Fort Mountain State Park

DIRECTIONS

Go north from Chatsworth on U.S. 411 for 4 miles to Eton. Turn right at the traffic light onto F.R. 18. Go east for 10 miles and turn left on F.R. 68. You will pass Barnes Creek Picnic Area after 4 miles and reach Lake Conasauga Recreation Area after another 6 miles.

LAKE RUSSELL
RECREATION AREA
CHATTOOGA RANGER DISTRICT

Hundred-acre Lake Russell is located at the base of Chenocetah Mountain, at the southeast corner of the wildlife management area named for it. Swimming at the grass beach, boating and fishing are all popular ways to enjoy the scenic lake. There are 21 picnic tables, a boat ramp and flush toilets in the recreation area. Boats must use electric motors on the lake.

The lake is named for Senator Richard B. Russell (1897–1971), who also has a bridge in Quitman County and a scenic highway in Union and White Counties named in his honor.

CAMPING

There are 42 campsites in the camping area, which is equipped with flush toilets, showers and a dump station. A fee is charged.

The 100-person Lake Russell Group Camp is available by reservation to organized groups. For more information or to make reservations, call the Chattooga Ranger District Office at 706-754-6221.

HIKING

There are two foot trails in and near the recreation area. The 4.6-mile Lake Russell Loop Trail follows the southern shore of the lake before cutting back through the woods on roads to the trailhead at the group-camp entrance. Because part of the return loop is on roads open to traffic, we suggest hiking out and back along the lakeshore for a 3.2-mile hike. The 2.7-mile Sourwood Trail loops to Nancytown Falls and back. It is an easy hike suitable for the whole family.

HORSEBACK RIDING

The 6.2-mile Ladyslipper Trail is open to both horse and foot travel. Lady's-slippers are among the many wildflower species found along this trail in the spring and early summer. The trailhead is at the group-camp entrance.

NEARBY ATTRACTIONS

Fern Springs Group Area
Lake Richard B. Russell Wildlife Management Area
Tallulah Gorge State Park

DIRECTIONS

Go north from Gainesville on GA 365 to GA 197. Then turn right onto Old GA 197. Turn right again at the second stop sign onto Dicks Hill Parkway. Go 0.8 mile to F.R. 59; turn left and continue 2 miles to the lake.

LAKE WINFIELD SCOTT RECREATION AREA

BRASSTOWN RANGER DISTRICT

This high mountain lake is on the edge of the 7,100-acre Coosa Bald Scenic Area. The 18-acre lake is a great place to picnic, swim, boat and fish; only boats without motors are allowed on the lake. There are 19 picnic tables and two group picnic shelters in the picnic area. The camping area has 36 campsites and nearby flush toilets and showers. Fees are charged for both day use and overnight camping.

The lake is named for General Winfield Scott (1786–1866), the commander of American forces during the Mexican War. Scott was also charged with removal of the Cherokee Indians in 1838. He made a public apology for the forced evacuation that began the Trail of Tears, a march to a Western reservation that left 4,000 Cherokees in unmarked graves in its wake. Scott made a failed bid for the United States presidency in 1852.

BOATING AND FISHING

Boats are limited to using electric motors on the mountain lake. Legal fishing is permitted, but persons over 16 must have a valid Georgia fishing license. The 0.4-mile Winfield Scott Trail loops around the lake and provides access for bank fishing, as well as a leg-stretching walk. Cooper Creek, which flows from the dam, is a good trout-fishing stream.

HIKING

Both of the trails leading away from the lake connect to the Appalachian Trail. Jarrard Gap Trail leads 1.2 miles to the A.T., while Slaughter Gap Trail leads 2.7 miles to the A.T. a mile south of Blood Mountain. It is possible to combine these two trails with the 2.1-mile section of the A.T. that connects Jarrard and Slaughter Gaps to make a 6-mile loop hike that starts and ends at the lake. The round trip to Blood Mountain (elevation 4,458 feet) adds another 2 miles to the hike but takes you to the top of one of the highest mountains in the state, for a rewarding but tough 8-mile hike. Parking for either trail is in the gravel parking lot at the head of the lake. Both trails pass through the Blood Mountain Wilderness.

NEARBY ATTRACTIONS

Appalachian National Scenic Trail
De Soto Falls Scenic Area
Vogel State Park

DIRECTIONS

From Blairsville, go south on U.S. 19/U.S. 129 for 10 miles. Turn right on GA 180 and continue 7 miles to the lake.

MORGANTON POINT CAMPGROUND
TOCCOA RANGER DISTRICT

Swimming, boating and fishing on the 3,290-acre Lake Blue Ridge are the attractions at this recreation area. There are eight picnic tables and a boat ramp. A fee is charged for the camping area, which has 37 sites with nearby flush toilets. Showers are provided.

NEARBY ATTRACTION

Lake Blue Ridge Campground

DIRECTIONS

From the town of Blue Ridge, go south on U.S. 515 for 4 miles to GA 60. Turn right and go 3 miles to Morganton. In Morganton, turn right onto County Road 616 and continue 0.5 mile to Morganton Point.

MULKY CAMPGROUND
TOCCOA RANGER DISTRICT

Situated on the banks of Cooper Creek, Mulky offers camping, fishing and hiking. Cooper Creek is stocked with trout. The recreation area has 10 campsites, flush toilets and drinking water. A usage fee is charged.

NEARBY ATTRACTION

Cooper Creek Campground

DIRECTIONS

Follow GA 60 north from Dahlonega for 26 miles. Turn right on F.R. 4 and follow it for 5 miles. Or you can take GA 60 south from Morganton for 15 miles, turn left on F.R. 4 and drive 5 miles.

PANTHER CREEK RECREATION AREA
CHATTOOGA RANGER DISTRICT

This recreation area on the banks of Panther Creek has 11 picnic sites, including two picnic shelters. Drinking water and flush toilets are available.

PANTHER CREEK FALLS AND TRAIL

Panther Creek Falls is reached via Panther Creek Falls Trail, which continues past the falls another 2 miles to its terminus near Yonah Dam. It is 3.5 miles one-way to the base of the large waterfall.

The western terminus of the trail is across U.S. 441 from the recreation area. The trail follows Panther Creek toward its confluence with the Tugaloo River. There is an area of high shoals after 2.3 miles that is often mistaken for the waterfall. Panther Creek Falls is quite breathtaking, dropping through a series of cascades before plummeting over a 50-foot drop.

Past the falls, the trail continues to the bridge that marks its end, passing large boulders and pools before ascending to a piney ridge and returning once again to Panther Creek. The eastern terminus is west on Yonah Dam Road.

Panther Creek Trail is known for its wide variety of plant life, particularly its ferns and wildflowers. In the spring, it is home to thousands of blooming gaywings, which often grow among partridge berries, forming a dense carpet of deep green and pink.

NEARBY ATTRACTIONS

Black Rock Mountain State Park
Rabun Beach Recreation Area
Tallulah Gorge State Park
Traveler's Rest State Historic Site

DIRECTIONS

Follow U.S. 23/U.S. 441 north from Clarkesville for 10 miles to Panther Creek Recreation Area.

THE POCKET
RECREATION AREA
ARMUCHEE RANGER DISTRICT

This pretty recreation area was a Civilian Conservation Corps camp in the 1930s. The picnic area surrounds a clear-flowing but small stream and a very large piped spring. Camping, picnicking and hiking are offered here. The Pocket Recreation Area has 17 picnic sites, including a picnic shelter, along with 27 campsites, flush toilets and drinking water. A usage fee is charged.

The picnic area and the campground are open from 6 A.M. until 10 P.M. There is no fee for use of the picnic tables, but a $25 reservation fee is required for the shelter, which is otherwise available on a first-come, first-served basis.

HIKING

The Pocket Trail is a 2.5-mile loop which circles "The Pocket," a horseshoe-shaped, mostly level piece of land surrounded on three sides by ridges of Horn Mountain and Mill Mountain. The trail remains fairly level at about 900 feet in elevation. The many spring-fed streams within The Pocket form the headwaters of Johns Creek, which flows out of the open end of the horseshoe.

The trail roller-coasters over steep areas, streams and dry areas. Because of the biological diversity of the area, hikers pass through a variety of forest types—sycamore, beech and sugar maple in the moist areas; black gum, several types of oak and sassafras in the drier areas; and pines and scrubby hardwoods in areas with poor soil. Keep an eye out for the loblolly pine; although not uncommon here, it is still not often seen. A tall loblolly stands next to a huge white oak on the right about 600 feet after you cross the second bridge.

The trail heads over a 65-yard-long boardwalk through a seepage area before passing through a couple of pine forests and reaching the end of the loop.

Because of the abundance of pink lady's-slippers, an interpretive sign can be found midway through the hike in the vicinity of an extensive colony of these native orchids.

An 0.5-mile nature trail has been incorporated as part of The Pocket Trail. There are a number of interpretive signs along this trail's route.

NEARBY ATTRACTIONS

Keown Falls Recreation Area
Hidden Creek Recreation Area

DIRECTIONS

Follow GA 136 east from LaFayette for 13.5 miles. Half a mile east of Villanow, turn right (south) on Pocket Road (a county road) and travel 8 miles to the recreation area.

POPCORN OVERLOOK
TALLULAH RANGER DISTRICT

This scenic viewpoint overlooks the mountains of northeast Georgia. It is unusual in that its picnic tables, benches and car stops are all made from recycled plastic and wood fiber. The overlook has four picnic tables and flush toilets.

NEARBY ATTRACTION

Southern Nantahala Wilderness Area

DIRECTIONS

Follow U.S. 76 west from Clayton for 12 miles.

RABUN BEACH
RECREATION AREA
TALLULAH RANGER DISTRICT

This recreation area on the shore of 835-acre Lake Rabun boasts the largest United States Forest Service camping area in the state, with 80 sites. Boating, picnicking, swimming and fishing are the area's main attractions. The mountainous setting provides a scenic backdrop for the lake.

Many geographic features in the area bear the name Rabun in honor of William Rabun (1771–1819), who was Georgia's governor from 1817 to 1819.

CAMPING

Some of Rabun Beach's 80 sites have electrical and water hookups. The campground has flush toilets, hot showers and a dump station. A usage fee is charged. The campground is open from mid-May through early November.

A separate group camping area accommodates approximately 30 people. It is available on a reservation basis.

WATERFALLS

The 1.3-mile Rabun Beach Trail crosses Joe Branch several times en route to Angel and Panther Falls. The trail first comes to the broad, 50-foot-tall Panther Falls, then turns steep as it climbs up switchbacks to a platform where you can view the 60-foot-tall Angel Falls. These waterfalls look their best in the spring or at other times when the water level on Joe Branch is high.

Near the recreation area is the 0.2-mile Fall Branch Trail, which leads to the impressive Minnehaha Falls. The 100-foot-tall falls is a series of falls and cascades half as wide as it is tall. To get to the trailhead for Minnehaha Falls, continue on Lake Rabun Road past the recreation area; after 1 mile, cross the bridge and follow the gravel Bear Gap Road for 1.7 miles to a small pull-off at the trailhead.

NEARBY ATTRACTIONS

Moccasin Creek State Park
Tallulah Gorge State Park

DIRECTIONS

From Clayton, go south on U.S. 441/U.S. 23 for 7 miles. Turn right onto an unnamed county road and drive 0.1 mile; turn left on GA 15 and follow it for 2 miles; then turn right on County Road 10 and proceed 5 miles.

RAVEN CLIFFS WILDERNESS AREA
CHATTOOGA RANGER DISTRICT

There are 9,649 acres at Raven Cliffs, which was protected by the Wilderness Act in 1984 and 1986 as part of the 1970s RARE II project, designed to establish wilderness areas.

There are four trails in the wilderness area—part of the 2,150-mile Appalachian Trail, the 2-mile Logan Turnpike Trail, the 1.1-mile Whitly Gap Trail and the 2.5-mile Raven Cliff Falls Trail.

HIKING

Logan Turnpike Trail is a 2-mile trail that follows a former 19th-century toll road and crosses some of Georgia's most rugged terrain. The trail parallels Town Creek. It offers an easy hike for the first mile, turning strenuous for the last mile. It accesses the A.T. near Cowrock Mountain.

The blue-blazed Raven Cliff Falls Trail follows Dodds Creek, which features several small waterfalls and the 90-foot falls the trail is named for. Wildflowers abound along the trail from mid-April to summer. The trailhead is on GA 348 some 2.8 miles south of its junction with GA 356 and GA 75 Alternate. The parking area is unmarked but well used.

FISHING

Native brook trout are found in Duke's Creek. Special fishing regulations apply. Check the Georgia fishing regulations booklet for current regulations.

NEARBY ATTRACTIONS

De Soto Falls Scenic Area
Appalachian National Scenic Trail

Raven Cliffs Wilderness Area is bordered to the west by U.S. 19 and U.S. 129 at De Soto Falls Scenic Area and to the northwest and west by GA 348.

RIDGE AND VALLEY SCENIC BY-WAY
ARMUCHEE RANGER DISTRICT

This is a 47-mile loop of roads posted with the United States Forest Service's Scenic By-Way signs. As the name implies, the route affords views of the long ridges and parallel valleys that are common in this part of the state. You will pass by Johns Mountain Overlook, The Pocket Recreation Area, Keown Falls Recreation Area and the Arrowhead Public Fishing Area on the drive. Each of these areas has at least one hiking trail, making for a pleasant drive-awhile, hike-awhile day trip.

NEARBY ATTRACTIONS

The Pocket Recreation Area
Keown Falls Recreation Area
Lake Arrowhead Public Fishing Area

DIRECTIONS

From U.S. 27 north of Rome, the byway turns right (northeast) on GA 136. In Villanow, at the intersection with GA 201, the byway turns left (southwest) and continues to U.S. 27, where it turns left and continues south to the intersection with GA 136 at the starting point.

RUSSELL/BRASSTOWN SCENIC BY-WAY
CHATTOOGA AND BRASSTOWN RANGER DISTRICTS

This 38-mile loop of roads is posted with the United States Forest Service's Scenic By-Way signs and interpretive signs. Andrews Cove is the only recreation area along this drive, but Brasstown Bald is 3 miles off the by-way on a spur road, and Anna Ruby Falls is also a short drive off the by-way.

NEARBY ATTRACTIONS

Andrews Cove Recreation Area
Anna Ruby Falls Recreation Area
Brasstown Bald Recreation Area
Moccasin Creek State Park
Unicoi State Park and Lodge
Vogel State Park

DIRECTIONS

From the town of Helen, go north on GA 75. Turn left on GA 180, then left on GA 348, then left on GA 75 Alternate to return to Helen.

SANDY BOTTOM CAMPGROUND
TALLULAH RANGER DISTRICT

Trout fishing and camping are the main activities here. There are 12 campsites with nearby flush toilets and drinking water at this fee area. The campground is open from mid-March through October.

DIRECTIONS

Go west from Clayton on U.S. 76 for 8 miles; turn right on an unnumbered county road and drive 4 miles; turn left on F.R. 70 and follow it for 5 miles to Sandy Bottom.

SOSEBEE COVE SCENIC AREA
BRASSTOWN RANGER DISTRICT

This picturesque tract of land has been set aside as a memorial to Arthur Woody, who served here from 1918 to 1945. The 175 acres of hardwood timber were a favorite place to Woody, who was known as "the Barefoot Ranger." Because he loved this peaceful cove, he negotiated its purchase by the United States Forest Service. The cove abounds in wildflowers, and the yellow poplars here are said to be among the best second-growth stand of this species in the United States.

HIKING

Sosebee Cove Trail is an 0.3-mile loop trail.

Logged early in the century, the trees at Sosebee Cove have not been touched again except for a power-line cut-through. The largest yellow poplar in the cove stands just to the right of where the loop trail heads to the left. Its girth measures 16 feet, four inches.

The cove also boasts one of the largest yellow buckeyes to be found—15 feet, three inches in circumference. This gigantic tree can be seen near the road where the trail passes along the lower edge of the GA 180 road bank.

The number and variety of wildflowers the cove supports are truly amazing. From early March through late September, you are bound to find at least one species of flower blooming in the cove.

NEARBY ATTRACTIONS

Vogel State Park
Appalachian National Scenic Trail
Lake Winfield Scott Recreation Area

DIRECTIONS

Follow U.S. 19/U.S. 129 south from Blairsville for 10 miles. Turn right (west) on GA 180 and travel 2 miles to Sosebee Cove.

SOUTHERN NANTAHALA WILDERNESS AREA
TALLULAH RANGER DISTRICT

More than half of this 24,515-acre wilderness area is in North Carolina, with the remainder hugging Georgia's northern boundary in Rabun and Towns Counties. It was created by the 1984 Georgia Wilderness Act and the 1984 North Carolina Wilderness Act. The name Nantahala comes from the Cherokee expression for "Land of the Noonday Sun," because the deep hollows stay in the shade for much of the day. Most of the area was logged before the United States Forest Service acquired it for Georgia's Chattahoochee National Forest and North Carolina's Nantahala National Forest. Like all wilderness areas, it is closed to bikes and other mechanized forms of transportation, with wheelchairs being the only exception.

HIKING

The Appalachian Trail is the only footpath in the Georgia section of Southern Nantahala Wilderness Area. The A.T., which follows the Tennessee Valley Divide through the wilderness area, connects Blue Ridge Gap (elevation 3,020 feet) to Bly Gap (elevation 3,840 feet) on the North Carolina line. It passes on the side of Wheeler Knob, Rocky Knob and Rich Knob as it climbs into North Carolina.

The nearest access to the A.T. here is at Dick's Creek Gap on U.S. 76 some 11 miles east of Hiawassee and 18 miles west of Clayton. From that trailhead, it is 5.6 miles north on the A.T. to the wilderness-area boundary at Blue Ridge Gap and another 2.2 miles to Bly Gap.

NEARBY ATTRACTIONS

Tallulah River Campground
Tate Branch Campground
Sandy Bottom Campground

DIRECTIONS

The wilderness area is on the northern boundary of Georgia in Rabun and Towns Counties. It is located within 0.5 mile of F.R. 70 on both sides of the road from about a mile north of Tate Branch to the state line.

TALLULAH RIVER CAMPGROUND
TALLULAH RANGER DISTRICT

The Tallulah River's name has many suggested sources. Among the theories are that it derives from the Choctaw word *talulu*, or "bell"; from the Cherokee word *tu-lu-lu-li*, or "the frog place"; or from a word meaning "terrible," with reference to the 1,000-foot falls on the river, located in Tallulah Gorge State Park. The Cherokees knew the river as *Terrora*, which might explain the latter interpretation.

Hiking, camping and fishing are among the opportunities at this recreation area, which is known for its rugged terrain. There are 17 campsites, drinking water and flush toilets. A usage fee is charged. The campground is open from mid-March through October.

HIKING

Oddly enough, the hiking offered at the Tallulah River Campground takes you into the Coleman River Scenic Area. Coleman River Trail begins about 150 yards north of the Tallulah River Campground at the Coleman River Bridge. Nearly a mile long, the trail follows the right bank of the Coleman River upstream. This trail boasts one of the largest white pines in North Georgia. It is more than 150 feet tall and about 10 feet in circumference.

NEARBY ATTRACTIONS

Coleman River Scenic Area
Tate Branch Campground
Sandy Bottom Campground

DIRECTIONS

Follow U.S. 76 west from Clayton for 8 miles. Turn right (north) on an unnumbered, paved county road and drive 4 miles, then turn left on F.R. 70 and follow it for 1 mile.

TATE BRANCH CAMPGROUND
TALLULAH RANGER DISTRICT

Located at the junction of Tate Branch and the Tallulah River, this recreation area features good trout fishing, exceptional fall foliage and remote mountain scenery. Camping and hiking are popular activities here. The recreation area offers 19 campsites, drinking water and flush toilets. A usage fee is charged. Tate Branch is open year-round.

NEARBY ATTRACTIONS

Coleman River Scenic Area
Tallulah River Campground
Sandy Bottom Campground

DIRECTIONS

Follow U.S. 76 west from Clayton for 8 miles. Turn right (north) on an unnumbered, paved county road and travel 4 miles. Turn left on F.R. 70 and follow it for 4 miles.

TRACK ROCK GAP ARCHAEOLOGICAL AREA
BRASSTOWN RANGER DISTRICT

This 52-acre area has been set aside to help preserve the ancient Indian petroglyphs here. This mountain gap received its name because most of the carvings resemble animal and bird tracks, human footprints and circles and crosses. The petroglyphs are carved in micaceous soapstone rocks and were probably made by the Indians for their own amusement. Indian legend says the tracks were made by a great army of birds and animals in the newly created earth's surface, which was still soft. The animals and birds, they say, were escaping some great danger from the west—perhaps, some say, a great "drive hunt" of the Indians.

The Cherokees called this place *Datsu nalas gun yi* ("Where There Are Tracks") and also *Degaleyunha* ("Printed Place"). Trails provide access to a closer view of this archaeological treasure.

NEARBY ATTRACTION

Brasstown Bald Recreation Area

DIRECTIONS

Follow U.S. 19 and GA 515 east from the Blairsville post office for 5.8 miles. Turn right (south) on Trackrock Gap Road. Travel 2.2 miles to the parking area just past the petroglyphs.

TRAY MOUNTAIN WILDERNESS AREA
CHATTOOGA RANGER DISTRICT

This 9,702-acre wilderness is named for 4,430-foot Tray Mountain, one of the tallest peaks in the state. It was once known as Trail Mountain for the paths leading to its summit. The present name is a corruption of the original. The 360-degree view from Tray Mountain's rocky summit is one of the best mountaintop views in the state.

Access to the mountain is on a mile-long section of the Appalachian Trail that leads from a dirt parking area to the summit. The short, strenuous climb is graded with switchbacks. It

is well worth the effort. To get to the trailhead for this short hike on the A.T., take GA 356 east from Robertstown. Go 5 miles and turn right on Chimney Mountain Road. Go 2 miles to F.R. 79. It is 7 miles north to Tray Gap, where the A.T. leads 1 mile to the Tray Mountain summit. F.R. 79 is a rough road and should only be driven by trucks and cars with good clearance.

NEARBY ATTRACTIONS

Unicoi State Park and Lodge
Anna Ruby Falls Recreation Area

DIRECTIONS

The wilderness area is east of GA 75 and GA 17 and north of Anna Ruby Falls Recreation Area. See the directions to the A.T. above to get to the wilderness area.

UPPER CHATTAHOOCHEE RIVER CAMPGROUND
CHATTOOGA RANGER DISTRICT

This recreation area features camping, picnicking, hiking and fishing. Located near the headwaters of the Chattahoochee River, it is adjacent to both Horse Trough Falls and the Mark Trail Wilderness Area. The area has campsites, flush toilets and drinking water. It is open year-round.

The river is believed to have been named after an early Indian settlement. The name's meaning is not certain. It could have derived from *Chatta Ochee*, which means "Sparkling Rocks" or "Flowered Rocks." The Yuchi Indians called the river *Tiah*.

WATERFALL

Though Horse Trough Falls is not in the recreation area itself, you may want to visit it while you are in the area. The 60-foot falls on Horse Trough Creek, a tributary of the Chattahoochee River, is a short distance from the campground. Below the falls, the river is 20 feet wide and a foot deep, but here the river rushes through a narrow channel in the rocks.

To get to the falls, go north from Helen on GA 75 for 8 miles. Turn left on F.R. 44 (Chattahoochee River Road) and go 5.4 miles to Upper Chattahoochee River Campground; turn right and follow the signs to the parking area. It is an easy 0.2-mile hike to the falls.

NEARBY ATTRACTIONS

Andrews Cove Recreation Area
Unicoi State Park and Lodge

DIRECTIONS

In addition to the route described in the Waterfall section, you can follow GA 75 north from Helen for 1.5 miles and turn left on GA 356 (GA 75 Alternate). Cross the river and turn right at the paved road next to the Chattahoochee Church. When the pavement ends, follow the same road for another 9 miles to the campground.

WARWOMAN DELL PICNIC AREA
TALLULAH RANGER DISTRICT

The name Warwoman honors Nancy Hart (1735–1830), a heroine of the Revolutionary War who lived in this area and was given the name by the Indians. This six-foot-tall patriot, wife and mother was an expert shot. She served as a spy for General Elijah Clarke during the war, often disguised as a man. When a band of six Tories came to her house demanding she cook for them, she killed one and captured the others, injuring one. Hart County and the towns of Hartwell and Hartford are also named in her honor. She is the only woman to have one of Georgia's 159 counties named for her.

This densely forested area on Warwoman Creek features an abundance of wildflowers in the spring and summer. It offers seven picnic sites, two group shelters, a latrine and drinking water. Open year-round, Warwoman Dell also boasts a nature trail.

HIKING

A 0.4-mile loop trail was built by a volunteer group of young adults during the summer of 1984. In the spring, the trail abounds in wildflowers. There is even a small waterfall along the route.

Bartram National Recreation Trail reaches its

midpoint at Warwoman Dell at about 37 miles. The trail crosses Warwoman Road and passes through the picnic area.

FISHING

Nearby Warwoman Creek is a popular and productive trout stream. An early start offers your only hope of finding room to fish this creek on the opening day of trout season.

WATERFALLS

There are several waterfalls off Warwoman Road that you may want to visit on a trip to Warwoman Dell.

The trailhead for Becky Branch Falls is across Warwoman Road from the picnic area. Follow the right side of the branch upstream for 500 feet to reach the Bartram Trail. The base of the falls is 100 feet farther upstream.

The 60-foot-tall Dick's Creek Falls is also near Warwoman Dell. Go 2.9 miles past the picnic area on Warwoman Road and turn right onto Sandy Ford Road, which is paved at its intersection with Warwoman Road. Go 0.6 mile and turn left, staying on the gravel Sandy Ford Road. Go 3.6 miles, crossing two shallow fords on your way to the Bartram Trail; there is a parking area in the woods on the left about 100 feet before the trail. Follow the Bartram Trail 0.35 mile to the falls, which drop into the Chattooga at a scenic bend in the river.

The last two waterfalls accessible from Warwoman Road are the 130-foot-tall Holcomb Creek Falls and the nearby Ammons Creek

Falls. To reach them, go east from Clayton on Warwoman Road for 10 miles; turn left on Hale Ridge Road and follow it 9 miles to the intersection with Overflow Road. The trailhead for the 1.3-mile loop hike is at the intersection.

NEARBY ATTRACTIONS

Black Rock Mountain State Park
Chattooga Wild and Scenic River
Tallulah Gorge State Park
Willis Knob Campground

DIRECTIONS

Where U.S. 76 turns west in Clayton, turn right (east) onto Warwoman Road (County Road 5) and travel 3 miles to Warwoman Dell Picnic Area.

WATERS CREEK RECREATION AREA
CHESTATEE RANGER DISTRICT

This creek-side recreation area is open year-round for camping, picnicking and fishing. There are eight campsites with flush toilets and drinking water. A usage fee is charged. Waters Creek is across the road from the game-checking station for the Chestatee Wildlife Management Area, making this a convenient camping area for hunters.

WATERFALL

Though not in the recreation area itself, Blood Mountain Falls is nearby. This 20-foot sluice on Blood Mountain Stream is reached by a short, unmaintained trail. From U.S. 19, the trailhead is 7.7 miles beyond Waters Creek Recreation Area on Dick's Creek Road (F.R. 34).

NEARBY ATTRACTIONS

Chestatee Wildlife Management Area
De Soto Falls Scenic Area
Dockery Lake Campground
Lake Winfield Scott Recreation Area

DIRECTIONS

From Dahlonega, go north on U.S. 19 for 12 miles and turn left on Dick's Creek Road. Waters Creek is 1 mile down the forest-service road.

WILLIS KNOB CAMPGROUND
TALLULAH RANGER DISTRICT

Equestrians will particularly enjoy this recreation area near the Chattooga River, with its horse camps and horse trails. There are eight campsites with nearby flush toilets and drinking water. A usage fee is charged. Reservations are required at this camp, which is open year-round.

NEARBY ATTRACTIONS

Black Rock Mountain State Park
Chattooga Wild and Scenic River
Tallulah Gorge State Park
Warwoman Dell Picnic Area

DIRECTIONS

From Clayton, go east on Warwoman Road for 11.6 miles to the gravel F.R. 157 (Goldmine Road). Turn right and follow the signs.

WOODY GAP RECREATION AREA
CHESTATEE RANGER DISTRICT

This roadside stop on GA 60 affords a nice view of the Yahoola Valley. There are 10 picnic tables and flush toilets. The 2,150-mile Appalachian Trail crosses the road in the gap. It is 1 mile north on the trail to Big Cedar Mountain, which offers a nice view from a rocky outlook.

NEARBY ATTRACTIONS

De Soto Falls Campground
Dockery Lake Campground
Lake Winfield Scott Recreation Area
Vogel State Park
Waters Creek Recreation Area

OCONEE NATIONAL FOREST

CENTRAL GEORGIA   **113,000 ACRES**

Though Oconee National Forest is much smaller than its sibling in North Georgia, it is home to many of middle Georgia's popular hunting and fishing spots. All USFS lands are managed as the Oconee Ranger District under the forest supervisor in Gainesville.

All of the recreation areas except Lake Sinclair are open year-round. A brochure with recreational opportunities and trail map for Oconee National Forest is available from the United States Forest Service. Donald W. Pfitzer's *Hiker's Guide to Georgia*, published by Falcon Press, has detailed descriptions of several hikes in both Oconee and Chattahoochee National Forests as part of his coverage of more than 100 trails in the state.

The Oconee River was named for a Creek

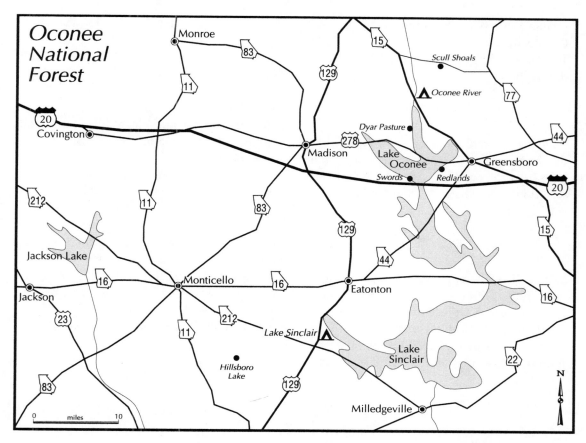

Indian town. The word's original meaning has been lost to time.

BURGESS MOUNTAIN TRAIL

This 1-mile trail begins at a forest road and ambles along an old roadbed to the highest point in Oconee National Forest—645 feet. Horses are allowed on the trail.

DIRECTIONS

From Eatonton, follow the Godfrey Highway (County Road 213) north for 4 miles to F.R. 1120. Turn left on F.R. 1120 and travel 1.4 miles to the trailhead.

DYAR PASTURE BOAT RAMP

Hiking and bird-watching are well suited for this boat ramp on Lake Oconee. A short trail leads from the parking lot to a waterfowl conservation area. There are flush toilets at the parking lot.

DIRECTIONS

From Greensboro, go west on U.S. 278 for 8 miles; turn right on Greshamville Road and go 1 mile to Greshamville. Turn right on Copeland Road and go 2.15 miles to a dirt road leading through a pasture to the boat ramp; the turnoff is just after the bridge over Greenbrier Creek.

HILLSBORO LAKE RECREATION AREA

This wooded area on a small lake has 23 picnic tables, five campsites and pit toilets. Legal fishing is allowed in the lake year-round.

DIRECTIONS

From GA 11 in Hillsboro, go southeast on County Road 1036 for 3 miles.

HITCHITI NATURE TRAIL

This 1.5-mile trail follows Falling Creek down to its confluence with the Ocmulgee River. The trail is in the Ernst Brender Demonstration Forest in Jones County. You can pick up a brochure outlining a self-guided nature hike on the trail at Jarrell Plantation State Historic Site, located near the trailhead.

Like much of middle and south Georgia, the trail was flooded in 1994. Flood damage can be seen along the trail, which has been cleared. The trail offers a scenic walk to the river. It has lots of ticks in the summer, so check yourself carefully for the pests after a hike.

A gated gravel road that also descends to the river parallels the trail at varying distances. While not as scenic as the trail, it offers a quicker walk back up from the river to complete a 3-mile loop.

DIRECTIONS

To get to the trailhead, take Exit 60 off I-75

and follow GA 18 for 17 miles. The trailhead is at the intersection with F.R. 908.

KINNARD CREEK TRAIL

This easy, 4.1-mile trail travels between two hunt camps through piney woods and bottoms, including a stand of old-growth loblolly pines. The trail begins at Concord Hunt Camp and ends at Horse Hunt Camp. It is great for both hiking and horseback riding.

DIRECTIONS

Follow GA 16 west from Monticello for 6.3 miles to Concord Church Road. Turn left and travel 1.6 miles to Concord Hunt Camp.

LAKE SINCLAIR RECREATION AREA

This 15,330-acre lake near Eatonton is a great spot for fishing and boating. The campground has 44 campsites, flush toilets, showers and a dump station. There are 12 picnic tables, a swimming beach and a boat ramp to help you make the most of the lake. A usage fee is charged. The 1.8-mile Twin Bridges Trail begins at the recreation area and offers an easy walk through a wooded area.

The lake and dam are named in honor of

Benjamin W. Sinclair, who was a manager of production for the Georgia Power Company.

DIRECTIONS

To get to the recreation area, go south from Eatonton on U.S. 129 for 10 miles; turn left on GA 212 and drive 1 mile; turn left on F.R. 1062, drive 2 miles and follow the signs to the recreation area.

OCMULGEE RIVER TRAIL

This 2.8-mile trail follows the Ocmulgee River through flat, piney woods. It is perfect for both hiking and horseback riding.

DIRECTIONS

Follow GA 83 south from Monticello for 13 miles to F.R. 1099. Turn north on the forest-service road and travel 1 mile to the Ocmulgee Flats Hunt Camp. The trailhead is behind the hunt camp.

OCONEE RIVER RECREATION AREA

This riverside recreation area in the Piedmont offers camping, hiking, picnicking and fishing. There are six picnic tables and seven campsites with nearby drinking water and pit toilets. Scull Shoals Trail winds along the Oconee River for 1 mile between the recreation area and Scull Shoals village. The remains of a historic boardinghouse are 0.3 mile beyond the village on Boarding House Trail.

DIRECTIONS

From Greensboro, go north on GA 15 for 12 miles to the recreation area.

REDLANDS BOAT RAMP

This boat ramp on Lake Oconee has three picnic sites, as well as flush toilets. A usage fee is charged.

DIRECTIONS

To reach the boat ramp, follow GA 278 west from Greensboro for 6 miles. Turn south on F.R. 1255 and drive 1 mile.

SCULL SHOALS HISTORIC AREA

This once-prosperous town now lies in ruins, its factories, bridges and buildings slowly returning to dust. Scull Shoals once supported Georgia's first paper mill, as well as one of the first cotton gins and an early textile factory.

HIKING

The 1-mile Scull Shoals Trail follows the Oconee River from Scull Shoals village to the Oconee River Recreation Area. It is a flat, easy hike.

The 0.3-mile Boarding House Trail begins at the parking lot in the Scull Shoals Historic Area and follows an easy course through piney woods to the remains of a historic boardinghouse.

Another short hike, the 0.3-mile Indian Mounds Trail leaves from the end of F.R. 1231A and crosses the Oconee River flood plain to two prehistoric Indian mounds. You can reach the trail by traveling 0.5 mile back from the Scull Shoals Historic Area toward the junction with F.R. 1234. Turn left on F.R. 1231A and travel about 0.5 mile to the trailhead. If you are at the junction of F.R. 1234 and F.R. 1231, bear left on F.R. 1231 and travel 0.5 mile to F.R. 1231A; bear right and travel another 0.5 mile to the trailhead.

NEARBY ATTRACTIONS

Oconee River Recreation Area
Lake Oconee

DIRECTIONS

Follow GA 15 north from Greensboro for 10 miles. Turn right on Macedonia Church Road and drive 2 miles before turning left on F.R. 1234. Follow the signs for 2 miles to F.R. 1231, turn left and travel 1 mile to Scull Shoals.

SWORDS BOAT RAMP

There are two picnic sites at this boat ramp on Lake Oconee, along with flush toilets. A usage fee is charged.

DIRECTIONS

To reach the boat ramp, take GA 278 west from Greensboro for 6.5 miles. Turn south on County Road 1135 and travel 4 miles.

TOWN CREEK BIKE TRAIL

This 15-mile loop trail was designed primarily for motorbikes, although it can also be used by all-terrain vehicles. For safety and environmental reasons, this trail is not recommended on wet days.

DIRECTIONS

Follow Penfield Road north from Greensboro to Shiloh Church. Turn right on the dirt county road and follow it until it ends. Turn left on another unpaved county road and travel 0.75 mile to a hunt camp on the left. Signs mark the trail.

WISE CREEK TRAIL

Part of a proposed trail along the western edge of Oconee National Forest, this 2.5-mile trail passes through piney woods and hardwood bottoms and follows the Ocmulgee River before it climbs back through piney woods. An easy hike, it is perfect for horseback riding, too.

DIRECTIONS

Follow GA 83 south from Monticello for 6.6 miles to Clay Road. Turn right and travel 2.5 miles to McElheney's Crossroads; turn left on the single-lane, gravel county road. Travel 1.2 miles, turn right and travel 0.1 mile. Turn left onto F.R. 1019 and follow it for 1.8 miles to F.R. 1098. Follow F.R. 1098 for 1.3 miles to the Wise Creek Hunt Camp on the Ocmulgee River, where the trail begins.

NATIONAL PARK LANDS

A tent under live oak trees in the early morning light of the Stafford Beach campsite on Cumberland Island

The National Park Service lands in Georgia preserve areas of historical significance. At Fort Frederica, on the coast, you can relive Georgia's colonial past, while at Cumberland Island National Seashore, you get a glimpse of a 19th-century island retreat. As you continue your tour through time at the national parks and monuments, you will find yourself in Plains, where former president Jimmy Carter began a successful bid for the United States presidency.

As a bureau of the Office of Fish, Wildlife and Parks within the Department of the Interior, the National Park Service is charged with protecting and interpreting important natural and historic sites. The more than 350 parks, monuments, national preserves, historic sites, seashores, memorials and battlefields scattered around the country attract 260 million visitors each year.

As you visit the parklands, remember that disturbing plants, animals, historical objects and geologic specimens is prohibited by law. You are not allowed to have metal detectors in the historic sites. The only exception to these rules is Cumberland Island, where visitors are permitted to collect seashells on the beach and the shark teeth that are scattered along the island's main road.

ANDERSONVILLE NATIONAL HISTORIC SITE

ANDERSONVILLE   475 ACRES

PP

This historic site is unique among the many units of the National Park Service, as it is set aside as a memorial to not just the thousands who died here at Camp Sumter during the Civil War, but to all Americans ever held as prisoners of war. Its purpose is to interpret the role of prisoner camps in history and to commemorate Americans who lost their lives in this and similar camps.

In 1864, the Confederate army created Camp Sumter to move the thousands of prisoners kept in the Richmond area to a camp with improved security and a more secure food supply. Over the

This memorial at Andersonville National Historic Site stands watch over row upon row of Civil War graves.

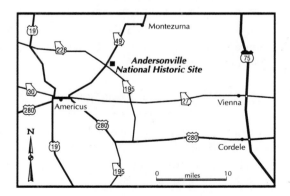

next 14 months, 13,000 of the 45,000 prisoners sent to Andersonville died of disease, poor sanitation, malnutrition, overcrowding and exposure.

In the late summer of 1865, Dorence Atwater and Clara Barton worked with soldiers and laborers to mark the graves at Andersonville. Atwater used records he copied while he was a prisoner in the camp to identify and properly mark all but 460 of the 13,000 graves.

Captain Henry Wirz, Camp Sumter's

The Georgia memorial at Andersonville National Historic Site provides an artistic window on the suffering of prisoners of war.

commandant, was tried by a military tribunal, convicted and hanged in Washington, D.C., in November 1865 for war crimes stemming from how he ran the camp. He was convicted of taking part in a conspiracy to injure the health of the prisoners in the camp. There was no evidence of a conspiracy, but public outrage in the North was so great that only a scapegoat such as Wirz could placate the angered citizenry.

The former prison site was privately owned until 1890, when it was purchased by a Union veterans' group called The Grand Army of the Republic. It was later run by the G.A.R.'s Woman's Relief Corps, then by the War Department and the Department of the Army before the National Park Service took over administration of the site in 1971.

Today, you can visit the national cemetery and the prison site, where the story of this and other prison camps is told. Andersonville offers picnicking, audiotapes for auto tours, walking tours, commemorative monuments, interpretive exhibits, a visitor center and a museum. There is a 12-minute slide show in the museum. The site is open daily from 8 A.M. until 5 P.M., with extended hours until 7 P.M. on Memorial Day. There is no entrance fee. Automobiles are restricted to the parking area and the auto tour roads.

NEARBY ATTRACTIONS

Georgia Veterans Memorial State Park
Jimmy Carter National Historic Site

DIRECTIONS

Andersonville is 10 miles northwest of Americus on GA 49 and can be reached via I-75 south of Macon.

FOR MORE INFORMATION

Superintendent, Andersonville National Historic Site, Route 1, Box 80085, Andersonville, GA 31711 (912-924-0343)

CHATTAHOOCHEE RIVER NATIONAL RECREATION AREA
ATLANTA
48-MILE STRETCH OF THE CHATTAHOOCHEE RIVER

Fishing, picnicking, hiking, jogging, bird-watching, photography, horseback riding and numerous river activities including rafting and canoeing are among the favorite pastimes along this stretch of the Chattahoochee. Opportunities to learn about the area's rich human and natural history are available throughout the 14 land units that make up this recreation area, which extends into northwest Atlanta. Watercraft rentals and shuttle services are offered from mid-May through September. The park is open daily.

While there is no entrance fee, vehicles are restricted to parking areas and roads. Glass containers are not permitted on the river, although snacks, soft drinks and sandwiches can be purchased within the park.

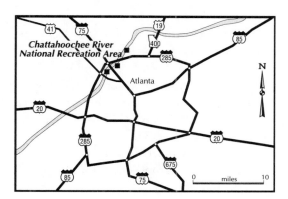

RAFTING

Paddling down the Chattahoochee in rafts and canoes is a favorite activity among visitors. The popular trip is to put in just below Morgan Falls Dam near Sandy Springs and float all day to the West Palisades Unit of the park at U.S. 41 near Cumberland Mall and the Galleria. Rafts, canoes, kayaks and all necessary gear can be rented for the trip from concessionaires at Johnson Ferry and Powers Island. Buses will return you to the starting point at the end of your float if you take advantage of the commercial service.

The sun on the river can be brutal. Don't forget to take plenty of water and sunscreen in your boat.

FISHING

Rainbow and brown trout populations are maintained in the Chattahoochee River near Atlanta. Persons over 16 years of age must have a valid Georgia fishing license and a trout stamp.

HIKING

There are eight trails in six of the recreation area's units.

The 968-acre Cochran Shoals Unit has a 2.5-mile handicapped-access fitness trail, the 1.5-mile Sope Creek Trail and the 1.5-mile Gundy Creek Trail. The fitness trail has 22 workout stations. The two hiking trails are good spots for finding wildflowers from April through June. Sope Creek Trail takes in both the creek

Joe and Monica Cook paddle on the 526-mile Chattahoochee River.

and the ruins of the Marietta Paper Mill. Biking and jogging paths are also located in this unit. Parking for this unit is along I-285 on Interstate North Parkway between New Northside Drive and Powers Ferry Road.

The 393-acre East Palisades Unit has 5 miles of riverside trail. From Northside Drive at I-285, go south to Indian Trail Road. It is 0.5 mile down this road to the parking area.

The park headquarters is the trailhead for 3 miles of interconnecting loops. The trailhead is at the parking area on Island Ford Parkway in Dunwoody.

The 108-acre Johnson Ferry Unit offers Mulberry Creek Loop Trail. This 2.5-mile trail goes north on the riverbank before forming a loop and returning to the trailhead on the first 0.25 mile of the hike. To reach this trail from Sandy Springs, go north on Johnson Ferry Road; the parking area is on the right after you cross the river.

The 43-acre Medlock Bridge Unit has interconnecting trails totaling 3 miles. The trailhead is just south of Medlock Bridge on GA 141.

The West Palisades Unit offers 4.5 miles of hiking trails in its 302 acres. The parking area is on Cobb Parkway (U.S. 41) at the Chattahoochee River. This unit offers a picnic area, restrooms and a raft ramp by the parking lot. This is a popular takeout point for rafters.

NEARBY ATTRACTIONS

Kennesaw Mountain National Battlefield Park
Martin Luther King, Jr., National Historic Site
Pickett's Mill Battlefield State Historic Site

DIRECTIONS

This recreation area is located in 14 separate land units along 48 miles of the Chattahoochee River in the vicinity of Atlanta.

FOR MORE INFORMATION

Chattahoochee River National Recreation Area, 1978 Island Ford Parkway, Atlanta, GA 30350-3400 (404-399-8070)

CHICKAMAUGA AND CHATTANOOGA NATIONAL MILITARY PARK

FORT OGLETHORPE, GEORGIA, AND LOOKOUT MOUNTAIN, TENNESSEE

During the fall of 1863, some of the hardest fighting in the Civil War was concentrated on the areas within this park. In June of that year, the Union's Army of the Cumberland, with 60,000 men, moved from Murfreesboro, Tennessee, to take the Confederacy's key rail center in Chattanooga. Some 43,000 Confederate soldiers under the leadership of General Braxton Bragg were arrayed about 20 miles from the town. For the next several months, the two armies marched and drew up new battle lines, with the Confederates eventually forced south from Chattanooga.

Then the Confederates, bolstered with reinforcements, moved 66,000 men south to engage the Union troops. On September 18, General Bragg tried to block the Union advance into Chattanooga by placing his troops on the banks of Chickamauga Creek. The next morning, the Union army encountered the Confederate cavalry at Jay's Mill, and the battle soon spread south for nearly 4 miles.

Unlike most of the battles of the Civil War, which were fought in fields, the Battle of Chickamauga blazed through dense woods that confounded the generals' attempts to keep track of the engagement and maneuver their men. The desperate and bloody attacks often ended in costly hand-to-hand combat.

On September 20, the battle continued with General Bragg's attempt to cut the Union army off from Chattanooga. When a gap opened in the Union line, General James Longstreet pressed the advantage and routed half of Union general William Rosecrans's army. General George Thomas took command of the remaining Union troops along a new battle line at Snodgrass Hill. Repeatedly, Thomas held his ground against fierce Confederate assaults. General Thomas earned the nickname "Rock of Chickamauga" for his stubborn opposition.

When darkness fell, the Union troops retreated to Chattanooga. The Confederate army lost 18,000 men and the Union army 16,000. Confederate general William Bate called Chickamauga a "River of Death." On one day alone, the 22nd Alabama Regiment lost more than half its soldiers and nearly half its officers in the fierce fight.

THE PARK

In 1895, Chickamauga became the first national military park, setting the pattern for the other military and battlefield parks to follow. It was placed under the supervision of the War Department until 1933, when it was transferred to the National Park Service. The park has been maintained as close as possible to its appearance in 1863 to aid historians and visitors in picturing the natural obstacles which shaped the battle. Its main purpose is to preserve the significant resources of the Civil War battles of Chickamauga and Chattanooga and to educate the public about the events memorialized here.

VISITOR CENTERS

There are several rare and unique pieces among the 355 weapons on display in the Chickamauga Visitor Center. They are from a collection of American military shoulder arms which Claude and Zenia Fuller donated to the National Park Service in 1954. Outside the center is an artillery display showing the various cannons used during the Civil War. The exhibits inside describe the battle and show its significance to the Civil War. A 26-minute video dramatically orients visitors to the battle. Tickets can be purchased in the visitor center bookstore.

The primary exhibit at the Lookout Mountain Visitor Center is the James Walker painting *Battle Above the Clouds*. The exhibit includes an audio orientation to the painting and the battles for Chattanooga.

Both visitor centers are open daily except for Christmas.

Tours of the historic Cravens House on Lookout Mountain are conducted seasonally. The Cravens House, where the fiercest fighting took place, was badly damaged by Union gunfire. It was used by Confederate officers as a headquarters.

AUTO TOUR

A 7-mile self-guided auto tour takes visitors by the major sites of the battle. An audiotape tour is available for rent at the visitor center.

HIKING

The park has trails ranging in length from 5 to 20 miles. There are two trails under 10 miles—the 6-mile Confederate Line Trail and the 5-mile General Bragg Trail. The four longer trails are the white-blazed, 12-mile Memorial Trail; the yellow-blazed, 14-mile Cannon Trail; the pink-blazed, 14-mile Historical Trail; and the blue-blazed, 20-mile Perimeter Trail.

The paint blazes are particularly important in this park, as the trails interconnect, often sharing footpaths with each other. There are times when you may hike on a trail that is marked with up to three different blazes as the trails briefly share the same footpath.

NEARBY ATTRACTION

Cloudland Canyon State Park

DIRECTIONS

From I-75, take GA 2 to Fort Oglethorpe. The park is south of Fort Oglethorpe on U.S. 27. The Lookout Mountain Unit is located at the entrance to Point Park.

FOR MORE INFORMATION

Chickamauga and Chattanooga National Military Park, P.O. Box 2128, Fort Oglethorpe, GA 30742 (706-866-9241)

CUMBERLAND ISLAND NATIONAL SEASHORE/ CUMBERLAND ISLAND NATIONAL WILDERNESS AREA

ST. MARYS   8,840-ACRE WILDERNESS AREA

Thousands of years of history are crammed into this tiny island 18 miles long and only 3 miles across at its widest point. This barrier island, established in 1972 as one of the nation's first national seashores, was home to Timucuan Indians for more than 4,000 years. The Indians called the island *Wissoe*, or "Sassafras," but no one has seen that plant on the island recently.

The Indians were superseded by the Spanish in 1566 when they arrived to build Fort San Pedro and establish a Franciscan mission to convert the Indians. For the next 200 years, England, France and Spain vied for control of the Southeast. Under the direction of General James Oglethorpe in 1736, the island was renamed Cumberland, and forts—Fort St. Andrews and

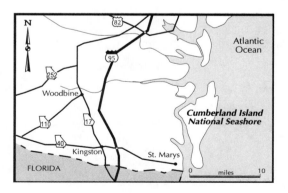

Fort Prince William—were built at either end of the island. The English also built a hunting lodge called Dungeness.

In 1783, Revolutionary War hero Nathanael Greene purchased a large part of the island in order to harvest its live oaks for ships' timber. He died three years later. His widow, Catharine, married Phineas Miller and built a four-story tabby mansion, which she called Dungeness. In 1818, General Light-Horse Harry Lee, a Revolutionary War friend of the Greenes, died on Cumberland after a short illness.

During the Civil War, the island's slaves were removed to Amelia Island by Union troops. After the war, many returned and settled near Halfmoon Bluff at the northern end of the island. Only a church remains from this settle-

ment. It was during this period that the second Dungeness was destroyed by fire.

Andrew Carnegie's brother, Thomas, bought the Dungeness property in 1881 and built himself a mansion, also called Dungeness. Carnegie died shortly after the mansion was completed. His widow, Lucy, eventually acquired most of the island. Dungeness was eventually abandoned and was later completely destroyed by fire.

Plum Orchard, a mansion built by Lucy for her son, George, was donated to the National Park Foundation by Carnegie family members in 1971. Their contribution, as well as funds from supporting foundations, helped win congressional approval for establishing Cumberland Island as a national seashore.

The island is now home to an abundance of

Terns fly just off the sand at Cumberland Island National Seashore.

wildlife. From armadillos to feral hogs and horses, all manner of animals inhabit the island. You will find deer and alligators, bobcats and river otters, loggerhead turtles and diamondback rattlesnakes, egrets, herons, ducks and many other birds. You will also find biting insects such as ticks, so check yourself carefully when hiking through the maritime forest.

CAMPING

Cumberland Island has only one established campground. Sea Camp features 16 sites with water, restrooms and showers (cold water only). The sites have a picnic table and a raccoon box, or visitors can use the hooked pole for storing supplies. Reservations are required, and all food and equipment must be hand-carried the 0.5 mile from the dock to Sea Camp. Pets are not allowed on the island.

BACK-COUNTRY CAMPING

Cumberland Island has four primitive camping areas, three of which are located within the national wilderness. As with Sea Camp, reservations are required. The first site, Stafford Beach Camp, is a 3.5-mile hike from Sea Camp dock. This camp is only a short distance from the beach. Hickory Hill Camp, a 5.5-mile hike, and Yankee Paradise Camp, a 7.4-mile hike, are both located within the island's inland forests. Brickhill Bluff Camp, a 10.6-mile hike, is located on the Brickhill River.

Campsites are assigned once you reach the island and cannot be reserved in advance for any camp except Sea Camp. Fires are not permitted in the back country; a camp stove is required for cooking. All drinking water must be boiled, filtered or treated. Also, because of problems with raccoons and squirrels, you will want to bring enough rope to suspend your pack, food and litter from a tree.

HIKING

More than a dozen trails provide ample hiking opportunities. From South Point Trail at the southern end of the island to Terrapin Point Trail in the north, miles of trail lead you past all the island's habitats—beaches, dunes, interdune meadows, ponds, maritime forests and salt marshes. Back-country maps are available at the visitor center.

FISHING

Year-round fishing on Cumberland Island is open to children and to persons over 16 years of age who have a valid freshwater fishing license. All Georgia fishing laws apply.

HUNTING

Cumberland Island has four managed deer hunts and hog hunts each year. For more information, call 912-882-4338.

SWIMMING

Swimming is allowed on the public beaches; some areas are private property. Lifeguards are not provided. There is a gradual slope offshore; sharks may be present in the surf. Swim at your own risk.

GREYFIELD INN

This Carnegie mansion is operated privately as an inn. Reservations can be made by calling 904-261-6408.

PLUM ORCHARD

This Georgian Revival–style mansion was a wedding present from Lucy Carnegie to her son, George. Tours of the 30-room home, built in 1898, are available to island visitors for a fee of $6, the cost of the ferry ride from Sea Camp dock to Plum Orchard. Reservations are appreciated and can be made by calling at the times and number listed in the Reservations section below.

As of 1995, the National Park Service was discussing plans to allow a private group to lease Plum Orchard with the intent of placing an artist colony in the mansion.

RESERVATIONS

Reservations may be made 11 months in advance, starting on the first working day of each month. They are not absolutely necessary if you plan to make a day trip but are mandatory if you plan to camp. If you don't make reservations, you will be put on standby. Reservations may be made by calling the park office

from 10:00 A.M. to 4:00 P.M. Monday through Friday.

The ferry departs St. Marys at 9:00 A.M. and 11:45 A.M. and returns from Cumberland Island at 10:15 A.M. and 4:45 P.M. During peak season—March 15 through September—there is an additional ferry run. During the off-season, there is no ferry service on Tuesdays and Wednesdays. The cost is $10.07 for adults, $5.99 for children 12 and under and $7.97 for those 65 and older; prices include tax. Camping is free of charge.

NEARBY ATTRACTIONS

Crooked River State Park
Hofwyl-Broadfield Plantation State Historic Site
Okefenokee National Wildlife Refuge and Wilderness Area

DIRECTIONS

The ferry to Cumberland Island departs from the park office in St. Marys. To get to St. Marys, take Exit 2 off I-95 and travel east on GA 40 for 16 miles. GA 40 ends in St. Marys. Turn right; the park office is on your immediate left.

FOR MORE INFORMATION

Cumberland Island National Seashore, P.O. Box 806, St. Marys, GA 31558 (912-882-4335)

FORT FREDERICA NATIONAL MONUMENT

ST. SIMONS ISLAND

Situated on the banks of the Frederica River, this archaeological site is all that remains of what was once a flourishing military town. From 1736 until 1749, Fort Frederica was the center of British military operations on the Georgia frontier. This planned town was built by the immigrants that James Edward Oglethorpe welcomed to his new settlement along the Savannah River. Three years after Oglethorpe reached Georgia, he began construction on the town with the help of 44 men (mostly craftsmen) and 72 women and children. The town was named for the only son of King George—Frederick.

The fort was built before the town because of the continued threat of attack by the Spanish, who occupied Florida. Once the fort was completed, Oglethorpe staked out 84 lots, each measuring 60 feet by 90 feet. Each family was granted a lot plus 50 acres in the country on

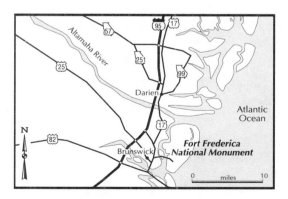

which to plant crops. The simple palmetto huts were soon replaced by homes built of wood, tabby and brick. The town was completed by a 75-foot-wide avenue called Broad Street, which ran from the fort to the town gates. This thoroughfare was made more picturesque by the orange trees that lined it.

A baker, a blacksmith and a wheelwright were among those Oglethorpe hired to ply their trade. The only thing missing from the town of Fort Frederica was a church, but that didn't stop the town from prospering. By the mid-1740s, the population reached about 500. Because Oglethorpe had banned slavery, the farmers worked their own fields. Local game such as deer supplemented the diet of the townsfolk.

After settling Fort Frederica in 1736, Oglethorpe returned to England to round up troops for the war he knew he would soon have to fight. He returned in 1738 with approximately 600 men—eight companies of infantry and one company of grenadiers. He garrisoned most of the men at Frederica but sent some to the southern end of the island to the recently built Fort St. Simons. The very next year, the war between Britain and Spain began. Not willing to wait for the Spanish to reach St. Simons, Oglethorpe built an earthen wall and a palisaded moat around Fort Frederica. He then set out to capture Castillo de San Marcos at San Augustine in Florida. But even with 900 troops and 1,100 Indian allies, his siege failed, and he returned to Fort Frederica.

Two years later, on July 7, 1742, the Spanish began their attack on St. Simons. They failed, only catching a glimpse of the fort before being forced back by the British. When the Spanish commander heard of this event, he sent several hundred more soldiers to cover his troops' retreat. These men were ambushed by Oglethorpe at Bloody Marsh, so called because it is said the marshes ran red with blood. The British routed these men as well. Within a week, the Spaniards made their way back to Florida, never to return.

The demise of Fort Frederica began with the end of the threat from Spain. Oglethorpe returned to England in 1743, and his regiment was disbanded in 1749. With the loss of several hundred soldiers, the economy of the military town soon faltered. The town struggled on for another decade or so, but by 1755, it had already lost the appearance of a thriving town, due to its empty houses, empty barracks and overgrown streets. Before the country began its war for independence against the British, Fort Frederica lay in ruins.

FORT FREDERICA TODAY

Fort Frederica National Monument is administered by the National Park Service. It can be toured for a small fee. From the visitor center, it is still possible to walk up the old military road which once connected the fort to Fort St. Simons at the southern end of the island. Visitors can pass through the once-guarded town gate, then walk along Broad Street, eventually passing the sites of the Calwell House, where John Calwell made soap and candles, and the Hawkins-Davison House, half of which was built by Thomas Hawkins, surgeon and apothecary,

and the other half by Samuel Davison, tavern keeper and town constable. At the end of Broad Street is the site of the tabby fort, which was square and had bastions at each corner.

Also on the tour are the site of the barracks, which held several hundred men; the northeast bastion, a remnant of the time when Oglethorpe fortified the town against the Spanish; and the burying ground, which lies outside the palisade to the east of the town.

The hours of operation are from 8 A.M. until 5 P.M. There is no campground in the park.

NEARBY ATTRACTIONS

Hofwyl-Broadfield Plantation State Historic Site
Jekyll Island
Fort King George State Historic Site

DIRECTIONS

Fort Frederica is 12 miles from Brunswick. It can be reached via U.S. 17 and the F. J. Torras Causeway. A toll is charged to cross over to the island.

FOR MORE INFORMATION

Superintendent, Fort Frederica National Monument, Route 9, Box 286-C, St. Simons Island, GA 31522 (912-638-3639)

FORT PULASKI NATIONAL MONUMENT
COCKSPUR ISLAND, EAST OF SAVANNAH
OVER 5,000 ACRES

The massive brick walls of Fort Pulaski seem immovable even today. Standing by one of the cannons on the outer wall, you get a commanding view of the salt marsh surrounding Cockspur Island. It is difficult to imagine anyone staging an assault on this imposing fortress. That feeling of invincibility ran strong in the Confederate army, too, until that fateful April day when the fort's walls were blown open by artillery attack. The white flag of surrender waving over Fort Pulaski changed the way that all fortifications were built from that day forward.

Cockspur Island was selected as the site of a new fortification in the early 1800s because of its strategic importance in defending the port in Savannah. It was named in honor of Count Casimir Pulaski, the Polish hero of the American Revolution who was mortally wounded in the attack on Savannah in 1779.

Construction began on the marshy site in 1829. It would take 18 years and $1 million to complete the fort, which was considered an engineering marvel. The 7½-foot thick outer walls were backed with massive masonry piers to create an impenetrable barrier to artillery attack. At the time the fort was built, it was an established fact that smoothbore cannons and mortars were of little practical use from more than 1,000 yards, and there was no firm ground within a mile of Fort Pulaski to erect an artillery battery to stage an attack. United States chief of engineers Joseph Totten was so sure of the stout fortress that he asserted an enemy "might as well bombard the Rocky Mountains."

When the fort was completed, there was no threat of war and little money in the national treasury. As a result, there weren't enough funds to arm Fort Pulaski or garrison soldiers there. As fate would have it, the United States Army would have to take Pulaski in battle before Federal troops would man the fort.

Only two soldiers were stationed at the fort in January 1861. Their task was maintenance, not coastal defense. On January 3, Georgia governor Joseph Brown ordered the Georgia Militia to garrison Fort Pulaski. After the state seceded from the Union on January 19, the fort was transferred to the Confederate States of America.

On November 7, 1861, a combined navy and army force struck 15 miles north of Fort Pulaski at Port Royal Sound, South Carolina. Federal

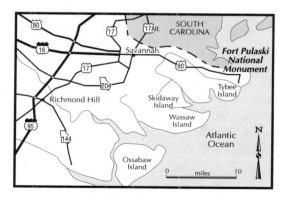

Looking through the drawbridge into Fort Pulaski on the coast of Georgia.

ships bombarded Forts Walker and Beauregard and landed an unopposed force on Hilton Head Island. Three days later, shaken by the Federal assault, the Confederates abandoned Tybee Island at the mouth of the Savannah River, leaving Fort Pulaski as the only defense for Savannah. The Federal army quickly prepared for the siege of the fort by erecting 11 artillery batteries on Tybee Island. Among the 36 cannons and mortars on Tybee were 10 experimental cannons with rifled barrels. The spiraled grooves inside the cannons' barrels were designed to spin the bullet-shaped shells and cause them to fire with greater accuracy, range and penetration.

On April 10, engineer captain Quincy Gillmore demanded that Pulaski be surrendered to the Federal army. Confederate colonel Charles Olmstead confidently refused. By noon the following day, it was obvious to both armies that warfare would never be the same again. The rifled cannons had bored large holes in the thick outer walls, and the Federal army began to drop explosive shells dangerously close to the 40,000 pounds of gunpowder stored in the northwest magazine. With defeat assured and a devastating explosion imminent, Colonel Olmstead waved a white flag to end the siege after just 30 hours. The battle necessitated a radical rethinking of fortification design, just as the sea battle between the ironclads *Monitor* and *Merrimack* changed naval architecture forever.

Federal troops were stationed at Fort Pulaski for the duration of the war. By 1864, parts of the fort were being used as a prison for Confederate officers. Following the Civil War, political prisoners were held here.

The fort was made a national monument in 1924. Restoration work began in 1933, when the fort was transferred to the National Park Service.

FORT PULASKI TODAY

Visitors can tour the entire fort and view several rooms arranged to show what life was like for soldiers stationed at Fort Pulaski. Park rangers give talks and conduct special programs. Call the office for more information.

The visitor center has interpretive displays on Fort Pulaski. A number of artifacts from the fort are on display. A short video is shown in the center to orient visitors to Fort Pulaski's history. Restrooms are located both at the visitor center and inside the fort.

The picnic area may be accessed either by car from the road into the monument or by the 0.6-mile trail leading from the parking lot near the visitor center.

A boat ramp and 5,000 acres of salt marsh provide recreational opportunities for fishing, crabbing and oystering by permit.

HOURS AND FEES

Fort Pulaski is open daily except for Christmas from 8:30 A.M. to 5:30 P.M., with extended hours during the summer. There is a $2 per-person park entrance fee, which covers all activities. The maximum fee for immediate family is $4.

DIRECTIONS

Fort Pulaski is located on U.S. 80 some 15 miles east of Savannah and west of Tybee Island.

FOR MORE INFORMATION

Fort Pulaski National Monument, P.O. Box 30757, Savannah, GA 31410-0757 (912-786-5787)

JIMMY CARTER NATIONAL HISTORIC SITE
PLAINS

In 1976, the eyes of the nation turned to an unlikely small town in southwest Georgia—Plains. Native son Jimmy Carter was running for president, and Plains was at the center of the media attention surrounding his successful bid for that office. The railroad depot served as his campaign headquarters. The press played

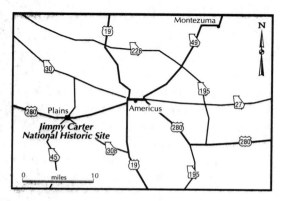

The train depot in Plains, Georgia, served as Jimmy Carter's presidential campaign headquarters during his successful bid for office in 1975.

softball games against Carter and his campaign staff, while tourists packed his brother Billy's gas station to learn more about the farmer who would be statesman.

James Earl Carter was born in Plains on October 1, 1924, and grew up on his family's farm 3 miles out of town. After graduating from Plains High School, he attended Georgia Southwestern College and Georgia Tech for a year each while waiting for his appointment to the United States Naval Academy. After graduating from the academy in 1946, he married Plains native Rosalynn Smith and worked for the next seven years on nuclear submarines in the navy. When his father died in 1953, Carter resigned his naval commission and returned home to run the family's farms and farm-supply store. He soon

became involved in his church, the local planning commission and the local school board. In 1963, he was elected to the Georgia Senate, where he served two terms. He ran unsuccessfully for governor against Lester Maddox in 1966, but ran again in 1971 and won. After one term as governor (governors could serve only one four-year term in Georgia at that time), he began making plans for his presidential campaign.

After his loss to Ronald Reagan in the 1980 presidential race, he returned to Plains. Since then, he and Rosalynn have written several books and given countless lectures. He is on the faculty at Emory University and works for world peace in various ways through his Carter Center in Atlanta. He regularly teaches Sunday school at Maranatha Baptist Church in Plains; visitors are encouraged to attend. A sign in the park's visitor center notes the next date when Carter will be teaching at the church.

Today, Plains is once again a sleepy southwest Georgia town, but those hectic days are not so far away. Here and there around the town are the signs of that successful campaign. The railroad depot is now the visitor center for Jimmy Carter National Historic Site, where pictures from the 1976 campaign and Carter's four years as president remind visitors of the town's recent history. The park is limited to interpreting Carter's early years and presidential campaign. The Carter Center in Atlanta covers his years as our 39th president.

In March 1995, the National Park Service publicized plans to begin reconstruction work at Plains High School and its hopes to complete the restoration before the 1996 Olympics, to be held in Atlanta. The high school is where Jimmy and Rosalynn Carter attended first through 11th grades. After the high school is renovated, the National Park Service hopes to begin work on Carter's boyhood home. These projects mark the beginning of many changes at the historic site. When the work is completed, Plains High School will be turned into a visitor center and museum, which will more fully interpret President Carter's life, as well as the history of the town of Plains.

Though visitors are not allowed to see the former president's home, which is protected by the United States Secret Service, the visitor center offers a video of the Carters giving a tour of their home.

HOURS

The visitor center is open daily from 9 A.M. to 5 P.M. except for Christmas and New Year's. There is no entrance fee.

NEARBY ATTRACTIONS

Andersonville National Historic Site
Georgia Veterans Memorial State Park
Providence Canyon State Conservation Park

DIRECTIONS

The park office is in the old railroad depot, located just across the railroad tracks from U.S. 280 in downtown Plains, 10 miles west of Americus.

FOR MORE INFORMATION

Jimmy Carter National Historic Site, P.O. Box 392, Plains, GA 31780 (912-824-3413)

KENNESAW MOUNTAIN NATIONAL BATTLEFIELD PARK
KENNESAW, COBB COUNTY

From May to August 1864, Union general William T. Sherman waged a series of battles and flanking maneuvers as he and Confederate general Joseph E. Johnston played a deadly game of chess. The important railroad hub of Atlanta was the sought-after prize as Sherman's 100,000

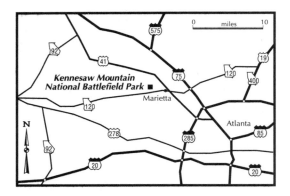

troops squared off time and again with the 65,000 soldiers under Johnston's command.

June 1864 was a sloppy, wet month in Georgia. The constant rain bogged down the roads into barely passable, muddy tracks in some places, hindering Sherman's troop movements.

The Confederate army was prepared to defend the heavily guarded slopes of Kennesaw Mountain, from which it could see the rail lines that Sherman depended on for his supplies. Every possible point of attack against the mountain was protected by cannon and rifle fire.

As he had done many times already during the Atlanta Campaign, Sherman choose not to meet the well-entrenched army head on, but to outflank it. On June 22, Johnston dispatched 11,000 soldiers under General John Bell Hood to counter the Union's flanking maneuver. They met at Kolb Farm in a bloody fight that failed to turn the Federal army back.

The muddy roads continued to limit Sherman's choices. Five days later, he called for a diversionary attack against the mountain while a greater force attacked the center of Johnston's

A display of cannons guard the museum at Kennesaw Mountain.

forces along Burnt Hickory Road. Under a rain of fire and a barrage of rocks rolled down Little Kennesaw Mountain by the Confederates, the Federals first attacked and then were recalled from Pigeon Hill. A second offensive south of Dallas Road pitted 8,000 Union troops against Johnston's two best divisions. The stubborn fighting was a close-quarters attack that ended in a short hand-to-hand fight atop the Confederate earthworks at Cheatham Hill.

The Federals lost 3,000 men to the Confederates' 800, but the diversionary movement at the Confederate left gave Sherman an important intersection and placed his army closer to the Chattahoochee River than Johnston's. On July 2, the Confederate army was forced to abandon Kennesaw Mountain.

The campaign for Atlanta continued in a series of battles and flanking maneuvers. On September 2, Sherman telegraphed Washington, "Atlanta is ours, and fairly won." A week after Lincoln's reelection, Sherman began his devastating March to the Sea.

Just 200 to 300 yards north of the entrance to Kennesaw Mountain National Battlefield Park is the site of an old Indian route that led from the heart of the Cherokee nation to Standing Peachtree, a Creek village that grew into a trading post and fort just south of the Chattahoochee River. Pioneers called this route Peachtree Road or Montgomery Ferry Road (Montgomery's Ferry was located here). This same route was later used by the Confederates and the Federals as they fought in the area in 1864. With the advent of automobiles, this road became the Dixie Highway and U.S. 41.

SELF-GUIDED AUTO TOUR

The park's major historic areas are located on the driving tour. A map of the tour can be obtained at the visitor center. Each stop on the tour has a parking area with interpretive signs. There are also short interpretive trails leading from the auto tour to the tops of Kennesaw Mountain and Cheatham Hill.

HIKING

The park's East Trail and West Trail offer a total of 16 miles of trail. Hikes of a number of lengths are possible. The most popular is the 1-mile hike from the visitor center to the top of Kennesaw Mountain. East and West Trails meet five times. The longest hike uses the two trails to form a loop between the visitor center and Kolb Farm on Powder Springs Road. A good shorter loop connects the visitor center and Burnt Hickory Road, crossing Big Kennesaw and Little Kennesaw Mountains and Pigeon Hill for a 5.5-mile loop.

A trail map is available in the visitor center. Pets must be on a leash at all times on the trails.

HORSEBACK RIDING

The park has 13 miles of trails open to equestrians. The only trails closed to horses are East Trail between the visitor center and Burnt Hickory Road and the first 0.5 mile of West Trail as you hike south from the visitor center. There is a parking area for horse trailers at the pull-off on Cheatham Hill Road near Kolb Farm. You cannot ride or graze horses in the park's open fields. Horses are also not allowed near parking lots, park buildings, picnic areas and roadsides except at trail crossings.

ACTIVITY AREAS

The park's activity areas are popular places for playing Frisbee and ball, flying kites, picnicking and sunbathing. The three open fields are spread through the park. Activity Area #1 is on Old U.S. 41, Activity Area #2 on Stilesboro Road just west of the visitor center and Activity Area #3 at the south end of the park on Cheatham Hill Road. No alcoholic beverages are allowed in these areas or any part of the park.

PICNICKING

In addition to the activity areas, there are picnic tables at the visitor center. There are also barbecue pits at the picnic area near the visitor center on Stilesboro Road.

PARK HOURS

The park is open daily from 8:30 A.M. until 5:00 P.M. except for Christmas. No fee is charged to enter the park.

NEARBY ATTRACTIONS

Pickett's Mill Battlefield State Historic Site
Etowah Indian Mounds State Historic Site

Allatoona Lake
Red Top Mountain State Park and Lodge

DIRECTIONS

From Kennesaw, go south on U.S. 41 to Old U.S. 41. The visitor center is on Stilesboro Road at its junction with Old U.S. 41. From I-75, take Exit 116 and follow the signs for 4 miles to the park.

FOR MORE INFORMATION

Kennesaw Mountain National Battlefield Park, 900 Kennesaw Mountain Drive, Kennesaw, GA 30144-4854 (404-427-4686)

MARTIN LUTHER KING, JR., NATIONAL HISTORIC SITE
ATLANTA

The birthplace and boyhood surroundings of Martin Luther King, Jr., the nation's foremost

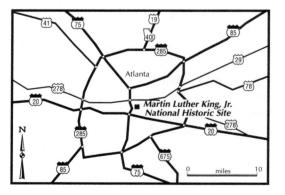

civil-rights leader, are preserved in this close-knit community called "Sweet Auburn." The neighborhood was given the nickname by John Wesley Dobbs, a political leader. Dobbs was referring to the unique grouping of more than 100 neighborhood businesses owned or operated by blacks, including a library and a business college. This created a pocket of opportunity for blacks in a city controlled by segregation laws.

King's birthplace, his grandfather's home, is just down the street from Ebenezer Baptist Church, where he returned in 1960 to serve as co-pastor with his father. Dr. King's mother was assassinated here in 1974 while sitting at the church organ. King's grave site is on Auburn Avenue in front of Freedom Hall at the Martin Luther King, Jr., Center for Nonviolent Social Change.

THE SITE

At present, the National Park Service owns 19 historical structures at this site. Twelve of these have been restored to their original 1930s appearance, and plans call for the restoration of the remaining seven. A number of these structures are used for administrative purposes, with the remainder rented for residential use.

Park rangers conduct tours of the site every half-hour daily throughout the year except for Christmas and New Year's. Tours begin at the Bryant-Graves House at 522 Auburn Avenue. Each tour is limited to 15 people. The tours are filled on a first-come, first-served basis, with the first tour beginning at 10 A.M. and the last at 5 P.M. One of the highlights of the tour is 501

Patrick Morelli's sculpture, "Behold," at the Martin Luther King, Jr., National Historic Site was inspired by the ancient Aftrican ritual of holding a new born child to the heavens and proclaiming, "Behold, the only thing greater than yourself." Atlanta's skyscrapers can be seen in the background.

Auburn Avenue, where Dr. King was born and spent his first 12 years. The nine-room Queen Anne–style house was built in 1895. Only the first floor of the home is accessible, but the second floor can be seen by way of pictures in a photo album.

An interpretive video is shown at the visitor contact station, a kiosk located across Auburn Avenue from the Freedom Hall complex; the video is captioned for the hearing-impaired. The site's official brochure is available in Braille and on audio cassette.

Other tours are offered on a seasonal basis by both the National Park Service and private organizations. These tours are held at such key sites as Ebenezer Baptist Church, the Martin Luther King, Jr., Center for Nonviolent Social Change and the African-American Panoramic Experience (APEX). Both the King Center and Ebenezer Baptist Church are open to the public.

The National Park Service and the King Center were involved in a well-publicized dispute in early 1995 over the park service's right to offer tours at the site. The King family ordered the park service off the site and demanded increased payments to the center, as well as the donation of park-service land to the family. The park service's plan to build a visitor center on land opposite the site in time for the 1996 summer Olympics in Atlanta was also a matter of controversy. The differences have been worked out, with a new visitor center to be built in late 1995.

NEARBY ATTRACTIONS

Chattahoochee River National Recreation Area

Kennesaw Mountain National Battlefield Park

DIRECTIONS

From I-75/I-85 South, exit at Butler Street and follow the signs. From I-75/I-85 North, exit at Edgewood Avenue/Auburn Avenue and follow Auburn Avenue east for 0.6 mile to the site.

FOR MORE INFORMATION

Martin Luther King, Jr., National Historic Site, 526 Auburn Avenue N.E., Atlanta, GA 30312 (404-331-5190)

OCMULGEE NATIONAL MONUMENT
MACON

More than 10,000 years of human habitation are represented at Ocmulgee National Monument. From Ice Age hunters to the Creek Indi-

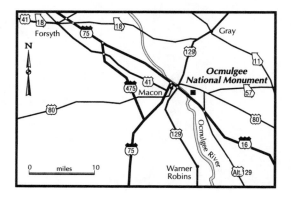

Griffin Logue looks inside the earthlodge at Ocmulgee National Monument. The reconstructed ceremonial building recreates a structure that stood on this site around A.D. 1000.

ans, this site offers information on many distinct cultures, particularly the skillful farmers known as the Mississippians, who lived here from 900 to 1100 A.D.

The Dunlap House, located opposite the monument, is the site of the only battle fought in Macon during the Civil War.

ACTIVITIES

A museum, a self-guided tour, walking trails, an auto tour, a picnic area and fishing are among the offerings at this site. A 12-minute movie is shown regularly, and special events are scheduled throughout the year. The monument is open from 9 A.M. until 5 P.M. daily except for Christmas and New Year's. There is no entrance fee, but parking and driving are restricted.

NEARBY ATTRACTIONS

Oconee National Forest
Jarrell Plantation State Historic Site
Piedmont National Wildlife Refuge

DIRECTIONS

The monument can be reached by taking Exit 4 off I-16 and following U.S. 80 east for 2 miles to the park entrance.

FOR MORE INFORMATION

Ocmulgee National Monument, 1207 Emery Highway, Macon, GA 31201 (912-752-8257)

CORPS OF ENGINEERS RESERVOIRS

A father and son boating on West Point Lake near the Georgia/Alabama state line.

Millions of visitors boat, fish, ski and swim each year on the Corps of Engineers reservoirs in Georgia. Three of the ten lakes—Allatoona, Clarks Hill and Sidney Lanier—are on the short list of the most-visited Corps of Engineers projects in the country.

Authorized by Congress primarily to control flooding, generate power and aid navigation, the lakes are also a great recreational resource. They offer more than 1,000 campsites to choose from. Hundreds of boat ramps give access to the 295,970 acres of lakes impounded by Corps of Engineers dams in Georgia and along its boundaries with Alabama, South Carolina and Florida. Many of the lakes, including Seminole and

Clarks Hill, are noted as some of the best fishing spots in the Southeast.

A map of each lake is available through the lake's resource manager's office, which is also a good source of boating and fishing information.

FEES

A fee is charged to camp in developed campgrounds and to use some of the lakes' developed recreational facilities. All Corps of Engineers lakes, however, have a number of free access points to the water.

Golden Age Passports for persons age 62 and older and Golden Access Passports for the handicapped entitle their holders to reduced fees at federally operated facilities. These passports are available at the resource manager's office of any of Georgia's Corps of Engineers lakes.

FOR MORE INFORMATION

United States Army Engineer District, Mobile, P.O. Box 2288, Mobile, AL 36628-0001 (205-690-2505)

ALLATOONA LAKE
BARTOW, CHEROKEE AND COBB COUNTIES
12,010-ACRE LAKE

This is the oldest Corps of Engineers lake in the Southeast, as well as one of the most visited, with about 13 million visitors each year. Just 30 miles north of Atlanta, this large, irregularly shaped lake sprawls across three counties, reaching not just up the Etowah River, but well

up its many tributary creeks as well. The lake collects the runoff from a 1,100-square-mile drainage area, and lake levels can fluctuate greatly with rainfall. A daily increase of three to four feet is not uncommon during heavy rains. The lake not only generates electricity, but also serves an important function in reducing flood heights in Rome and the lower Etowah Valley. During dry periods, stored water is released to produce power and add to the diminished stream flow. As a result, the lake level can be quite low at times, especially from November to February.

The area around Allatoona Lake is quite significant historically. The Allatoona Pass, where the ridges from east and south meet, was an easy crossing point and developed into a travel hub in pioneer days. Sandtown Road, or Tennessee Road, from the south and Old Alabama Road from the east met at the pass, crossed the ridges and then separated, with Sandtown Road crossing the Etowah River and heading toward Tennessee and Old Alabama Road heading west on the south side of the Etowah River near the current dam.

The dam is also the site of an ironworks that was destroyed by General Sherman during the Civil War. The iron furnace was owned by Mark Anthony Cooper, a Georgia politician, and was located in what is now the parking lot of the powerhouse. South of the reservoir manager's office is the Mark Anthony Cooper Friendship Monument. This monument was erected in 1860 in honor of the 38 men who helped Cooper pay a $100,000 debt rather than lose the Etowah Ironworks. On a hilltop to the east is the site of

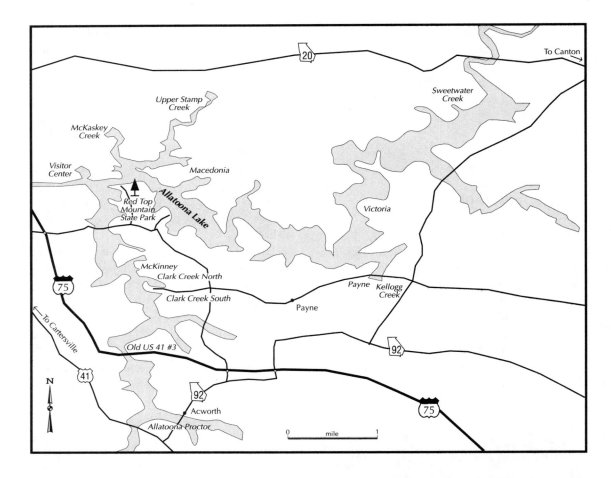

a fort built by Sherman to protect the Etowah River Bridge; the historical marker is visible from the parking lot.

Construction on Allatoona began in 1941, but the work was soon discontinued at the start of World War II. The lake was not completed and placed into operation until 1950.

The Corps of Engineers operates 11 campgrounds (with more than 700 campsites) and 19 day-use areas on the lake. Red Top Mountain State Park and six city and county parks are also located on Allatoona, which is served by eight commercial marinas. In addition to the day-use areas and campgrounds listed below, there are several boat ramps that offer no facilities. For a map showing all of the facilities on the lake (including all 33 boat-launching lanes), contact the resource manager's office.

ALLATOONA PROCTOR DAY-USE AREA

Picnic sites and two group shelters are available at this handicapped-accessible picnic area, located near U.S. 41 on Allatoona Creek in Cobb County.

BLOCKHOUSE DAY-USE AREA

This area has a boat ramp and a fishing jetty. Water and restrooms are also provided at this handicapped-accessible area.

CLARK CREEK NORTH CAMPGROUND

This full-featured fee campground has hookups, tables and grills at each site, along with a dump station. The bathhouse is equipped with hot showers, flush toilets and coin-operated laundry facilities. A group camping area is also available here. The campground is accessed via Exit 121 off I-75.

CLARK CREEK SOUTH CAMPGROUND

Like the campground on the north side of Clark Creek, this is a full-featured fee campground with hookups, tables and grills at each site, along with a dump station. The bathhouse is equipped with hot showers, flush toilets and coin-operated laundry facilities. There is also a boat ramp here. The campground is accessed via Exit 121 off I-75.

COOPER FURNACE DAY-USE AREA

This handicapped-accessible picnic area has picnic tables with grills, picnic shelters, restrooms and water. There is also a hiking trail at this day-use area, which is located near the resource manager's office just below the dam. This is the site of Cooper Iron Works. The furnace is still standing.

COOPER'S BRANCH #1 AND #2

This handicapped-accessible day-use area near the dam is well equipped for picnickers. The boat ramp has nearby picnic tables and picnic shelters. A playground, water, restrooms and a hiking trail are also offered here.

DALLAS ROAD DAY-USE AREA

This day-use area has a boat ramp, a swimming area, restrooms, water and picnic tables with nearby grills. It is just northwest of the town of Acworth off GA 92.

GALTS FERRY DAY-USE AREA

This day-use area has a lot to offer. For boaters and fishermen, there are a boat ramp and a fishing jetty. For picnickers, there are picnic shelters, tables and grills. For swimmers, there is a swimming area. This handicapped-accessible area also has restrooms and water. It is located near the commercial Galts Ferry Marina north of the community of Payne.

KELLOGG CREEK DAY-USE AREA

This day-use area has a swimming area with picnic shelters, tables and grills. Restrooms and water are also available at this site near Payne, west of Bells Ferry Road in Cherokee County.

MACEDONIA CAMPGROUND

The Corps of Engineers does not charge a fee to use this campground, located on the edge of the Allatoona Wildlife Management Area. It has a boat ramp, latrines and water. Primitive campsites are nearby. Picnic tables and grills are also provided at this site, located on Clear Creek off GA 20 in Bartow County.

MCKASKY CREEK CAMPGROUND

This fee campground has a swimming area and a boat ramp in addition to a full array of features including campsites with tables, grills and full hookups. A dump station is provided. The bathhouses have hot showers, toilets and coin-operated laundry facilities. Playground equipment is also available at this campground, located east of Cartersville.

MCKINNEY CAMPGROUND

This fee campground has campsites with full hookups, tables and grills. The bathhouses have showers, toilets and coin-operated laundry facilities. A dump station is available for RVs. A boat ramp and a swimming area round out the list of features at this campground, located west

of the community of Payne. Access is via Exit 121 off I-75.

OLD U.S. 41 CAMPGROUND #3

This fee campground is located on the north side of I-75, the opposite side of the interstate from the day-use areas listed above. There are tables, grills and full hookups for each campsite. There is a dump station for RVs. The bathhouses have showers, toilets and coin-operated laundry facilities. A swimming area, a playground and a boat ramp are also located in the campground.

OLD U.S. 41 DAY-USE AREAS #1 AND #2

These day-use areas have a boat ramp, a swimming area, picnic tables, grills, restrooms and water. They are located on GA 293 northwest of Acworth, alongside I-75. There is no exit off the interstate at this part of the lake; the nearest access is via Exit 121.

PAYNE CAMPGROUND

This fee campground just north of the community of Payne has full hookups, picnic tables and grills at each site. The bathhouses have showers, toilets and coin-operated laundry facilities. There is a dump station in the campground. This handicapped-accessible facility also has a swimming area, a playground and a boat ramp.

Completed in 1950, the 190-foot tall Allatoona Dam impounds 367,500 acre-feet of water on the Etowah River, creating 270 miles of shoreline. The powerhouse (at right in foreground) generates about 140 million kilowatt hours of electricity each year.

RIVERSIDE PARK

This handicapped-accessible day-use area has picnic shelters, tables, grills, a boat ramp, restrooms and water. There is also a trailhead for a hiking trail. This area near the powerhouse is accessed from U.S. 41 near Exit 122 off I-75.

SWEETWATER CREEK CAMPGROUND

This fee campground offers more features than any other Corps of Engineers site on the lake. The campsites have full hookups, tables and grills. The bathhouses have showers, toilets and coin-operated laundry facilities. A dump station is provided. This handicapped-accessible facility has a swimming area in its day-use area, a playground, a boat ramp and a separate group-camping area. A hiking trail is also offered at this site, located west of Canton off GA 20.

TANYARD CREEK DAY-USE AREA

A boat ramp and a swimming area with restrooms and water are offered at this area, located just north of I-75 near Exit 121.

UPPER STAMP CREEK CAMPGROUND

A fee is charged at this campground, which has tables, grills, restrooms, water and a boat ramp, as well as electrical and water hookups at most sites. The campground is accessed from GA 20 east of Exit 125 off I-75.

VICTORIA CAMPGROUND

This is a full-featured, handicapped-accessible fee campground with an accompanying day-use area. The campsites have full hookups, tables and grills. The bathhouses have showers, toilets and coin-operated laundry facilities. There is a dump station for RVs. A boat ramp, a swimming area and a fishing jetty are located in the day-use portion of this site, as are restrooms and water. The campground is accessed from Bells Ferry Road south of the Little River Bridge in Cherokee County.

HUNTING

Allatoona Wildlife Management Area is lo-cated on the north shore of the lake. For complete information, see the Public Fishing and Wildlife Management Areas section of this book. A Georgia hunting license is required for hunters age 16 and over.

FISHING

Legal fishing is permitted year-round at the lake, but a valid Georgia fishing license is required for persons age 16 and over.

NEARBY ATTRACTIONS

Red Top Mountain State Park and Lodge
Etowah Indian Mounds State Historic Site

A family sitting on a rock outcrop at a Lake Allatoona picnic area

FOR MORE INFORMATION

Allatoona Lake Resource Manager's Office, P.O. Box 487, Cartersville, GA 30120 (404-382-4700)

CARTERS LAKE
GILMER AND MURRAY COUNTIES
3,220-ACRE LAKE

Collecting more than 375 square miles of runoff water on the Coosawattee River is the primary job of this mountain reservoir. Authorized by Congress in 1945, it was built between 1962 and 1977 as part of the development of flood control for the Alabama River–Coosa River System. Power generation and recreation were side benefits of this project. Electricity is only generated during peak-use periods.

Though recreation was not the purpose of the lake, its 62 miles of shoreline and more than 3,000 acres of water provide great opportunities for boating, fishing, swimming, water-skiing, camping, picnicking and hiking. The area around the lake is less developed than its closest Corps of Engineers neighbor, Lake Allatoona.

DAMSITE RECREATION AREA

The Carters Lake Visitor Center is located in this area on the south side of the dam. The visitor center is open year-round Monday through Friday from 8:00 A.M. to 4:30 P.M. and on weekends and holidays from 10:00 A.M. to 6:00 P.M.

The boat ramp and picnic area have nearby restrooms. There is a small picnic shelter (six tables) in the picnic area. It can be reserved for group use for a small fee.

Adjoining this recreation area is the commercial Carters Lake Marina and Resort, which offers boat rentals and repairs, slip rentals and cabin and room rentals, as well as a full-service marina with fishing supplies, gas and a snack bar. Contact the marina at 706-276-4891 for more information.

Two trails—Big Acorn Nature Walk and Talking Rock Nature Trail—form a 2-mile loop that starts below the visitor center.

The north bank of the dam site has a dam overlook, picnic tables and two picnic shelters, one with twelve tables, the other with six. The shelters can be reserved for group use for a small fee.

To reach this recreation area from Chatsworth, go south on U.S. 411 for 13 miles to GA 136. Turn left (east) and go 2.5 miles to the sign for the dam; turn left and follow the signs for 2 miles to the visitor center.

DOLL MOUNTAIN RECREATION AREA

Located on a thin peninsula jutting into the main body of the lake, Doll Mountain has a picnic area and a campground. There is a large shelter with 12 tables in the picnic area; it can be reserved for a fee. A small per-car fee is charged for this recreation area.

There are 57 campsites on the peninsula. All are alongside the lake and come with water hookups. Thirty-eight of the sites have electrical hookups as well. There are two comfort stations in the campground, each with showers, flush toilets and laundry facilities. Other campground amenities include a boat ramp, an amphitheater and a dump station. To reserve a campsite at Doll Mountain, call 706-276-4413 from the first Friday in May to the Sunday after Labor Day, the period when the campground is open.

To reach this recreation area, take Exit 133 off I-75 and go east for 15 miles on GA 136. Cross U.S. 411 and continue to the intersection with GA 382; turn left onto GA 382 and follow the signs about 4 miles to the recreation area. Doll Mountain is the second recreation area on the left.

HARRIS BRANCH RECREATION AREA

A public swimming beach is the big draw for this recreation area. There are no lifeguards on duty, and swimming is at your own risk. The beach closes daily during the summer at 9 P.M. A short nature trail connects the campsites at one point on the peninsula to the swimming beach on the other.

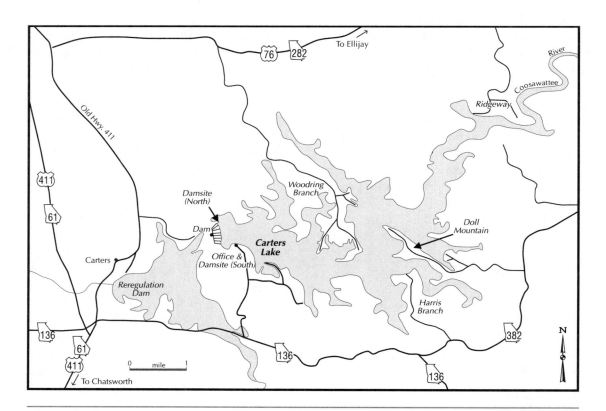

There are 10 primitive campsites in the campground, six of which can accommodate a pop-up camper or small RV. The other four sites are walk-in tent sites. The comfort station near the gatehouse has showers, flush toilets and laundry facilities. To reserve a campsite, call 706-276-4545 from the first Friday in May to the Sunday after Labor Day, the period when the campground is open.

There is a group tent-camping area near the main campground. It offers six tables, a large grill, 10 tent pads, two pit toilets and water. Organized groups can contact the resource manager's office for more information.

To reach this recreation area, take Exit 133 off I-75 and go east for 15 miles on GA 136. Cross U.S. 411 and continue to the intersection with GA 382; turn left onto GA 382 and follow the signs to the recreation area. The turnoff for Harris Branch is about 0.75 mile from the intersection of GA 136 and GA 382.

REREGULATION DAM RECREATION AREA

Located downstream from the dam along Talking Rock Creek, this recreation area at the reregulation dam has a picnic area, a fishing deck and a hiking trail. The reregulation dam is a secondary dam that regulates the flow of water from the main lake to provide a continuous outflow from the project and storage for pump-back operations. The reregulation reservoir varies in size from 60 acres at minimum storage to 1,030 acres at maximum capacity.

The fishing deck is open year-round to legal fishing. The 0.6-mile Hidden Pond Trail is an easy loop hike; its trailhead is in the recreation area. The picnic area has picnic tables and a large, 12-table picnic shelter available by reservation for a small fee.

To reach this site, take Exit 133 off I-75 and go east on GA 136 for 15 miles. Cross U.S. 411 and turn left (north) on Old U.S. 41 almost immediately. From that turn, it is about a mile to the reregulation dam.

RIDGEWAY RECREATION AREA

There are 22 primitive campsites at this recreation area along the Coosawattee River's junction with the lake. Pit toilets and water from a hand-operated pump are provided. Trails, picnic tables and a paved boat ramp are also located in the recreation area.

The 0.5-mile Tumbling Waters Nature Trail has several short side trails leading to lookouts. The trail gets its name from a 12-foot cascade on Tails Creek that can be seen from the trail. The trailhead is in the parking area. A new 5-mile bike trail is now a part of this recreation area also.

To reach this site from Ellijay, go west on U.S. 76/GA 282 for 8.5 miles to the turn for the recreation area. A winding dirt road leads down to the lake and turns to pavement as you cross into the recreation area.

WOODRING BRANCH RECREATION AREA

This recreation area has a boat ramp, a picnic area and a nearby campground on a peninsula jutting south into the main body of the lake.

In addition to the regular picnic tables, there is a six-table shelter in the picnic area that can be reserved for a small fee. A small per-car parking fee is charged at this recreation area.

All of the campground's 42 sites are near the water. Thirty-one of them are equipped with water and electrical hookups. The remaining sites are walk-in tent sites. The well-equipped campground has a boat ramp, a playground, horseshoes pits, an amphitheater, a dump station and a comfort station with flush toilets, showers and laundry facilities. There are 12 boat-access sites in the campground. Sixteen campsites are open year-round, with water the only service provided. The 42 main sites operate as a full-service campground from the first Friday in April through the last Sunday in October. Call 706-276-6050 to reserve a site.

To reach Woodring Branch, go west from Ellijay on U.S. 76/GA 282 for about 16 miles. Turn left at the sign and go an additional 5 miles to the recreation area.

CAMPING

Campsite reservations can be made from 9 A.M. to 9 P.M. Sunday through Thursday. You will be charged a small reservation fee, but you do not have to pay that fee or the fee for the site until you arrive in camp. Reservations must be made by the person occupying the site. There is a maximum stay of 14 consecutive days. Except for the group camping area at Harris Branch, all of the campsites are available on a first-come, first-served basis when not reserved.

Quiet hours are in effect from 10 P.M. to 6 A.M. daily. The entrance gates are locked from 10 P.M. to 9 A.M., and you can only leave in an emergency during those hours. Pets are allowed in the campground, but they must be caged or on a leash no more than six feet long.

HIKING

There are five trails at Carters Lake. The 0.5-mile Hidden Pond Trail begins at the entrance to the management area. A 200-foot boardwalk over a beaver pond leads to a good area for viewing both beavers and waterfowl. At the visitor center is the trailhead for Big Acorn Nature Walk and Talking Rock Nature Trail, which form a 2-mile loop hike. Interpretive signs note the names of trees along the broad path. Tumbling Waters Nature Trail offers a mile-long round-trip hike at Ridgeway Recreation Area; there are views of a 12-foot cascade on Tails Creek on this hike. A 5-mile bike trail has been added to Ridgeway Recreation Area.

PICNIC SHELTERS

The six picnic shelters around the lake can be reserved for a fee by calling the resource manager's office. When not reserved, these shelters are available on a first-come, first-served basis.

FISHING

Legal fishing is permitted year-round on the lake and in the reregulation dam area. The lake is stocked with species including walleye and striped bass. The Corps of Engineers has an information sheet with fishing predictions and suggestions for Carters Lake. It is available from the resource manager's office.

NEARBY ATTRACTIONS

Fort Mountain State Park
Chief Vann House State Historic Site
New Echota State Historic Site

DIRECTIONS

The lake is located south of U.S. 76/GA 282 between Chatsworth and Ellijay.

FOR MORE INFORMATION

Carters Lake, Resource Manager's Office, P.O. Box 96, Oakman, GA 30732-0096 (706-334-2248)

CLARKS HILL LAKE
ELBERT, LINCOLN AND COLUMBIA COUNTIES
71,000-ACRE LAKE

Clarks Hill Dam impounds water 40 miles up the Savannah River and 26 miles up the Little River to form 1,200 miles of shoreline in Georgia and South Carolina. There are nine Corps of Engineers campgrounds, three state parks and five recreation areas on the Georgia side of the lake.

This schizophrenic lake is known by different names in Georgia and South Carolina. The Corps of Engineers officially calls it J. Strom Thurmond Lake at Clarks Hill. That last phrase is not tacked on as an afterthought but because this, the largest Corps of Engineers project east of the Mississippi, was originally named Clarks Hill Reservoir. For 40 years, it was named for the South Carolina town near the dam. In 1991, South Carolina changed the name to honor its ranking senator. Georgia refused to change the name, and the lake remains known as Clarks Hill on the Georgia side.

The name derives from Revolutionary War colonel Elijah Clarke, who led the colonists in their only decisive victory in Georgia, at Kettle Creek. He lived nearby. His grave and a reproduction of his cabin are in Elijah Clark State Park, which is on the lakeshore near Lincolnton. His son, a fellow Revolutionary War hero and a two-time governor of Georgia, dropped the *e* from the family name, which explains the current spelling.

The lake has further ties to Georgia's colonial past. Revolutionary War forts James and Charlotte once stood on sites now covered by the massive lake. A memorial stone that once stood near Fort James is located in Bobby Brown State Park.

This lake was authorized by Congress as part of the Flood Control Act of 1944. The dam was the first Corps of Engineers flood-control project on the Savannah River. The mile-long, 200-foot-high dam contains more than a million cubic yards of concrete. It cost $79 million to complete. Corps of Engineers studies estimate

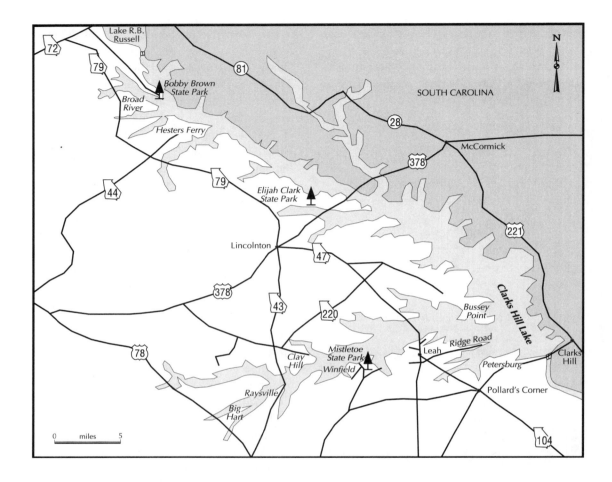

that $25.8 million in flood damage was prevented by the dam through 1990. Sediment traveling downstream to Savannah Harbor has also been reduced by 22 percent since the dam was built.

Clarks Hill has about 8 million visitors annually, making it one of the country's 10 most-visited Corps of Engineers lakes.

AMITY RECREATION AREA

This fully equipped recreation area has a boat ramp, a fishing pier, a beach, a playground and restrooms. The picnic area has picnic tables, in addition to picnic shelters which may be reserved. There is also a fish-cleaning station.

This recreation area is at the southern tip of

Lincoln County along the Little River part of the lake, off GA 43.

BIG HART CAMPGROUND

This campground on Hart and Big Creeks offers everything. The campsites have full water and electrical hookups. There is a bathhouse with hot showers and flush toilets, a fish-cleaning station and a dump station. There is a group camping area, too. Campsites can be reserved by calling 706-595-8613. A fee is charged for using this area.

The day-use portion has a picnic area, a beach, restrooms, a boat ramp, a fishing pier, a playground and hiking trails. The picnic shelters may be reserved.

Big Hart Campground is located off U.S. 78 about 3 miles northwest of its junction with GA 43.

BROAD RIVER CAMPGROUND

This fee camping area has full water and electrical hookups, a bathhouse with flush toilets and hot showers, a dump station and a fish-cleaning station. There is a boat ramp at Broad River. Campsites may be reserved by calling 706-359-2053.

The campground is at the northern tip of Lincoln County on GA 79. It is the northernmost Corps of Engineers site on the Georgia side of the lake.

BUSSEY POINT CAMPGROUND

There is no fee to use this primitive camping area at the confluence of the Savannah and Little Rivers. Here, the lake stretches for 40 miles from South Carolina on the Savannah River well into Georgia on the Little River. There are hiking trails, a boat ramp and a picnic area at Bussey Point. The campground is west of Lincolnton at the end of U.S. 220 Spur.

CLAY HILL CAMPGROUND

These campsites have full water and electrical hookups and a nearby bathhouse with hot showers and flush toilets. The campsites at Clay Hill may not be reserved. There is a boat ramp at this fee camping area. The campground is on the Little River a mile west of GA 220, about 0.5 mile west of that highway's junction with GA 43.

GILL POINT RECREATION AREA

This recreation area between Pistol and Newford Creeks has a beach, a picnic area, a boat ramp and restrooms. The picnic shelters are available by reservation. The recreation area is off GA 79 some 3 miles north of its junction with GA 44.

HESTERS FERRY CAMPGROUND

This fee campground on the Savannah River has campsites with full water and electrical hookups. A dump station, bathhouses with hot showers and flush toilets, a boat ramp and a playground are provided. To reach the campground from Washington, take GA 44; it is 17 miles from Washington, straight ahead where GA 44 ends at GA 79. Call 706-359-2746 to reserve a campsite.

LAKE SPRINGS RECREATION AREA

This day-use area is on a peninsula reaching into the main body of the lake near the dam. It offers a boat ramp, a fishing pier and a fish-cleaning station. The picnic area has both tables and shelters. The shelters may be reserved for group use. There is a swimming beach with restrooms, along with a nearby playground. The recreation area is off U.S. 221 between Pollard's Corner and the dam, just past Tradewinds Marina and Yacht Club.

PETERSBURG CAMPGROUND

The campsites in this fee campground have full water and electrical hookups and nearby bathhouses. A dump station, a fish-cleaning station, a playground, a boat ramp, a beach and hiking trails are also offered. Campsites may be reserved by calling 706-541-9464. Petersburg Campground is off U.S. 221 about 2 miles northeast of Pollard's Corner.

RAYSVILLE CAMPGROUND

This fee campground lies near Raysville Bridge Marina, where Hart and Big Creeks join the

Little River. The campsites have full water and electrical hookups. A dump station, a fish-cleaning station, bathhouses with hot showers and flush toilets, a boat ramp and a playground are also offered. Call 706-595-6759 to reserve a site. Raysville Campground is on GA 43 about 12 miles south of Lincolnton.

RIDGE ROAD CAMPGROUND

This fee campground west of Leah is on a peninsula where Chigoe Creek joins the main body of the lake. The campsites, which may be reserved, have full water and electrical hookups. A dump station, a fish-cleaning station, bathhouses with hot showers and flush toilets, a beach, a playground and a boat ramp are also offered. This campground is on Ridge Road, which is 4 miles west of Leah off GA 104. Call 706-541-0282 for reservations.

WEST DAM RECREATION AREA

Here, picnic tables and shelters look out on the lake, which is more than 3 miles wide at this point. A beach, a playground, a fishing pier and restrooms are among the area's facilities. This is the only Corps of Engineers facility in Georgia without a boat ramp. The picnic shelters may be reserved. The recreation area is on U.S. 221 at the South Carolina state line.

WINFIELD CAMPGROUND

This fee campground is near Mistletoe State Park. The campsites, which may be reserved, are equipped with full water and electrical hook-ups. A dump station, a fish-cleaning station, a bathhouse with hot showers and flush toilets, a beach, a playground and a boat ramp are also offered. Call 706-541-0147 for reservations. From GA 150 in the community of Winfield, it is 3 miles on Mistletoe Road to the turnoff for this campground.

HUNTING

Deer and turkeys are the most popular game on Clarks Hill Lake, but quail, doves and other small game are prolific as well. The flocks of Canada geese on the lake have not yet grown to sufficient size to permit hunting.

Bussey Point usually has two annual hunts each for turkeys and deer. There are limits on the number of hunters admitted and the amount of game taken. The deer and turkey hunts are often arranged on a first-come, first-served basis. During the hunts, game may be taken by bow and arrow and muzzleloader only. Notice of upcoming hunts is announced in the local newspapers. Call the resource manager's office for the current hunting schedule.

FISHING

Legal fishing is permitted year-round on the lake. Through a reciprocal agreement, either a Georgia or a South Carolina fishing license may be used for fishing on any part of Clarks Hill. The lake is home to a large population of bass, including white, striped, hybrid and largemouth.

Other game fish include bluegill, crappie and sauger. There are 30 fish attractors in the lake. More information on fishing is available through the resource manager's office.

MARINAS

There are four commercial marinas on the Georgia side of the lake: Mike's Marina is 1 mile northeast of Leah; Soap Creek Lodge is about 4 miles northeast of Lincolnton off U.S. 378; Raysville Bridge Marina is at Raysville Bridge over the Little River on GA 43; and Tradewinds Marina and Yacht Club is off U.S. 221 near the dam.

PICNIC SHELTERS

The picnic shelters at Gill Point, Lake Springs, West Dam and Amity Recreation Areas may be reserved by calling the resource manager's office.

NEARBY ATTRACTIONS

Bobby Brown State Park
Elijah Clark State Park
Mistletoe State Park
Lake Richard B. Russell State Park
Hartwell Lake

DIRECTIONS

The lake is west of Lincolnton on the Georgia/South Carolina state line.

J. Strom Thurmond Lake at Clarks Hill, Resource Manager's Office, Route 1, Box 6, Clarks Hill, SC 29821-0010 (706-722-3770)

HARTWELL LAKE
FRANKLIN, HART AND STEPHENS COUNTIES
56,000-ACRE LAKE

One of the South's most popular lakes, Hartwell sees more than 14 million visitors annually. The lake was named for the nearby Georgia town, which was in turn named for Nancy Hart (1735–1830), a heroine of the Revolutionary War who lived in this area. The six-foot-tall patriot, wife and mother of eight was an expert shot. She served as a spy for Colonel Elijah Clarke during the war, often disguised as a man. When a band of six Tories came to her house demanding she cook for them, she killed one and captured the others, injuring one. When her husband and friends returned home, they told her that the survivors should be shot. Nancy declared that shooting was too good for them and had all five hanged. She was called *Wahatche*, or "War Woman," by the Indians.

Another quaint story involving the lake is the number of creeks that enter it which are named after miles. Six-Mile, Twelve-Mile, Twenty-Three-Mile and Twenty-Six-Mile Creeks all flow into Lake Hartwell. Local legend says the creeks were named by the Cherokee maiden Issaqueena, who, while riding to Fort Ninety-Six to warn settlers of an impending attack, named the streams she encountered for the number of miles she had covered.

Hartwell Lake extends 49 miles up the Tugaloo River and 45 miles up the Seneca River under normal conditions. The dam is located 7 miles below the point at which the Tugaloo and the Seneca join to form the Savannah River. With 962 miles of shoreline, the entire Hartwell project comprises more than 76,000 acres of land and water. Because the lake is bisected by I-85, it is easily accessible to visitors. Construction on Hartwell began in 1955, and the lake was opened to the public in 1963.

Public tours of the dam and powerhouse are given free of charge at 2:30 P.M. on Wednesdays, Sundays and holidays from June 1 through Labor Day. Call the project manager's office for more information.

BIG OAKS RECREATION AREA

Big Oaks features a launching ramp, a comfort station, drinking water, a picnic area, a picnic shelter and facilities for the handicapped. It can be reached by taking GA 181/U.S. 29 east out of Hartwell and watching for the signs.

ELROD FERRY RECREATION AREA

A boat ramp, a comfort station, drinking water, a picnic area, a picnic shelter and facilities for the handicapped are all available at Elrod Ferry. This recreation area can be reached by following GA 181/U.S. 29 east from Hartwell and following the signs.

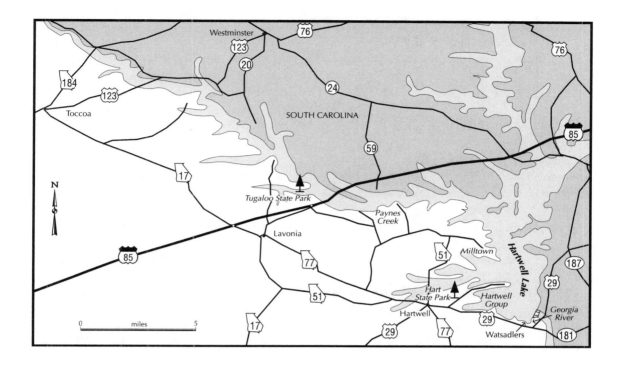

GEORGIA RIVER RECREATION AREA

This campground is open year-round but offers minimal facilities—a comfort station, drinking water, a picnic area and facilities for the handicapped. A fee is charged for camping here from May 1 to September 9. The sites have neither electrical nor water hookups. The park is located off U.S. 29 east of Hartwell, just before you enter South Carolina.

HARTWELL GROUP CAMP

This group camp is open from April through October 31. There is a fee for camping. Restrooms, drinking water, a dump station and a picnic shelter are offered. The group camp is located east of Hartwell off GA 181/U.S. 29 between Elrod Ferry Recreation Area and Big Oaks Recreation Area. The camp must be reserved in advance by contacting the project manager's office at the address listed below.

LONG POINT RECREATION AREA

A boat ramp, a comfort station, drinking water, a picnic area, a picnic shelter and facilities for the handicapped are offered at Long Point.

To reach the recreation area, follow GA 181/U.S. 29 east from Hartwell and take the road that leads to the Powderbag Creek and Duncan Branch Accesses and Long Point Recreation Area. Signs will guide you.

MARY ANN BRANCH RECREATION AREA

A boat ramp, drinking water and a picnic area are provided here. The recreation area can be reached by following GA 51 north from Hartwell to Reed Creek, then continuing north out of Reed Creek on GA 51 and following the signs.

MILLTOWN CAMPGROUND

Milltown is operated seasonally from May 1 through September 9. It offers a boat ramp, a comfort station, a shower house, drinking water and a dump station, but there are no electrical or water hookups for RVs. A park attendant is on hand to collect the campground fee and provide information. There are facilities for the handicapped here. To reach the campground, follow GA 51 north from Hartwell to Reed Creek, then follow the signs east to the campground.

PAYNES CREEK CAMPGROUND

Operated seasonally from May 1 through September 9, Paynes Creek has a boat ramp, a comfort station, a shower house, drinking water, a dump station and facilities for the handicapped, as well as electrical and water hookups at all sites. There is a fee for camping. An attendant

is on duty. You can reach the campground by following GA 77 south from Lavonia and turning left on the road that leads through the Mount Olivet community. From Mount Olivet, follow the signs to the campground.

POPLAR SPRINGS RECREATION AREA

Poplar Springs offers a boat ramp, a comfort station, drinking water, a picnic shelter and a picnic area, as well as facilities for the handicapped. It can be reached by taking GA 328 north from Lavonia and following the signs.

STEPHENS COUNTY RECREATION AREA

A boat ramp, a comfort station, a picnic area, a fishing pier and facilities for the handicapped are provided at this recreation area. To reach it, follow U.S. 123 east from Toccoa. The park is on the right just before you cross into South Carolina.

WATSADLERS CAMPGROUND

Open from March 1 through November 30, Watsadlers offers a boat ramp, a comfort station, a shower house, drinking water and a dump station, as well as facilities for the handicapped. All sites have electrical and water hookups. A park attendant is on duty during the campground's months of operation, and a fee is charged for camping. The campground is located east of Hartwell off GA 181/U.S. 29. Follow the signs.

BOAT ACCESS

Corps of Engineers boat ramps providing access to Hartwell Lake are scattered along the shoreline from Walker Creek, north of Toccoa, to Powderbag Creek and Duncan Branch, east of Hartwell. Other access points include Spring Branch, Jenkins Ferry, Rock Springs and Crawfords Ferry, all of which follow the Tugaloo River south to where it flows into the Savannah. Carters Ferry, New Prospect, Cleveland and Gum Branch are on the Savannah River.

There are four boat ramps on Hartwell Lake provided by the state or local municipalities—Holcomb, Franklin County, Rocky Ford and Bradberry. These are located in Stephens County, Franklin County and Hart County.

Bruce Creek Recreation Area, located south of U.S. 123 on the Tugaloo River, offers a boat ramp and a picnic area.

MARINAS

There are two marinas on Hartwell Lake in Georgia. Harbor Light Marina is off I-85 east of Lavonia; for information, contact Harbor Light Marina, Route 1, Lavonia, GA 30553 (706-356-4119). Hartwell Marina is located just north of Hartwell; for information, contact Hartwell Marina, 1500 North Forest Avenue, Hartwell, GA 30643 (706-376-5441). Both marinas offer boat and motor rentals and a boat ramp.

NEARBY ATTRACTIONS

Traveler's Rest State Historic Site
Tugaloo State Park
Hart State Park
Lake Richard B. Russell State Park
Victoria Bryant State Park

DIRECTIONS

Hartwell Lake can be accessed via I-85 and through the towns of Toccoa, Lavonia and Hartwell.

FOR MORE INFORMATION

Office of the Project Manager, Hartwell Lake and Powerplant, P.O. Box 278, Hartwell, GA 30643-0278 (706-376-4788)

LAKE GEORGE W. ANDREWS
CLAY AND EARLY COUNTIES
1,570-ACRE LAKE

Though this 29-mile-long lake has just 65 miles of shoreline along its relatively narrow width, it offers a wealth of fishing opportunities. Along with Walter F. George Lake, which is located just upstream, Andrews helps provide a navigable channel up the Chattahoochee River to Columbus. Boating activities are limited due to the narrow channel, which must be shared with commercial barge traffic. Fishing is the primary attraction at this lake.

215

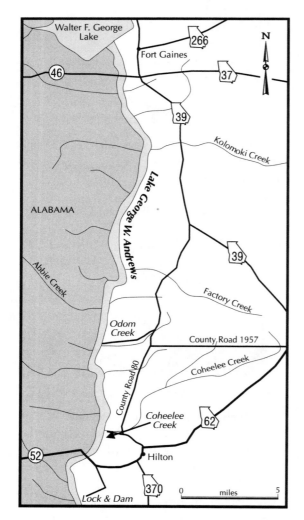

COHEELEE CREEK PARK

This boat ramp has picnic tables and pit toilets. There is also a free camping area.

GEORGE W. ANDREWS LOCK AND DAM

A boat ramp and restrooms are available at this site just below the lock and dam. The tailwater below the lock and dam is a prime fishing spot. To check on the power generation schedule, call 912-768-2424.

ODUM CREEK PARK

This boat ramp has picnic tables and pit toilets. It is located north of the town of Coheelee, which is northwest of Hilton.

FISHING

Largemouth bass, white bass, bream, channel catfish and crappie are among the game fish in the lake. Under an agreement between the two states, either a valid Alabama or Georgia fishing license is valid on all areas of the lake. Licenses are required for all persons over age 16. The mouths of creeks and the tailwater of the dam are among the better fishing spots on this narrow lake.

NEARBY ATTRACTIONS

Florence Marina State Park
George T. Bagby State Park and Lake
Walter F. George Lodge

Kolomoki Mounds State Historic Park
Providence Canyon State Conservation Park

DIRECTIONS

The recreational areas and the lake can be accessed from GA 39 and GA 1691 between the towns of Fort Gaines and Hilton.

FOR MORE INFORMATION

Resource Manager's Office, Lake George W. Andrews, Route 1, Box 175, Fort Gaines, GA 31751 (912-768-2516)

LAKE RICHARD B. RUSSELL
ELBERT COUNTY   26,000-ACRE LAKE

Clovis points, pottery shards, burial mounds and the site of an 18th-century fort are among the finds made by archaeologists while investigating the area to be covered by the waters of Lake Richard B. Russell. Some of these archaeological artifacts were dated at more than 10,000 years old. A number of sites—and in particular the Gregg Shoals site—provided scientists with a Rosetta stone of the Savannah River Valley area, making it possible for scientists to piece together a picture of the valley's changing landscape over the past 10,000 years.

Georgia's newest lake was opened to the public in 1985 following years of cultural and archaeological investigation. Construction began in 1976, but the lake didn't begin to fill until 1983. By the winter of 1984, it had reached its standard operating elevation at 475 feet above sea level. The lake covers 26,650 acres. More than 52,000 acres were purchased in Georgia and South Carolina as part of the lake itself and for road and railroad relocations, project operations and recreational areas.

The major recreational area for the lake in Georgia is Lake Richard B. Russell State Park, known at first as Coldwater State Park because of its location on Coldwater Creek. Other than a boat ramp at Elbert Park, the Corps of Engineers has yet to build any other recreational facilities in Georgia, although boat ramps, fishing piers and beach areas are planned.

The resource manager's office at the dam houses a museum that features local history and ecology. Entrance to the museum is free.

Lake Richard B. Russell was built for the purposes of power generation, recreation and flood control. It is located between Hartwell Dam, to the north, and Clarks Hill Dam, to the south.

ELBERT PARK

Located off of GA 72 before it crosses the lake into South Carolina, this park offers a boat ramp, a large parking area and latrines.

FISHING

Lake Richard B. Russell is primarily a fisherman's lake. Lake levels remain mostly stable throughout the year, fluctuating no more than five feet either way. Largemouth bass and crappie are the primary sport of anglers, although bluegill, white bass, bream, yellow perch, catfish and trout are also popular.

Statistics claim that the fishing here averages a harvest of about 0.5 bass per hour, at an average weight of 1.6 pounds. The lake's nearly 1,500 acres of standing timber and topped trees—many were topped at what is now 13 to 35 feet below the lake's surface—add to its enjoyment as a fisherman's paradise. Because of its miles of un-

developed shoreline, the lake sees an abundance of wildlife as well.

Fishing can be done by boat or at the pier below the dam, which provides excellent access and facilities for anglers interested in fishing the tailrace for white, hybrid and striped bass, as well as other species.

A couple of maps are available to those interested in more detailed information. A contour map can be purchased for $2, a pre-impound-

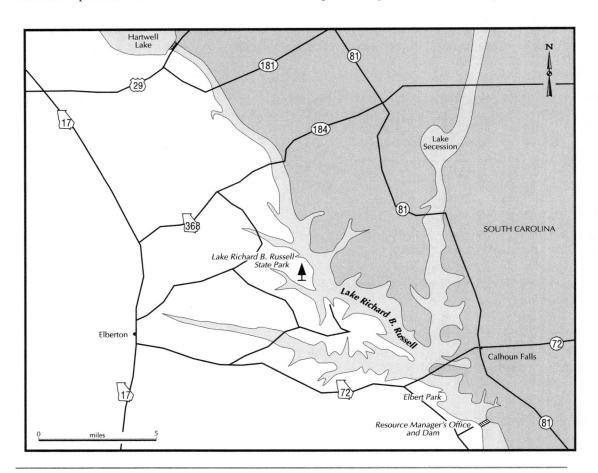

The boat ramp at Elbert Park is the only Corps of Engineers-operated facility on the Georgia side of Lake Richard B. Russell.

ment map with contours for $11. These maps can be purchased through the natural resource manager's office.

HUNTING

Public hunting is offered at certain areas around the lake, with a buffer zone of 300 feet surrounding the lake itself. Deer hunting is allowed at Elbert Park south of GA 72, as well as at the Pickens Creek Access and Heardmont Park. A game-management stamp is required. For more information, contact the natural resource manager's office.

The Beverly Park area is open to bowhunters on some occasions. For more information, contact the natural resource manager's office.

A hunt for handicapped sportsmen is planned each year at Lake Richard B. Russell State Park. For more information, call the Southeastern Paralyzed Veterans Association (800-292-9335), the Georgia Handicapped Sportsmen Association (404-246-9810) or the natural resource manager's office.

Closed to hunting are all public boat ramps and fishing piers, all project lands south of Shuck Pen Eddy Boat Ramp and Lake Richard B. Russell State Park.

All hunting must be done in compliance with Georgia game laws.

CAMPING

Although there are no Corps of Engineers campgrounds in Georgia, campers may use Bobby Brown State Park, which is just 4 miles south of the dam on Clarks Hill Lake (J. Strom Thurmond Lake). For more information, see the write-up on Bobby Brown State Park in this book. Campgrounds operated by the Corps of Engineers at nearby Hartwell and Clarks Hill Lakes are also possibilities. For more information, see their respective entries.

Accommodations may also be found in the nearby towns of Elberton and Hartwell. Contact the local chambers of commerce for more information: Elbert County Chamber of Commerce, 148 College Avenue, Elberton, GA 30635 (706-283-5651); or Hart County Chamber of Commerce, P.O. Box 793, Hartwell, GA 30643 (706-376-8590).

NEARBY ATTRACTIONS

Lake Richard B. Russell State Park
Bobby Brown State Park
Elijah Clark State Park
Hartwell Lake
Clarks Hill Lake (J. Strom Thurmond Lake)

DIRECTIONS

Lake Richard B. Russell can be reached via GA 72, Russell Dam Drive and Bobby Brown State Park Road.

FOR MORE INFORMATION

Lake Richard B. Russell Natural Resource Manager's Office, 4144 Russell Dam Drive, Elberton, GA 30635-9271 (706-283-8731)

LAKE SEMINOLE
SEMINOLE AND DECATUR COUNTIES
17,150-SQUARE-MILE LAKE

With a reputation as an unsurpassed fishing lake, Seminole lies at the confluence of the Chattahoochee and Flint Rivers. Hiding in the tree stumps and grass beds of the lake are bass that anglers dream of. Largemouth, hybrid, striped and white bass are abundant. Bream, crappie and catfish are also found in the lake's waters. There are hundreds of islands and thousands of acres of lily pads, grass beds, tree stumps and lime sinks for anglers to try.

The lime sinks, sloughs and flat pinelands that dominate the lake's terrain are built up over a layer of Tampa limestone. The exception is Seminole's southeast corner, which is bordered by the Apalachicola River Bluffs. The bluffs extend downstream along the Apalachicola for 25 miles. Ravines and small rivers joining the lake cause breaks in the bluffs on both sides of the state line. The ravines, like the bluffs themselves, are home to a variety of plant life.

The lake is formed behind Jim Woodruff Lock and Dam. The $46.5-million Corps of Engineers project was authorized by Congress in 1946 as part of a package to improve navigation on the Chattahoochee and Flint Rivers and to provide hydroelectric power. Before the dam was built, the water in the two rivers was about three feet deep. Since the construction of Jim Woodruff Dam and two other dams on the Chattahoochee, a nine-foot-deep, 100-foot-wide channel has been maintained north on the Chattahoochee to Columbus and northeast on the Flint to Bainbridge.

Completed in 1957, the 57-foot-tall, 3,600-foot-long dam backs up water 47 miles on each of the two rivers, for more than 376 miles of shoreline. More than 50,000 homes get their power from the lake, thanks to electricity sold through Florida Power Corporation.

A complete listing of all of the lake's boat ramps is available from the resource manager's office.

BUTLER'S FERRY LANDING

This is a full-featured boat ramp where you can buy bait and supplies, rent a boat and motor or grab a bite to eat before getting out on the water. There are restrooms and a picnic area as well. The landing is located where GA 253 dead-ends at the lake.

CHATTAHOOCHEE PARK

Swimming, picnicking and water-skiing are popular activities at this park 1.5 miles north of the dam. A boat ramp and a swimming beach with bathhouses are in the park, which is located on Booster Club Road 2 miles north of Chattahoochee, Florida, on Lake Seminole Road.

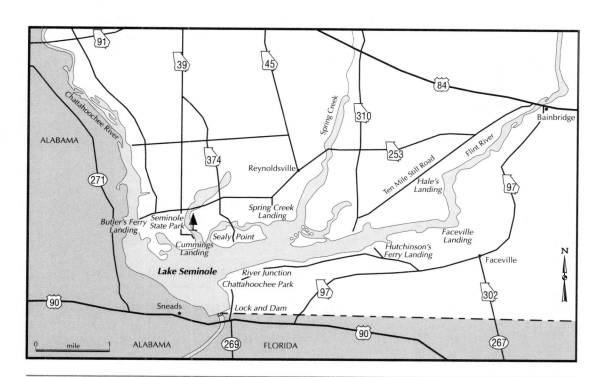

CUMMINGS LANDING

This boat ramp has a picnic area, restrooms with showers and a tent and trailer camping area, but no dump station. The landing is 17 miles south of Donalsonville on GA 39.

FACEVILLE LANDING ACCESS AREA

This boat ramp is on the Flint River 14 miles upstream from the dam. It has a picnic area, restrooms and a tent and trailer camping area, but no dump station. The access area is on Faceville Landing Road off GA 97 about 3 miles east of that route's intersection with GA 310.

HALE'S LANDING ACCESS AREA

This boat ramp on the Flint River offers a tent and trailer camping area and restrooms with showers. To get to the landing, go southwest from Bainbridge on GA 253. Bear left onto Ten Mile Still Road at the fork about 4 miles from town. The landing is on the left after another 3 miles.

HUTCHINSON'S FERRY LANDING

This full-service landing has a boat ramp offering boat docking and mooring, boat rentals, bait and supplies. Restrooms, bathhouses, a playground, a tent and trailer camping area and a snack bar are also located here.

The landing is home to the well-known Wingate's Lodge. Jack Wingate is one of the nation's premier bass fishermen. He also holds an annual carp shoot for bowhunters. The lodge offers a variety of unpretentious accommodations, including standard motel rooms, duplexes with a kitchenette and trailer rentals. The lodge's restaurant will also cook the day's catch. For more information on the lodge, call 912-246-0658.

JIM WOODRUFF DAM

The dam's east bank has a tent and trailer camping area with a dump station. A boat ramp, a picnic area, restrooms, bathhouses and a playground are the other amenities at this popular area. The deck alongside the tailrace below the dam is open for fishing; big catfish and bass are often caught there. Restrooms are nearby. This public area is less than a mile north of Chattahoochee, Florida, on Lake Seminole Road.

RIVER JUNCTION ACCESS AREA

This boat ramp on the Flint River side of the confluence has a tent and trailer camping area, a picnic area and restrooms with showers. It is located off Lake Seminole Road a little over 3 miles north of Chattahoochee, Florida, and 9 miles west of Recovery, Georgia.

SEALEY POINT ACCESS AREA

This boat ramp offers restrooms. It is located at the south end of GA 374, which dead-ends at the lake.

SPRING CREEK LANDING

Full service is provided for boaters at this landing. A boat ramp and dock, boat and motor rentals, bait and supplies are offered. A tent and trailer camping area, a picnic area and restrooms with showers make this a popular spot. It is located just over a mile off GA 253 southwest of Reynoldsville, where Spring Creek joins the Flint River.

FISHING

A valid Georgia fishing license is required for all persons over age 16. Bass are the big draw—with largemouth, hybrid, striped and white bass all in abundance—but catfish, crappie and bream are caught as well.

NEARBY ATTRACTIONS

George T. Bagby State Park and Lake Walter F. George Lodge
Kolomoki Mounds State Historic Park
Lake George W. Andrews
Walter F. George Lake
Lapham-Patterson House State Historic Site
Seminole State Park

DIRECTIONS

Lake Seminole is in the southwest corner of the state, bordering Alabama and Florida. Many of the recreation areas are off GA 253 or GA 97, both of which branch away from Bainbridge at the northeast end of the lake.

FOR MORE INFORMATION

Lake Seminole Resource Manager's Office, P.O. Box 96, Chattahoochee, FL 32324 (912-662-2001)

LAKE SIDNEY LANIER
LUMPKIN, DAWSON, HALL, FORSYTH AND GWINNETT COUNTIES
38,000-ACRE LAKE

Lake Sidney Lanier receives its waters from two rivers, the Chattahoochee and the Chestatee, extending 44 miles up the former and 19 miles up the latter. A number of creeks and other tributaries supply water as well. This is the largest man-made lake in Georgia, with 540 miles of shoreline. It is also the second-most-visited Corps of Engineers project in the nation, with millions of visitors annually. Located close to Atlanta, the lake offers a well-developed network of roads, with several highway crossings over the main body of the lake.

Buford Dam and Lake Sidney Lanier were authorized by Congress in 1946 and completed in 1957 at a cost of $45 million. Among the purposes of the lake are power production, navigation, recreation, flood control, water supply and fish and wildlife management. The lake collects runoff from a 1,040-square-mile area, storing water in wet periods and releasing reserve water during dry spells. Buford Dam, located over the original river channel, is connected to a powerhouse that provides electricity sent to

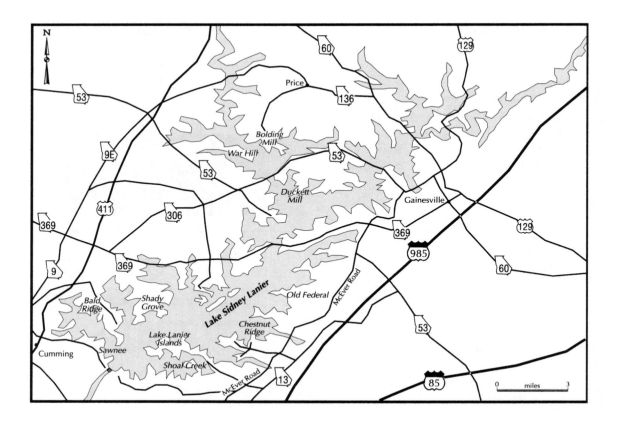

preferred government customers. The remainder of the electricity is purchased by Georgia Power Company.

Located in the foothills of the Blue Ridge Mountains, the lake is named for American poet Sidney Clopton Lanier (1842–81), who made the area famous with his "Song of the Chattahoochee." This scenic lake offers nine camping areas, all of which are accessible to the handicapped. All the campgrounds charge a usage fee and offer boat ramps and a swimming area as well. There are 42 day-use areas, as well as 10 state, city and county parks. There are 10 marinas and 54 boat-launching areas with parking facilities. The lake boasts more than 100 islands where boaters can seek privacy. Fishermen are offered a wide variety of game fish, including striped bass, largemouth bass, smallmouth bass, crappie and more. There is even trout fishing below Buford Dam, with brook, rainbow and brown trout available.

But don't get too distracted by your fishing.

Water is released periodically for the generation of power, so visitors must exercise caution. Horns are sounded prior to the release of water, but for current information, keep your radio tuned to 1610 AM.

For more information on Lake Sidney Lanier or a map that shows all its facilities, contact the resource manager's office.

BALD RIDGE CAMPGROUND

This campground offers electrical and water hookups, a dump station, a playground, tables, showers, restrooms, a telephone and laundry facilities. Bald Ridge is located off GA 400 at Exit 16.

BALUS CREEK DAY-USE AREA

This handicapped-accessible day-use area offers a boat ramp, water and restrooms; a fee is charged to use the boat ramp. Balus Creek is located off McEver Road via Exit 4 from I-985. Follow GA 53 west to McEver Road, which GA 53 joins briefly heading north. Follow the signs to Balus Creek.

BELTON BRIDGE DAY-USE AREA

This day-use area offers only a boat ramp. It is located at the far northeast corner of the lake off I-985.

A jet skier cuts up the water on Lake Sidney Lanier, one of the nation's most visited Corps of Engineer's lakes.

BETHEL DAY-USE AREA

This day-use area offers only a boat ramp, picnic tables and restrooms. It is reached by taking GA 306 off GA 400 at Exit 17. Head north and follow the signs to the day-use area, located south of GA 306.

BIG CREEK DAY-USE AREA

This handicapped-accessible area features a boat ramp, picnic tables, water, restrooms and a telephone; a fee is charged to use the boat ramp. The day-use area is located off McEver Road via Exit 2 from I-985. Turn west off the exit, then turn left onto GA 13, then take your next right. This road will take you to the day-use area after you cross McEver Road.

BOLDING MILL CAMPGROUND

Walk-in campsites and sites with electrical and water hookups can be found at Bolding Mill. The campground offers a dump station, a playground, tables, showers, a restroom, a telephone and laundry facilities. Bolding Mill is located off GA 400 on GA 136. Turn south at the town of Price and follow the signs.

BOLDING MILL DAY-USE AREA

This handicapped-accessible day-use area located alongside Bolding Mill Campground offers picnic shelters and tables, a boat ramp, a playground, water, a telephone, a swimming area

and restrooms. It, too, is located off GA 400 on GA 136, south of the town of Price.

BUFORD DAM PARK

This handicapped-accessible day-use area offers picnic shelters, a playground, water, a restroom, a telephone and a swimming area. A fee is charged to use this park, including the swimming facilities. The park is located off Buford Dam Road, which can be reached by taking GA 20 from Exit 14 off GA 400 or Exit 1 off I-985.

BURTON MILL DAY-USE AREA

This day-use area offers only a boat ramp, picnic tables and a restroom. It is located off McEver Road. Take Exit 2 off I-985, turn west from the exit, then turn right onto GA 13. From GA 13, take your first left, cross McEver Road and take your next left to the day-use area.

CHARLESTON DAY-USE AREA

This handicapped-accessible day-use area features a boat ramp, a playground, picnic tables, water, a telephone and restrooms. It can be reached by taking GA 369 east off GA 400 and following the signs.

CHESTNUT RIDGE CAMPGROUND

This campground features electrical and water hookups, a dump station, a playground, tables, showers, restrooms, a telephone and laundry facilities. It is located off McEver Road, which can be accessed via GA 13. Take Exit 2 off I-985, turn west, then turn right onto GA 13, then take your next left. This road will take you to the campground after it crosses McEver Road.

DUCKETT MILL CAMPGROUND

This campground offers everything but group camping and picnic shelters. It has walk-in sites, sites with electrical and water hookups, a dump station, showers, a restroom, a boat ramp, a swimming area, a playground, water, a telephone and laundry facilities. Duckett Mill is located south of GA 53 and north of Little Hall Day-Use Area.

DUCKETT MILL DAY-USE AREA

Located with Duckett Mill Campground, the day-use area offers handicapped access and a boat ramp. It, too, is south of GA 53 and north of Little Hall Day-Use Area.

KEITH'S BRIDGE DAY-USE AREA

This day-use area has been upgraded. It now offers a boat ramp, picnic tables, restrooms, a playground, drinking water and a swimming area. It is handicapped-accessible as well. The area is south of GA 53 just west of where it crosses the Chestatee branch of the lake on Bolling Bridge.

LITTLE HALL DAY-USE AREA

This handicapped-accessible day-use area features picnic shelters, a boat ramp, a playground, picnic tables, water, a swimming area and restrooms. It is located south off GA 53 right after it crosses the Chestatee branch of the lake on Bolling Bridge.

LITTLE RIVER DAY-USE AREA

This handicapped-accessible day-use area features a boat ramp, picnic tables, water and restrooms. It is located off GA 11 and U.S. 129 between Bell's Mill Bridge and Longstreet Bridge.

LONG HOLLOW DAY-USE AREA

This handicapped-accessible day-use area features a boat ramp, a playground, picnic tables, water, a swimming area and restrooms. It is located off GA 306 just south of where it intersects GA 53.

LOWER OVERLOOK DAY-USE AREA

This handicapped-accessible day-use area provides only picnic tables, water and restrooms. It is located at Buford Dam off Buford Dam Road, which can be reached via GA 20 from Exit 1 off I-985 and Exit 14 off GA 400.

LOWER POOL DAY-USE AREA

This handicapped-accessible day-use area

features a boat ramp, picnic tables, water and a restroom. It is located near Buford Dam off U.S. 19 in Cumming.

MARY ALICE DAY-USE AREA

This handicapped-accessible day-use area offers picnic shelters, a boat ramp, a playground, water, a swimming area, restrooms and a telephone. A fee is charged to use the boat ramp and the swimming area. Mary Alice Day-Use Area is located off U.S. 19 near Cumming.

MOUNTAIN VIEW DAY-USE AREA

This day-use area features a boat ramp, picnic tables, water and restrooms. Mountain View is located off GA 369 just east of where it crosses Brown's Bridge.

NIX BRIDGE DAY-USE AREA

This handicapped-accessible day-use area offers a boat ramp, a picnic table, water and restrooms. It is located off GA 226 south of GA 136.

OLD FEDERAL CAMPGROUND

Electrical and water hookups, showers, restrooms, a dump station, a playground, a boat ramp, picnic tables, water, a swimming area, a telephone and laundry facilities are among the features of this campground. Old Federal can be reached by taking Exit 3 off I-985, driving west to McEver Road and following the signs to the campground, located on Chattahoochee Bay.

OLD FEDERAL DAY-USE AREA

This handicapped-accessible day-use area offers a boat ramp, water, a swimming area, restrooms and a telephone. Located just east of Old Federal Campground, it can be reached by taking Exit 3 off I-985 and driving west to McEver Road. From there, follow the signs to the day-use area, also located on Chattahoochee Bay.

POWERHOUSE DAY-USE AREA

This handicapped-accessible day-use area provides only restrooms and a telephone. The powerhouse, part of Buford Dam, is used to generate electricity. It is located next to the dam off Buford Dam Road. It can be reached via GA 20 west from Exit 1 off I-985 or east from Exit 14 off GA 400.

ROBINSON DAY-USE AREA

This day-use area provides only a boat ramp, picnic tables and restrooms. It can be reached via GA 53. It is located south of GA 53 between where it crosses Bolling Bridge and where it crosses Lanier Bridge.

SARDIS CREEK DAY-USE AREA

This handicapped-accessible day-use area offers a boat ramp, picnic tables, water and restrooms. It can be accessed via GA 136 east of Price.

SAWNEE CAMPGROUND

Electrical and water hookups, showers, restrooms, a dump station, a playground, a boat ramp, picnic tables, water, a swimming area, a telephone and laundry facilities are among the features of this campground. It is located off U.S. 19 near Cumming.

SHADY GROVE CAMPGROUND

Walk-in sites, sites with electrical and water hookups and group camping are all available at this campground. Showers, restrooms, a dump station, a playground, a boat ramp, picnic tables, water, a swimming area, a telephone and laundry facilities are offered as well. Shady Grove is one of only two campgrounds around Lake Sidney Lanier that offer group camping. It is located off GA 369 just south of where it intersects GA 306.

SHOAL CREEK CAMPGROUND

Shoal Creek is the only other campground around Lake Lanier to offer group camping. It also has sites with electrical and water hookups. Showers, restrooms, a dump station, a playground, a boat ramp, picnic tables, water, a swimming area, a telephone and laundry facilities are among the features of this campground. Shoal Creek can be reached by taking Exit 1 off I-985 and heading west along GA 20 to McEver Road. Turn right on McEver Road and follow the signs.

SHOAL CREEK DAY-USE AREA

A fee-use boat ramp and pit toilets are the only amenities at this day-use area. Shoal Creek can be reached by taking Exit 1 off I-985 and heading west along GA 20 to McEver Road. Turn right on McEver Road and follow the signs.

THOMPSON CREEK DAY-USE AREA

This handicapped-accessible day-use area offers picnic shelters, a boat ramp, water and restrooms. Thompson Creek is on GA 318.

TIDWELL DAY-USE AREA

This handicapped-accessible day-use area provides a fee-use boat ramp, water, restrooms and a telephone. Tidwell can be reached by driving east from Exit 16 off GA 400 and following the signs.

TOTO CREEK DAY-USE AREA

A boat ramp, picnic tables, water, primitive camping and restrooms are offered at Toto Creek Day-Use Area; a fee is charged for camping. The area is located just north of the Toto Creek Bridge off GA 136.

TWO MILE DAY-USE AREA

This day-use area provides a boat ramp, picnic tables, water and restrooms. Two Mile can be reached via GA 369; it is located east of Four

Mile Creek Bridge and west of Two Mile Creek Bridge.

UPPER OVERLOOK DAY-USE AREA

This handicapped-accessible area, located at Buford Dam, offers picnic shelters, a playground, water, picnic tables, restrooms and a telephone. Upper Overlook is off Buford Dam Road. It can be reached via GA 20 by taking Exit 1 off I-985 or Exit 14 off GA 400.

VAN PUGH DAY-USE AREA

This handicapped-accessible day-use area offers picnic shelters, a boat ramp, a playground, picnic tables, water, a swimming area, restrooms and a telephone. Van Pugh is located off McEver Road. It can be reached by taking Exit 2 off I-985, driving west to GA 13, turning right and then left and following the signs.

VANN'S TAVERN DAY-USE AREA

This handicapped-accessible day-use area provides a boat ramp, water, restrooms and a telephone. Vann's Tavern is off GA 369 just east of Two Mile Bridge.

WAR HILL CAMPGROUND

Camping at War Hill is limited to unimproved sites, although there are picnic tables, water, restrooms, a boat ramp and a swimming area. A fee is charged to camp here. War Hill is located off GA 53 just south of where it crosses GA 318.

WAR HILL DAY-USE AREA

This handicapped-accessible day-use area offers a boat ramp, picnic tables, water, a swimming area and restrooms. It is located with War Hill Campground off GA 53 just south of where it crosses GA 318.

WEST BANK DAY-USE AREA

This handicapped-accessible day-use area provides picnic shelters, a playground, a boat ramp, picnic tables, water, a swimming area, restrooms and a telephone. A usage fee is charged for swimming. West Bank can be reached off U.S. 19 near Cumming.

YOUNG DEER DAY-USE AREA

This handicapped-accessible day-use area features picnic shelters, a boat ramp, a playground, picnic tables, water, a swimming area, restrooms and a telephone. Young Deer is located off GA 369 just east of Six Mile Creek Bridge.

MARINAS

A number of marinas are on Lake Sidney Lanier.

Aqualand Marina is located off I-985; take Exit 3 and drive west.

Bald Ridge Marina is located off GA 400; take Exit 15 and drive east.

Gainesville Marina is located off GA 53 just east of the Lanier Bridge.

Habersham Marina is located off GA 19 near Cumming.

Holiday Marina is located off McEver Road; take Exit 2 off I-985, head west to GA 13, turn left, take your first right and follow this road to Holiday.

Lan Mar Marina is located off GA 369 just west of Brown's Bridge.

Lanier Harbor Marina is located off GA 20; take Exit 1 off I-985 or Exit 14 off GA 400. Follow the signs to Lanier Park and Gwinnett Park; Lanier Harbor Marina is just east of these two parks.

Lazy Days Marina is located off McEver Road; take Exit 2 off I-985, head west to GA 13, turn left, take your first right and follow this road to Lazy Days.

Starboard Marina is located off McEver Road near Flowery Branch Park; take Exit 3 off I-985, drive west and follow the signs.

To reach Sunrise Marina, take Exit 4 off I-985 and follow GA 53 to McEver Road; turn left on McEver Road, then right on Oakwood. Follow this road to the marina.

NEARBY ATTRACTION

Lake Lanier Islands (state-park concession)

DIRECTIONS

Many state and U.S. highways can be used to access Lake Lanier, including I-985, GA 400, GA 20, GA 53, GA 19 and others.

FOR MORE INFORMATION

Resource Manager's Office, Lake Sidney Lanier, P.O. Box 567, Buford, GA 30518 (404-945-9531)

WALTER F. GEORGE LAKE
CHATTAHOOCHEE, STEWART, QUITMAN AND CLAY COUNTIES
45,180-ACRE LAKE

With 640 miles of shoreline, this lake provides plenty of opportunities for fishing, camping, boating, swimming, picnicking and more. Stretching for 85 miles down the Alabama-Georgia state line, it offers eight recreational areas in Georgia.

The 132-foot-tall Walter F. George Dam and its accompanying lock were built as part of several Corps of Engineers projects designed to enhance navigation, power generation and stream-flow regulation. The lake—sometimes referred to as Eufaula Lake, after the Alabama town on its western shore—has been in operation since 1963. The lock provides access to the Chattahoochee River for both pleasure-boat and barge traffic. It takes 28 million gallons of water to lower a boat through the lock to the river below.

The lock, dam and lake are named for a Georgia senator who served for 34 years. Born on a tenant farm in southwest Georgia in 1878, Walter F. George was very active in legislation concerning vocational education, among other things.

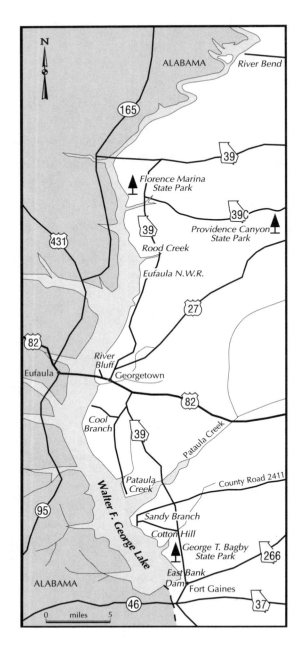

COOL BRANCH PARK

This park just south of the town of Georgetown offers a boat ramp and a picnic area. Drinking water and restrooms with showers are provided.

COTTON HILL PARK

This full-featured park is on the opposite side of Sandy Creek from George T. Bagby State Park and is convenient to that park's marina, with its boating and fishing supplies and fuel. Cotton Hill offers a fee camping area with full water and electrical hookups, a dump station, restrooms with showers and laundry facilities, a boat ramp and a picnic area with a playground near the swimming beach. This is the best-equipped Corps of Engineers park on the Georgia side of the lake.

EAST BANK PARK

This southernmost park on the lake is next to the dam, just north of the town of Fort Gaines. It offers a boat ramp and a fishing pier with restrooms and drinking water. A picnic area with tables, a picnic shelter, a playground and a basketball court round out the facilities at this park, located on the broadest section of the lake.

PATAULA CREEK PARK

This park lies at the confluence of Pataula Creek and the main body of the lake. It offers a boat ramp and a picnic area with picnic tables, a picnic shelter and nearby restrooms.

RIVER BEND PARK

This is the northernmost park on the Georgia side of the lake. It offers a boat ramp, a picnic shelter and picnic tables with nearby pit toilets. The park is located in Chattahoochee County just south of Fort Benning.

RIVER BLUFF PARK

This park on the northern edge of the town of Georgetown offers a fishing pier, a boat ramp and a picnic area with restrooms and drinking water.

ROOD CREEK PARK

A boat ramp, a free camping area and a picnic area with drinking water and pit toilets are offered at this park. It is located just south of Florence Marina State Park on GA 39 in Stewart County.

SANDY BRANCH PARK

This boat ramp has a picnic area and pit toilets.

POWERHOUSE

The powerhouse can generate enough power for a city of 40,000. Through a microwave hookup, the control room monitors water levels and power generation on the lower Chattahoochee River, including the dams and powerhouses at Walter F. George Lake and West Point Lake. To arrange a tour of the powerhouse and dam, call 912-768-2154.

BOATING

There are no motor restrictions on the lake, and water-skiing is permitted. A $2 launch fee is now charged at most Corps of Engineers boat ramps; an annual pass may be purchased at the resource manager's office for $25.

FISHING

Largemouth bass, white bass, bream, channel catfish and crappie are among the species of game fish in the lake. Since 1981, several government agencies have been strategically placing old tires and dead cedar trees in the lake to attract fish. These areas are marked with pilings. A map of their locations is available from the resource manager's office.

Under an agreement between the two states, either an Alabama or a Georgia fishing license is valid on all areas of the lake. Licenses are required for all persons age 16 and over.

PICNICKING

Picnic shelters may be reserved for a fee by calling the resource manager's office.

NEARBY ATTRACTIONS

Florence Marina State Park
George T. Bagby State Park and Lake
    Walter F. George Lodge
Kolomoki Mounds State Historic Park
Providence Canyon State Conservation Park

DIRECTIONS

All of the recreational facilities in Georgia are accessed from GA 39 via the towns of Fort Gaines and Omaha.

FOR MORE INFORMATION

Resource Manager's Office, Walter F. George Lake, Route 1, Box 176, Fort Gaines, GA 31751 (912-768-2516)

WEST POINT LAKE
TROUP AND HEARD COUNTIES
25,900-ACRE LAKE

PP

Along with power generation and flood control, recreation was a major consideration when the Corps of Engineers dammed the Chattahoochee River to form West Point Lake. It shows in the many day-use areas and campgrounds. West Point Lake boasts amenities not commonly found at Corps of Engineers reservoirs, including tennis courts, basketball courts and fish attractors placed under the handicapped-accessible fishing piers.

Spreading 35 miles upstream on the Chattahoochee and extending into Alabama, the lake serves as a reservoir to manage seasonal water flow from 3,400 square miles of drainage area. From December to mid-April, the lake is maintained at 625 feet above sea level; during the rest of the year, it is kept at about 635 feet above sea level. The lake also helps maintain the water level along the navigable section of the Chattahoochee from Columbus south to Florida.

The project was approved by Congress as part of the Flood Control Act of 1962. Construction of the dam began in 1962, with impoundment of the lake beginning 12 years later. The powerhouse generates enough power to supply 24,000 homes.

AUTRY DAY-USE AREA

Autry offers only a boat ramp. It can be reached by taking GA 109 west from LaGrange, turning right on Rock Mills Road, then turning right again on Antioch Road. Autry Day-Use Area is on the right at the end of Antioch Road.

BRUSH CREEK CAMPGROUND

This is one of the two parks on West Point Lake run by Heard County. Brush Creek is a full-service park with a boat ramp, picnic grounds, restrooms, a campground, a shower house, drinking water, a playground, a ball field, hiking trails and a dump station. It can be reached by taking Bevis Road out of Franklin. The road to Brush Creek turns left off Bevis Road.

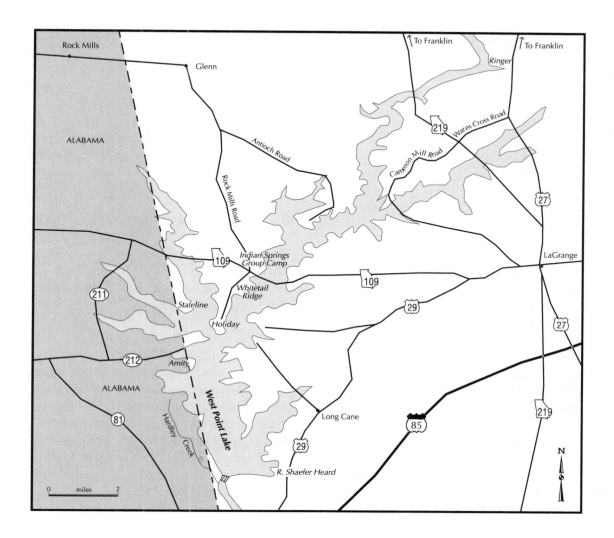

CLARK DAY-USE AREA

Clark has a boat ramp and a picnic area. It can be reached by following U.S. 27 north from LaGrange. Clark Day-Use Area is right off U.S. 27. Watch for the sign.

CROSSROADS PARK

Crossroads Park is one of the two facilities run by the Troup County Parks and Recreation Department. It offers only a boat ramp. It can be reached via Wares Cross Road off U.S. 27 north of LaGrange. Wares Cross Road is a left turn off U.S. 27. The next right turn takes you to Crossroads Park.

EAGLE VIEW PARK

Eagle View offers a picnic shelter available for reservation, restrooms and drinking water. It is located in the vicinity of West Point Dam and can be reached by following the signs on U.S. 29 at the southern end of the lake.

EARL COOK RECREATION AREA

Among the amenities at this recreation area are a boat ramp, a beach, a bathhouse, picnic grounds, picnic shelters, shelters that can be reserved for group functions, restrooms, drinking water, a playground and areas for playing basketball and softball. Earl Cook features facilities for the disabled. This fee area can be reached via U.S. 29 south of LaGrange by taking a right on Lower Glass Bridge Road.

EVANSVILLE PARK

A boat ramp and a picnic area are available at this park. Evansville Park can be reached by following GA 109 west into Alabama and taking your first right on Old State Line Road. Evansville Park is at the end of Old State Line Road where it crosses back into Georgia.

GEORGIA PARK

This park offers only a boat ramp and drink-ing water. It is located off GA 219 just south of the bridge over West Point Lake.

GLASS BRIDGE PARK

This park offers a boat ramp, picnic grounds, a picnic shelter, restrooms and drinking water. It can be reached by following U.S. 29 south from LaGrange and taking a right on Upper Glass Bridge Road.

HALFMOON CREEK PARK

Only a picnic area is available at this park. It can be reached by taking Cameron Mill Road west from LaGrange. The park is on the right after you pass Whitaker Road.

HARDLEY CREEK PARK

Hardley Creek features a fishing pier, a pre-teen and handicapped fishing pond, a picnic area and a shelter that can be reserved for group use. It also has facilities for the disabled, restrooms, drinking water, a playground and areas for playing tennis, basketball and softball. Hardley Creek Park can be reached by taking Stateline Road north from West Point.

HIGHLAND MARINA

This commercial marina, the only marina on the Georgia side of the lake, offers a boat ramp, boat repairs, a fuel dock and slip, boat, ski and tube rentals. It also has a store, a restaurant, a campground, a shower house, hotel/cabin rentals, a playground and a dump station. Highland Marina can be reached by taking GA 109 west from LaGrange and turning right on Whitaker Road, then taking a left on Seminole Road.

HOLIDAY CAMPGROUND

The campground has 88 sites with hookups, 51 campsites without hookups and two double-unit campsites with hookups. All campsites can accommodate tents. Shower houses and restrooms are located throughout the campground. There are two group camps as well. The campground also features a boat ramp, a playground, hiking trails, a dump station, an amphitheater and areas for playing basketball, softball and tennis. A fee is charged to use the campground. To reserve a site, call 706-884-6818. Holiday Campground is located off GA 109 just east of the Alabama state line.

HORACE KING PARK

This park offers a boat ramp, picnic shelters, drinking water and a shelter that can be reserved for group use. It can be reached by following GA 109 west from LaGrange. The park is the first left off GA 109 after the bridge across the Chattahoochee River/West Point Lake.

INDIAN SPRINGS GROUP CAMPING AREA

This fee area has four group camping areas. It is located on GA 109; take the right turn following the bridge across the Chattahoochee River/West Point Lake.

LIBERTY HILL PARK

A boat ramp is available at Liberty Hill. To reach the park, take Rock Mills Road/Antioch Road south from Glenn. Follow Antioch Road as it branches off to the left; continue until it reaches Liberty Hill Road, to the left. Liberty Hill Road makes a hard turn to the north.

LONG CANE PARK

Long Cane features a boat ramp, a picnic area, picnic shelters and a shelter that can be reserved for group use. There are also restrooms and drinking water. Long Cane Park is just south of Long Cane off U.S. 29.

MCGEE BRIDGE PARK

This park features a fishing pier, a boat ramp, restrooms, drinking water and a picnic area with a shelter. The park is located off GA 109 west of LaGrange. Take Vernon Ferry Road to the right, then follow the right fork to the park.

PYNE ROAD PARK

Run by the Troup County Parks and Recreation Department, Pyne Road Park features a boat ramp, a picnic area, restrooms, a campground, showers, restrooms, drinking water, a ball field and a dump station. It is on the left off GA 109 just west of Pyne Road.

R. SHAEFER HEARD CAMPGROUND AND DAY-USE AREA

This fee area has electrical and water hookups at its campsites. It also offers a boat ramp, shower houses, drinking water, a playground, a dump station, an amphitheater and an area for playing tennis, basketball and softball. The day-use area features a picnic area and shelters, along with the playground and other amenities offered by the campground. Reservations can be made by calling 706-645-2404. R. Shaefer Heard is located off U.S. 29 south of Long Cane on the road that leads to West Point Dam.

RINGER CAMPGROUND AND PARK

Ringer Campground features drinking water, a playground and a hiking trail. The park has a boat ramp, a picnic area and restrooms. It shares drinking water, a playground and hiking trails with the campground.

RIVERSIDE PARK

This park, run by the Heard County Parks and Recreation Department, offers a boat ramp, a picnic area, restrooms, a ball field and hiking trails. Riverside Park is located off GA 100 in Franklin. It sits alongside the Chattahoochee River.

ROCKY POINT RECREATION AREA

A fishing pier, a boat ramp, a beach, a bathhouse, a picnic area and shelters are among the amenities at this fee-use area. There are facilities for the handicapped and a shelter that can be reserved as well. Restrooms, drinking water, a playground, a hiking trail and an area for playing tennis, basketball and softball are also offered. Although in Georgia, Rocky Point can only be reached through Alabama. Take AL 222 east from Fredonia to where it ends at Rocky Point.

SNAKE CREEK PARK

A boat ramp, restrooms and a picnic area with shelters are available at Snake Creek. To reach the park, take South River Road south from Franklin to where it ends at the park.

STATELINE CAMPGROUND

This campground features 52 campsites with hookups, 66 campsites without hookups and two double-unit sites with hookups. All the campsites can accommodate tents, and all are situated along a peninsula with a view of the lake. The campground has a boat ramp and a beach, as well as shower houses, restrooms, drinking water, a playground, tennis facilities, a hiking trail and a dump station. Reservations can be made by calling 706-882-5439. Although located in Georgia, the campground can be reached only through Alabama. From Fredonia, follow AL 222 east to New Stateline Road/ AL 266. Take a left on this road and follow it north to AL 278. Take a right on AL 278 and follow it to Old State Line Road; turn right. Follow Old State Line Road south to where it ends at Stateline Campground. Or if you prefer, you can travel west on GA 109 into Alabama, take a left on Old State Line Road and follow it south to where it ends at the campground.

SUNNY POINT PARK

A boat ramp, a picnic area with a shelter, restrooms and drinking water are the amenities at Sunny Point. To reach the park, take GA 219 south from Franklin or north from LaGrange. The park is located to the east just south of Wares Cross Road.

WEHADKEE PARK

A boat ramp is all that is offered at Wehadkee Park. The park can be reached by following GA 109 west from LaGrange. It is the last park to the left just east of the state line.

WHITETAIL RIDGE CAMPGROUND

This campground offers 58 campsites with hookups and three double-unit campsites with hookups. There are no primitive sites, but all sites can accommodate tents. A fee is charged for using the campground, which also features a boat ramp, two shower houses, drinking water, a hiking trail and a dump station. Reservations can be made by calling 706-884-8972. You can access the campground by following GA 109 west and turning left on Thompson Road. Take your first left off Thompson Road to reach Whitetail Ridge.

WHITEWATER PARK

This park offers only a boat ramp on Turkey Creek. It can be reached by taking GA 109 west from LaGrange and turning right on Rock Mills Road, then right again on Antioch Road. Turn right on Neely Road, which ends at the boat ramp.

YELLOW JACKET CREEK RECREATION AREA

This fee-use recreation area sits on the end of the peninsula where Yellow Jacket Creek meets the Chattahoochee River. It offers a picnic area with tables and a shelter that can be reserved by groups for a fee. A swimming beach, a boat ramp, a playground, tennis courts and restrooms are the other amenities. The recreation area is northwest of LaGrange on Cameron Mill Road.

CAMPING

To make reservations, call the individual campgrounds at the numbers shown above. Reservations are taken up to 30 days in advance Monday through Thursday (except holidays) from 9 A.M. to 8 P.M. Reservations are made for the campground, not for a specific site. No advance deposit is required to reserve a site, but you will have to pay an additional small fee for the reservation service at the time you check in. Sites are available on a first-come, first-served basis when not reserved.

Campground stays are limited to 14 consecutive days. Quiet hours are from 10 P.M. until 6 A.M. The gates are locked from 10 P.M. to 7 A.M. During that time, you can only get the gate opened for an emergency. Checkout time is 4 P.M. daily.

HUNTING

A West Point Lake hunting permit and a valid Georgia hunting license are required for hunting on Corps of Engineers game lands in Georgia. Hunting in the wildlife management area is managed by the Georgia Department of Natural Resources. Call the project management office at 706-884-3915 for more information on hunts and for a hunting map.

FISHING

With a dozen creeks and 525 miles of shoreline, West Point Lake is a popular fishing spot. Bass, bream, channel catfish, catfish and crappie are found in abundance. Handicapped-accessible fishing is offered at the public fishing piers.

PICNIC SHELTERS

Group shelters can be reserved up to 60 days in advance by calling the resource manager's office. The shelters are available on a first-come, first-served basis when not reserved.

POWERHOUSE TOURS

The Powerhouse Visitor Facility is open Monday through Friday from 8 A.M. to 4 P.M. Call 706-643-5391 to arrange a tour.

NEARBY ATTRACTIONS

John H. Tanner State Park
Little White House State Historic Site
Franklin Delano Roosevelt State Park

DIRECTIONS

West Point Lake is northwest of I-85 near the city of LaGrange, near the Alabama state line.

FOR MORE INFORMATION

West Point Lake, Resource Manager's Office, 500 Resource Management Drive, West Point, GA 31833-9517 (706-645-2937)

NATIONAL WILDLIFE REFUGES

An alligator at the north entrance of the Okefenokee National Wildlife Refuge in the Southeast corner of the state

Georgia's 10 wildlife refuges are under the management of the United States Fish and Wildlife Service. Four of the refuges are on barrier islands, with another three near the coast. Because of the refuges and other federal and state lands including Cumberland and Ossabaw Islands, Georgia has a relatively unspoiled coast.

The primary goal of the refuges is to manage good, healthy populations of wildlife. As part of the management of the refuges, hunts are held annually to maintain high-quality populations of deer, turkeys and other game. Some of the refuges also offer hiking, biking, boating and fishing.

Sapelo Island National Estuarine Reserve, run by the University of Georgia, is listed with the refuges. It is not associated with the United States Fish and Wildlife Service.

BANKS LAKE NATIONAL WILDLIFE REFUGE

LANIER COUNTY   4,049 ACRES

This lake was listed in *The Guinness Book of World Records* for the record-length boat jump a stuntman made here for the Burt Reynolds movie *Gator*. The movie was filmed on Banks

Cypress trees are scattered throughout Banks Lake National Wildlife Refuge.

Lake in the 1970s. Today, the quiet, cypress-filled waters are better known for their herons, falcons, alligators and fishing.

A boat ramp and a fishing pier are run by the refuge.

NEARBY ATTRACTIONS

Reed Bingham State Park
General Coffee State Park

DIRECTIONS

This refuge is on the outskirts of Lakeland.

FOR MORE INFORMATION

Banks Lake National Wildlife Refuge, Route 2, Box 3330, Folkston, GA 31537 (912-496-7836)

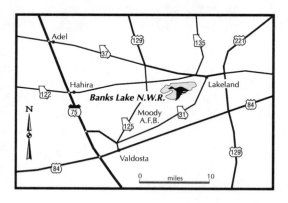

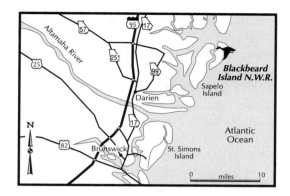

This island has been owned by the federal government since 1800, when the Navy Department

A baleen whale skull on the beach at Blackbeard Island National Wildlife Refuge. The refuge once provided shelter for the legendary pirate "Blackbeard."

bought it to harvest live oaks for shipbuilding. From 1830 to 1900, a tent hospital on the island's south end served as a quarantine station for yellow fever victims. In 1924, the island was given to the Bureau of Biological Service, now known as the United States Fish and Wildlife Service.

The dock on Blackbeard Creek is for loading and unloading passengers and for fishing. There are picnic tables near this dock. No motorized vehicles are allowed on the island. There are more than 20 miles of trails for hikers and mountain bikers to explore. Alligators are prolific. Raccoons, deer and numerous species of birds are often seen on this relatively untouched barrier island. Loggerhead sea turtles come ashore here to nest each summer. There was a virtually unheard-of confirmed sighting of a leatherback sea turtle attempting to nest on this beach in the early 1980s. The world's largest sea turtles, leatherbacks usually nest in South America.

The island's name comes from the notorious Edward Teach, nicknamed "Blackbeard." The British pirate used this island for his base of

243

operations from 1716 until his death in 1718. A spike through a tree at the island's north end is said to have been placed by Blackbeard as a clue to finding treasure buried on the island.

The refuge is open from sunrise to sunset daily except during the annual hunts, when only those with a permit to hunt may be on the island. Organized groups may camp on the island by permit only; no other camping is allowed.

HUNTING

Fall archery hunts for deer are held annually on the island. Call the refuge office for more information.

FISHING

Freshwater fishing is permitted in Flag Pond and North Pond in season. Saltwater fishing is allowed on the beach and in the saltwater creeks on the island. Freshwater anglers over 16 years of age must have a valid Georgia fishing license. A license is not required for saltwater fishing.

NEARBY ATTRACTIONS

Wolf Island National Wildlife Refuge
Fort Frederica National Monument
Fort King George State Historic Site
Hofwyl-Broadfield Plantation State Historic Site
Harris Neck National Wildlife Refuge
Sapelo Island National Estuarine Reserve

DIRECTIONS

Blackbeard Island is narrowly separated from Sapelo Island, to the south, by Blackbeard Creek. Refer to navigational charts for directions.

FOR MORE INFORMATION

Blackbeard Island National Wildlife Refuge, United States Fish and Wildlife Service, P.O. Box 8487, Savannah, GA 31412 (912-944-4415)

EUFAULA NATIONAL WILDLIFE REFUGE
STEWART COUNTY   11,184 ACRES

The refuge is named for the nearby Alabama town and lake, which in turn are named for the Abeika Indian town of Eufaula, which was in this area. Much of the refuge's acreage and its

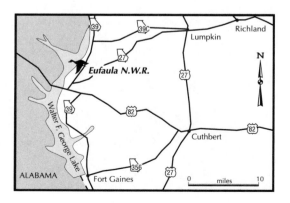

headquarters are in Alabama, but portions of the refuge in Georgia host deer and waterfowl hunts.

HUNTING

Fall hunts are scheduled for deer and waterfowl. Certain portions of Eufaula are within the Chattahoochee River system and are closed to waterfowl hunting. You must apply for deer hunts by the end of August and for waterfowl hunts by the end of October. Goose hunting is also allowed here.

There are quota hunts at the refuge, with selected hunters charged $12.50 for a permit.

NEARBY ATTRACTIONS

Providence Canyon State Conservation Park
Florence Marina State Park
Jimmy Carter National Historic Site
George T. Bagby State Park
Walter F. George Lake

DIRECTIONS

Eufaula National Wildlife Refuge can be reached via GA 39 south of Florence and north of Georgetown.

FOR MORE INFORMATION

Eufaula National Wildlife Refuge, Route 2, Box 97-B, Eufaula, AL 36027 (334-687-4065)

HARRIS NECK NATIONAL WILDLIFE REFUGE
MCINTOSH COUNTY   2,762 ACRES

This refuge served as an army airfield during World War II. It still occasionally makes the news as local African-American residents argue that the government broke faith with them when it gave the land to the United States Fish and Wildlife Service in 1962. They claim the land was taken during the war with an understanding that it should return to its previous owners if not used by the military. There are no signs that the refuge will be returned to the residents.

Some of the paved roads left from the refuge's time as an airfield are closed to vehicles but provide handicapped access to some prime viewing areas. Deer and armadillos are commonly seen. Hundreds of species of birds make this refuge popular with birders, especially during spring and fall migrations, when songbirds stop off here.

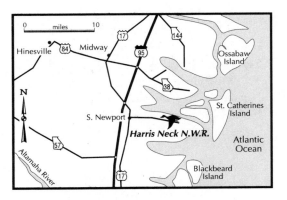

Harris Neck is a narrow isthmus on the Atlantic Intracoastal Waterway named for Harris Plantation, which once stood here.

The refuge is open seven days a week from sunrise to sunset. Organized conservation groups can arrange a tour by contacting the office in Savannah.

HUNTING

An annual deer hunt is scheduled for hunters with rifles or shotguns with slugs. Because this is a quota hunt, you must apply by the end of August. Selected hunters are charged a $12.50 permit fee. Call the refuge office for more information.

FISHING

There are two piers at the refuge entrance on GA 131. Barbour River Landing is open from 4 A.M. to midnight and has a high-tide boat ramp. The facility is closed from March 1 to April 31 due to the presence of wood stork nesting sites close to the landing.

NEARBY ATTRACTIONS

Fort Morris State Historic Site
Blackbeard Island National Wildlife Refuge
Fort King George State Historic Site
Fort Frederica National Monument
Hofwyl-Broadfield Plantation State Historic Site

DIRECTIONS

From Exit 12 off I-95, go south for 1 mile on U.S. 17 to GA 131. Turn east and drive 7 miles to the refuge entrance.

FOR MORE INFORMATION

Harris Neck National Wildlife Refuge, United States Fish and Wildlife Service, P.O. Box 8487, Savannah, GA 31412 (912-944-4415)

OKEFENOKEE NATIONAL WILDLIFE REFUGE/OKEFENOKEE NATIONAL WILDERNESS AREA
CHARLTON AND WARE COUNTIES
391,402 ACRES/353,981-ACRE WILDERNESS AREA

A huge saucer-shaped depression in what was once the ocean floor is the base for one of the nation's oldest and best-preserved freshwater areas—the Okefenokee Swamp. Since 1937, these vast wetlands have been protected as a refuge to block development of the once-endangered swamp.

The Okefenokee has been inhabited by man since about 2500 B.C. Indian mounds within the refuge are a testament to these inhabitants. As little research has been done on early Indian life in the swamp, most of what is known is speculation. We do know that the name *Okefenokee* comes from the white man's version of the Indian words meaning "Land of Trembling Earth." The name refers to the unstable

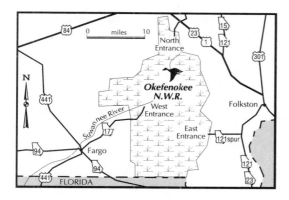

surface of the thick peat bogs which cover the swamp floor. Stamping on the bog can cause the surrounding trees and bushes to tremble. The Seminoles were the last tribe to seek refuge in the swamp. They were driven into Florida by an armed militia in 1850.

In 1891, the Suwannee Canal Company bought 238,000 acres of the Okefenokee from the state of Georgia. The canal company set to work at once building a canal to drain the swamp to aid in the logging and eventual farming of the land. After three years of work, it completed 11.5 miles of canal, which can still be used today at the refuge's east entrance. The canal company went bankrupt in the depression of the 1890s and sold its land to the Hebard Cypress Company. In 1909, a railroad into the western edge of the swamp was completed, and the logging of cypress began. Over the next 18 years, 431 million board feet of lumber were removed before logging ceased. In another 10 years, the swamp became a wildlife refuge.

Today, the swamp is home to 234 species of birds, 50 species of mammals, 64 species of reptiles and 37 species of amphibians. There are an estimated 9,000 to 12,000 of the refuge's trademark alligators in the swamp.

The swamp has about 60,000 acres of prairies, which attract herons, egrets, cranes (including the Florida sandhill crane) and other wading birds. These prairies were created when forested areas

The Chesser Cabin is still set up today as it was when the Chesser family lived there in the 1920s and 30s. It is on Swamp Island Drive at the east entrance to Okefenokee National Wildlife Refuge.

effected by a drought were burned out by forest fires. Chesser, Grand and Mizell Prairies can be reached by way of the Suwannee Canal at the east entrance. The small lakes in the prairies offer excellent freshwater fishing.

ENTRY FEE

There is a $4 per-vehicle fee for entering the refuge at the west and east entrances. The north entrance is operated as a concession by Okefenokee Swamp Park, which charges a per-person fee to visit its facilities.

EAST ENTRANCE—
SUWANNEE CANAL RECREATION AREA

This entrance offers direct access to the refuge at Suwannee Canal Recreation Area. The other two entrances have concessions, one operated by the state of Georgia and the other by a private, nonprofit concern. By using the Suwannee Canal, you can access the great open areas of the swamp from this entrance. The visitor center has some very good interpretive displays on the swamp habitat.

BOATING AND FISHING

Next to the visitor center is a boat dock, with canoe and johnboat rentals offered by a private concessioner. Boat tours of the swamp are also featured here. Legal fishing is permitted year-round in the refuge, but a current Georgia fishing license is required for all persons age 16 and over.

Wilderness canoe rides of two to five days can also be arranged, but a permit is required. Reservations are taken no more than two months in advance, and a fee is charged. Call 912-496-3331 to obtain a permit and to make reservations for a wilderness canoe trip.

HUNTING

Public hunting is permitted in the 1,240-acre Suwannee Canal unit. Youths wishing to hunt must show proof of having successfully completed a hunter safety course. A nontransferable permit is required for each hunter. To receive a permit application and a complete list of hunting regulations, write the refuge office. Applications are due each year by August 31. Successful applicants must pay $12.50 for issuance of a hunting permit.

WILDLIFE OBSERVATION DRIVE

Swamp Island Drive is a 4.5-mile wildlife observation drive. Along the route, you will pass through pine forests and beside small ponds. The drive makes an excellent bike route, as bikes travel quietly and stop easily to observe wildlife. Bike racks for locking up your bike while hiking are located at the major stops on the route. There is a parking lot with restrooms along the drive.

HIKING

The five trails in this recreation area cover a total of 4.5 miles. All of them have trailheads

A nature trail in Stephen C. Foster State Park at the west entrance to the Okefenokee National Wildlife Refuge

Family Homestead, which offers a glimpse at swamp life in the 1930s. Deerstand Trail cuts 0.5 mile through the pine trees to an observation tower. The fifth trail offers a 1.5-mile round-trip hike out over the swamp to an observation tower overlooking Seagrove Lake on the edge of Chesser Prairie.

DAYS AND DIRECTIONS

The east entrance is open daily year-round except for Christmas. It is located 8 miles south of Folkston off GA 121.

WEST ENTRANCE— STEPHEN C. FOSTER STATE PARK

Stephen C. Foster State Park is operated by the state of Georgia at the west entrance to the refuge. Canoe and motorboat rentals and a 0.5-mile nature trail are among the ways visitors can experience the swamp from this 80-acre park. For more detailed information, see the write-up on Stephen C. Foster State Park in the State Parks section of this book. The park is 18 miles northeast of the town of Fargo on GA Spur 177.

NORTH ENTRANCE— OKEFENOKEE SWAMP PARK

This entrance is through Okefenokee Swamp Park, a nonprofit organization that operates under a long-term lease with the government. The park offers easy access to the swamp experience, with alligators floating in the black water in

on Swamp Island Drive. The 0.5-mile Canal Diggers Trail loops around the forest along the Suwannee Canal; this trail can also be reached from the visitor center. The 0.2-mile Peckerwood Trail loops through the pine forest; it offers interpretive signs describing the habitat. Chesser Island Trail leads 0.5 mile past an Indian mound and to and around the Chesser

sight of the parking lot. A 25-minute boat tour of the swamp leaves from this area, which has a number of other attractions, including Pioneer Island, the Living Swamp Center, the Serpentarium and Wildlife Observatory and a 90-foot observation tower. A per-person fee is charged here. The park is 8 miles south of Waycross off U.S. 1. For more information, contact Okefenokee Swamp Park, Waycross, GA 31501 (912-283-0583).

NEARBY ATTRACTIONS

Crooked River State Park
Cumberland Island National Seashore
Laura S. Walker State Park
Stephen C. Foster State Park
Fort Frederica National Monument

FOR MORE INFORMATION

Okefenokee National Wildlife Refuge, Route 2, Box 3330, Folkston, GA 31537 (912-496-7836)

Pines and bottomland hardwoods now fill the one-time farmland at Piedmont National Wildlife Refuge.

PIEDMONT NATIONAL WILDLIFE REFUGE

JASPER AND JONES COUNTIES   34,903 ACRES

The land for this refuge was purchased in 1939 after area farmers abandoned their land. Years of heavy cotton farming caused extensive erosion, depleting the land of 1.5 feet of topsoil. The land became unproductive, and, coupled with the Depression, farmers could not sustain their farming practices. Insight into the farmlands that preceded the refuge can be gained at the adjacent Jarrell Plantation State Historic Site.

Today, the refuge is 35,000 acres consisting primarily of upland pine forest. The forest is managed for the resident, endangered red-cockaded woodpecker. These birds excavate cavities into living pine trees and drill resin wells around the cavities. Naturalists believe that these resin wells deter snakes and other predators from climbing into the nests.

The refuge's management benefits many Neotropical songbirds and other native wildlife, including beavers, bobcats, coyotes, fox squirrels, bats and white-tailed deer.

HUNTING

Public hunting is permitted on approximately 34,000 acres of the refuge. Small-game hunting (quail, rabbits and squirrels) is permitted except during refuge gun hunts for deer. Four weekend night hunts for raccoons and opossums are held each January. A refuge permit is required. There is no check-in.

Archery hunting for deer is permitted with a refuge permit. Check refuge regulations for dates. Gun hunts for deer and turkeys are quota hunts. Applications are available from the visitor center; the deadlines for applying are August 31 for deer and February 28 for turkeys. A public draw-

ing is held. Permits are $12.50. There is no check-in, but all deer and turkeys taken must be checked out.

A special gun hunt for deer is held each year for wheelchair-bound hunters. A special-use permit is required.

Contact the visitor center for a current brochure on hunting regulations for the refuge.

FISHING

The refuge has several ponds and creeks open to public fishing during daylight hours from May 1 to September 30. A Georgia fishing license is required for anglers over 15 years of age. Boats may be used on Allison Lake and Pond 2-A, but no gasoline motors are allowed. Boats may not be kept in the fishing areas overnight. All other ponds are open to bank fishing only. Pond 21-A on Little Rock Wildlife Drive is reserved for children 12 and under. Anglers must stay at least 30 feet away from wooden duck boxes. Contact the refuge office for a fishing-regulations brochure, which has a map of the refuge.

HIKING

Allison Lake Nature Trail is a mile-long loop that begins near the visitor center. A photo blind on the lake offers a sheltered view of waterfowl and other wildlife.

Red-Cockaded Woodpecker Trail is a 2.5-mile loop beginning at the same trailhead. About a third of this loop is along Allison Creek, but the main attraction is the loblolly pines marked with white bands. These trees are cavity sites

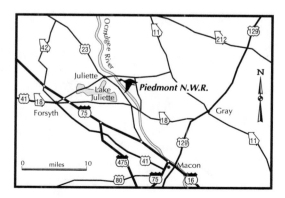

for red-cockaded woodpeckers. The best time to observe these woodpeckers is in May and June, when they are nesting.

A third trail connects the visitor center to Allison Lake Trail to form a 1.5-mile loop through hardwood bottom and upland pine habitats.

The 1.5-mile Hitchiti Nature Trail is located near the refuge; that hike is described in the write-up on Oconee National Forest in this book.

WILDLIFE DRIVE

The best way to explore the refuge by car is to get a copy of the self-guided tour brochure for Little Rock Wildlife Drive. This 6-mile gravel road offers an overview of the refuge's history, habitats and management programs. The drive is open year-round during daylight hours except during the annual gun hunts for deer. Brochures are available from the visitor center.

NEARBY ATTRACTIONS

Oconee National Forest
Jarrell Plantation State Historic Site
Ocmulgee National Monument
Lake Sinclair
Indian Springs State Park
High Falls State Park
Rum Creek Wildlife Management Area

DIRECTIONS

From Exit 61 off I-75, it is 18 miles east on Juliette Road to the visitor center.

FOR MORE INFORMATION

Piedmont National Wildlife Refuge, Route 1, Box 670, Round Oak, GA 31038 (912-986-5441)

SAPELO ISLAND NATIONAL ESTUARINE RESERVE
MCINTOSH COUNTY

The island of Sapelo has had a long and varied history. Beginning with its occupation by the Guale Indians, Sapelo has seen Spanish missionaries, English freebooters and French royalists fleeing a revolution. In 1802, the south end of the island was purchased by Thomas Spalding. This innovative planter, architect, businessman and statesman developed Sapelo into one of the South's most productive and efficient plantations before the Civil War. The ruins of his tabby sugar mill and other plantation buildings can still be seen on the island. Spalding

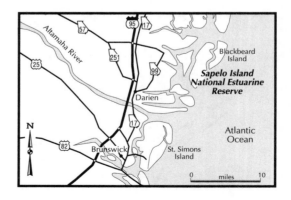

eventually owned all of Sapelo, along with 400 slaves and fields of sea-island cotton and sugarcane.

In 1912, the island was purchased by Howard E. Coffin, a Detroit automotive engineer. Coffin reestablished agricultural operations on the island and began a seafood business and a construction program as well. In 1925, he restored the South End Mansion, built by Spalding, and entertained two presidents—Calvin Coolidge and Herbert Hoover—there. Famous aviator Charles A. Lindbergh was also a guest of Coffin's.

Richard J. Reynolds, Jr., tobacco millionaire, was the next to purchase Sapelo. He owned the island from 1934 until his death in 1964. During his time on the island, he donated land and buildings to the University of Georgia for the creation of a marine research facility, where significant marsh and estuarine study has been conducted since 1954.

Today, visitors can experience virtually every facet of a typical barrier-island natural community—the diversified wildlife of the forest uplands, the vast expanses of salt marsh and the complex beach and dunes system.

Exhibits and displays can be found at the Long Tabby Interpretive Center, which features information on both the natural and cultural history of Sapelo. Public tours of the African-American community of Hog Hammock, the University of Georgia Marine Institute and the Coffin-Reynolds mansion are available. There are also marsh and beach walks, bird and wildlife observation tours and historic tours.

TOUR HOURS

Tours are held Wednesday from 8:30 A.M. to 12:30 P.M. and Saturday from 9:00 A.M. to 1:00 P.M. from September through May. Tours are also scheduled on Fridays from June through August. For ticket information, contact the Darien Welcome Center at 912-437-6684.

COFFIN-REYNOLDS MANSION OVERNIGHT LODGING

The mansion can accommodate groups of up to 28 persons for conferences, workshops and retreats. There is a minimum stay of two nights. Lodging rates include three meals per day, meeting facilities and transportation. For rates and other information, call 912-485-2299.

PIONEER CAMPING

Group camping is offered near the beach on Sapelo's Cabretta Island. There is a minimum two-night stay for up to 25 persons. A comfort station and a shower room are available, and transportation to and from the campground is provided. For more information, call 912-485-2299.

NEARBY ATTRACTIONS

Hofwyl-Broadfield Plantation State Historic Site
Fort Frederica National Monument
Fort King George State Historic Site
Blackbeard Island National Wildlife Refuge
Wolf Island National Wildlife Refuge

DIRECTIONS

The Sapelo ferry dock is located 8 miles northeast of Darien off GA 99.

FOR MORE INFORMATION

Sapelo Island National Estuarine Reserve, P.O. Box 15, Sapelo Island, GA 31327 (912-485-2251)

SAVANNAH NATIONAL WILDLIFE REFUGE

CHATHAM COUNTY   26,296 ACRES

Wildlife is easy to spot here, with alligators, eagles and other animals often in sight of the main road into the refuge. The 39 miles of dikes left from coastal Georgia's rice-plantation past can be hiked for access into the refuge for wildlife viewing.

In his book *Georgia Place Names*, Kenneth Krakow lists earlier names for the Savannah River, including *Isundiga*, meaning "Blue water"; *Westobou*, a Westoe Indian name meaning "River of the Westoes"; and *Grande*, a name given by the Frenchman Jean Ribault in 1562. The name Savannah probably derives from the Spanish name *Sabana*, for a group of Indians who once lived near the mouth of the river.

The refuge is open daily from a half-hour before sunrise to a half-hour after sunset.

HUNTING

Annual deer hunts are scheduled for hunters with rifles and shotguns with slugs. There is no check-in for these hunts. None of the hunts in the refuge are quota hunts.

Other hunts are for small game (squirrels only) and feral hogs. There is a check-in for both these hunts. Squirrels may be shot with shotguns only, feral hogs with shotguns with slugs. Call the refuge office for more information.

NEARBY ATTRACTIONS

Tybee Island National Wildlife Refuge
Wormsloe State Historic Site
Fort Pulaski National Monument
Skidaway Island State Park
Fort McAllister State Historic Park
Wassaw Island National Wildlife Refuge

DIRECTIONS

From Exit 5 off I-95, go east on U.S. 17 toward the airport. Laurel Hill Wildlife Drive is

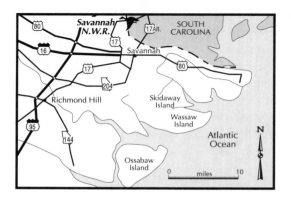

on the left at the entrance to the refuge after about 2 miles.

FOR MORE INFORMATION

Savannah National Wildlife Refuge, United States Fish and Wildlife Service, P.O. Box 8487, Savannah, GA 31412 (912-944-4415)

TYBEE ISLAND NATIONAL WILDLIFE REFUGE
CHATHAM COUNTY   100 ACRES

This small refuge is located on a sand bar used by the Corps of Engineers, which disposes of dredgings from the Savannah River here. Shorebirds rest here, and terns nest among the rattlesnake-infested vegetation. Strong currents make this a nearly unvisited refuge. It is open daily from sunrise to sunset but may be closed during tern nesting season.

Tybee's name was once spelled Tiby, from the Uchee Indian word for salt.

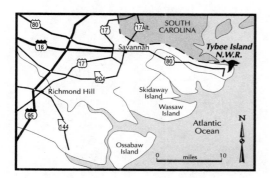

NEARBY ATTRACTIONS

Savannah National Wildlife Refuge
Wormsloe State Historic Site
Fort Pulaski National Monument
Skidaway Island State Park
Fort McAllister State Historic Park
Wassaw Island National Wildlife Refuge

DIRECTIONS

Consult navigational charts to find this refuge at the mouth of the Savannah River.

FOR MORE INFORMATION

Tybee Island National Wildlife Refuge, United States Fish and Wildlife Service, P.O. Box 8487, Savannah, GA 31412 (912-944-4415)

WASSAW ISLAND NATIONAL WILDLIFE REFUGE
CHATHAM COUNTY   10,070 ACRES

This island offers a glimpse at how the coast of Georgia must have looked before the Spanish arrived in the 1500s. The island was acquired by the Nature Conservancy in 1969 and donated to the United States Fish and Wildlife Service.

The 7-mile-long beach and nearly two dozen miles of inland trails offer visitors solitude, a rare commodity on the coast. The only man-made intrusion left from the island's

cessful applicants will be charged a $12.50 permit fee. Buckshot is not allowed on these hunts. Call the refuge office for more information.

NEARBY ATTRACTIONS

Savannah National Wildlife Refuge
Wormsloe State Historic Site
Fort Pulaski National Monument
Skidaway Island State Park

past is the remains of a tabby fort built in 1898. It has been severely deteriorated by time and tides.

The name Wassaw is said to come from the creek word *Wiso*, meaning "Sassafras."

TURTLE RESEARCH

The Caretta Research Project has operated here since 1973. From mid-May to early September, loggerhead sea turtles nest on the island. Volunteers identify the nesting females and later move the eggs to a protected hatchery. To participate in this rare opportunity for hands-on research, contact the Savannah Science Museum at 912-355-6705.

HUNTING

An archery deer hunt is scheduled each fall. While this is not a quota hunt, a check-in is required. Hunts are also scheduled in the fall for hunters with firearms; these are quota hunts with a required check-in. Applicants must file by the end of August for the firearms hunt. Suc-

Sea oats in silhouette at Wassaw National Wildlife Refuge

Fort McAllister State Historic Park
Tybee Island National Wildlife Refuge

DIRECTIONS

Wassaw is east of Skidaway Island and may be located with the help of navigational charts.

FOR MORE INFORMATION

Wassaw Island National Wildlife Refuge, United States Fish and Wildlife Service, P.O. Box 8487, Savannah, GA 31412 (912-944-4415)

WOLF ISLAND NATIONAL WILDLIFE REFUGE/WOLF ISLAND NATIONAL WILDERNESS AREA

MCINTOSH COUNTY   5,126 ACRES

This refuge at the mouth of the Altamaha River near Darien includes Wolf Island and the smaller Egg and Little Egg Islands. These islands have little solid land and offer scant recreation beyond fishing, birding and beachcombing. Wolf Island serves as an important nesting site for loggerhead sea turtles, which return each summer.

The refuge is open daily from sunrise to sunset but may be closed seasonally to protect nesting sites. Public use is permitted only on the beach.

NEARBY ATTRACTIONS

Sapelo Island National Estuarine Reserve
Fort King George State Historic Site
Hofwyl-Broadfield Plantation State Historic Site
Fort Frederica National Monument
Blackbeard Island National Wildlife Sanctuary

DIRECTIONS

These islands are south of Sapelo at the mouth of the Altamaha River. Directions may be found on navigational charts.

FOR MORE INFORMATION

Wolf Island National Wildlife Refuge, United States Fish and Wildlife Service, P.O. Box 8487, Savannah, GA 31412 (912-944-4415)

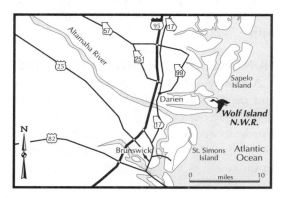

PUBLIC FISHING AREAS AND WILDLIFE MANAGEMENT AREAS

White-tailed deer were reintroduced to Georgia with great success. Well-managed herds now provide a bounty for big game hunters.

If you are looking for a place to hunt and fish, the state-managed public fishing areas and wildlife management areas (WMAs) provide a seemingly endless supply of possibilities. There are more than a million acres of hunting land within the managed game lands and 140 lakes with more than 5,000 acres of surface area in the state's fishing areas.

Much of the land is owned by either the state or the federal government, but the areas listed in this section also include state-managed game areas on private property. There are 20 companies and private landowners who own property within WMAs.

HUNTING AND FISHING REGULATIONS

A complete list of Georgia's hunting seasons and regulations is published each year by the Wildlife Resources Division of the Georgia Department of Natural Resources. The booklet also contains applications for permits to participate in quota hunts for deer, quail, waterfowl and

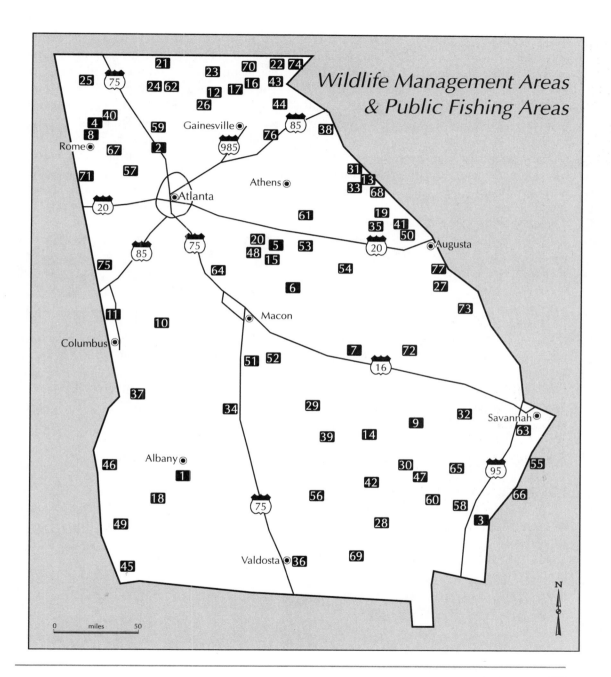

Wildlife Management Areas & Public Fishing Areas

turkeys. This free publication is available wherever hunting licenses are sold. A similar publication giving freshwater and saltwater sportfishing regulations is produced jointly by the Wildlife Resources Division and the Coastal Resources Division of the Georgia Department of Natural Resources. It is available free of charge wherever fishing licenses are sold.

Please note the special trout regulations in effect for Hoods Creek and Walnut Creek in the Warwoman WMA; Waters Creek in the Chestatee WMA; Jones Creek and Noontootla Creek in the Blue Ridge WMA; and Stanley Creek in the Rich Mountain WMA. These trout streams have specified minimum lengths.

CAMPING

Camping is permitted year-round at most of the areas listed in this section. On national forest lands managed as wildlife management areas, camping is allowed anywhere. At other WMAs, it is limited to designated campgrounds. The campgrounds have established quiet hours between 10 P.M. and 7 A.M. Organized groups of 10 persons or more must get a "right of entry agreement" from the nearest regional office.

FOR MORE INFORMATION

The wildlife management areas are managed by seven regional offices. The Armuchee office, which covers northwest Georgia, can be reached at 706-295-6041. The Gainesville office, which manages northeast Georgia, can be reached at 404-535-5700. The Thomson office, which covers the west side of the upper Piedmont, can be

telephoned at 706-595-4211. The Fort Valley office, which covers the east half of the upper Piedmont, can be contacted at 912-825-6354. The Albany office, which covers the southwest corner of the state below the fall line, can be reached at 912-430-4254. The Fitzgerald office, which covers the southeast corner of the state (but not including the coastline), can be contacted at 912-423-2988. The Brunswick office, which manages the coastal counties, may be contacted at 912-262-3173.

ALBANY NURSERY WILDLIFE MANAGEMENT AREA
DOUGHERTY COUNTY   300 ACRES

1

Deer, small game and doves may be hunted at this WMA, which also offers a handicapped-only hunt each year. Write to Wildlife Resources Division, 2024 Newton Road, Albany, GA 31708 for more information on the handicapped hunt.

DIRECTIONS

From Albany, go 11 miles west on GA 234 (locally marked as Gillionville Highway) and turn right on Tallahassee Road. It is 1.2 miles down that road to the entrance to the wildlife management area.

ALLATOONA WILDLIFE MANAGEMENT AREA
BARTOW AND CHEROKEE COUNTIES
15,000 ACRES

2

Deer, turkeys, small game, foxes, bobcats, raccoons, opossums and doves are all hunted at this large area on the north shore of Allatoona Lake.

DIRECTIONS

From Exit 125 off I-75, it is 5.5 miles to the check station.

ALTAMAHA WILDLIFE MANAGEMENT AREA
GLYNN COUNTY   27,078 ACRES

3

Deer, turkeys, small game, foxes, bobcats, raccoons, opossums, feral hogs, doves and waterfowl are all hunted at this area. There is a quota on waterfowl hunted on Butler Island. Airboats are prohibited inside of managed waterfowl impoundments. After waterfowl season, this area is closed to all firearms hunting.

DIRECTIONS

The check station is on the right 1.5 miles south of Darien on GA 17.

ARROWHEAD PUBLIC FISHING AREA
FLOYD COUNTY
NINE-ACRE AND 16-ACRE PONDS

4

Channel catfish, largemouth bass, bluegill and redear sunfish are the species found in these two ponds. No boats are allowed on the ponds, which

Canada Geese nest on platforms in the ponds at Arrowhead Public Fishing Area.

are open between March 1 and October 31 from sunrise to sunset on Wednesday, Saturday and Sunday. The ponds are also open on Memorial Day, the Fourth of July and Labor Day.

FACILITIES

Restrooms, picnic shelters and drinking water are available here. There is also a 2-mile nature trail leading around the ponds.

DIRECTIONS

From the intersection of U.S. 27 and GA 156 at a point 9 miles north of Rome, go east on GA 156. Turn north on Floyd Springs Road. The entrance is on the right.

B. F. GRANT WILDLIFE MANAGEMENT AREA
PUTNAM COUNTY   11,870 ACRES

5

Deer, turkeys, small game, foxes, bobcats, raccoons, opossums, doves and waterfowl are hunted at this WMA. Waterfowl hunting is not permitted in marsh ponds. For hunters using firearms, quality-buck regulations are in effect.

DIRECTIONS

From Eatonville, go 0.7 mile west on GA 16. Turn right at the experiment station and go 7 miles to the check station.

To get to the Carpenter Tract from Eatonville, go south on U.S. 129 for 3.9 miles to Old Macon Circle. Turn right, go 0.8 mile to Holder Road and turn right. The Carpenter Tract is to the right.

BALDWIN FOREST PUBLIC FISHING AREA AND WILDLIFE MANAGEMENT AREA
BALDWIN COUNTY
2,500 ACRES/FIVE PONDS RANGING FROM THREE ACRES TO 18 ACRES IN SIZE

6

Archery hunting of deer is permitted at this area. In the ponds, fishermen can catch channel catfish, largemouth bass (14-inch minimum size) and bluegill. From March through October, the fishing area is open from sunrise to sunset on Wednesday, Saturday and Sunday, as well as on Memorial Day, the Fourth of July and Labor Day.

FACILITIES

There are public restrooms at this area.

DIRECTIONS

The entrance is on the left 4 miles south of Milledgeville on U.S. 441.

BEAVERDAM WILDLIFE MANAGEMENT AREA
LAURENS AND WILKINSON COUNTIES
12,000 ACRES

7

Deer, turkeys, small game, foxes, bobcats, raccoons, opossums, feral hogs and doves are hunted at this area. Beaverdam is made up of two large tracts in separate counties—the Wilkinson Tract and the Laurens Tract.

DIRECTIONS

To get to the Wilkinson Tract, go north from Milledgeville on GA 112 for 14 miles. Turn left on the dirt road at the WMA sign and go 1.5 miles to the check station.

To get to the Laurens Tract, go north from Dublin on U.S. 441 for 4.5 miles to Toomsboro Road. Turn right and go 7.5 miles to the WMA sign. Turn right on the dirt road and go 2.5 miles to the check station.

BERRY COLLEGE WILDLIFE MANAGEMENT AREA
FLOYD COUNTY   25,860 ACRES

8

Deer, turkeys, small game and doves are hunted at Berry College Wildlife Management Area. There is a quota for deer except on ladies-only hunting days, which are offered each year. Hunters are not allowed to access the hunting area through the main college campus. There is no open season at the refuge.

DIRECTIONS

From Rome, go north on U.S. 27 to Old Summerville Road. Turn left and go 1.5 miles to the check station at the junction with CCC Road.

BIG HAMMOCK PUBLIC FISHING AREA AND WILDLIFE MANAGEMENT AREA
TATNALL COUNTY
6,177 ACRES/18 PONDS RANGING FROM ONE ACRE TO 12 ACRES IN SIZE

9

Deer, turkeys, small game, raccoons, opossums and feral hogs are hunted at this area. No deer hunting with firearms is allowed in the natural area, and archery hunters may not place a deer stand within 50 feet of the nature trail.

Largemouth bass, bream, catfish, crappie and chain pickerel are among the species you will find in these lakes. Some of the ponds can be reached only by foot. Boats are permitted, but no gas motors are allowed. The fishing area is open daily from sunrise to sunset. The access from County Road 441 to Bluff and Cedar Lakes is open only from April 1 to September 30, but the remainder of the area is open year-round.

This area is flood-prone. There is limited

A deer forages for food in the snow at Berry College Wildlife Management Area.

access in wet weather, and the area is closed when flooded. You can check on conditions at the area by calling the Bowens Mill Game Office at 912-423-2988.

FACILITIES

The only facilities here are the primitive boat ramps at some of the lakes.

DIRECTIONS

From Glennville, go south on GA 144 for 12 miles to the bridge over the Altamaha River. The yellow boundary signs mark off the area.

BIG LAZER CREEK PUBLIC FISHING AREA AND WILDLIFE MANAGEMENT AREA
TALBOT COUNTY
5,850 ACRES/195-ACRE LAKE

10

Deer, turkeys, small game, foxes, bobcats, raccoons and opossums are hunted at Big Lazer Creek. A quota is established each year for deer, except for archery hunters, special parent/child dates and dates for holders of honorary hunting licenses. You must apply in advance for a turkey-hunting permit for this area.

The public fishing area offers largemouth bass, bluegill, redear sunfish and channel catfish. It is open sunrise to sunset daily. Primitive camping is allowed at Big Lazer Creek.

FACILITIES

A concrete boat ramp, picnic tables, a handicapped-accessible fishing pier and restrooms are among the area's facilities.

DIRECTIONS

From Talbotton, take U.S. 80 east for 4 miles

to the junction with Po Biddy Road. Turn left and go 6.4 miles to Bunkham Road. Turn left again and drive into the area. It is 1.2 miles to the check station.

BLANTON CREEK WILDLIFE MANAGEMENT AREA
HARRIS COUNTY   **4,500 ACRES**

11

Deer, turkeys, small game, foxes, bobcats, raccoons, opossums and doves are hunted at Blanton Creek. A quota is established each year for hunting deer with firearms, but there are no quotas for archery season and parent/child hunting days. Waterfowl hunting is not allowed on marsh ponds.

DIRECTIONS

From West Point, go south on GA 103 for approximately 10 miles. Make a right-hand turn into the WMA to get to the check station.

BLUE RIDGE WILDLIFE MANAGEMENT AREA
CHATTAHOOCHEE NATIONAL FOREST
38,900 ACRES

12

Deer, bear, turkeys, small game, foxes, bobcats, raccoons, opossums and doves are all hunted in this area of Chattahoochee National Forest. No hunting is allowed at the managed waterfowl impoundment.

FISHING

Jones and Noontootla Creeks have special trout-fishing rules to maintain the high quality of fish in these streams. Artificial lures are the only lures permitted on the two creeks. Trout under 16 inches in length must be released immediately on Noontootla Creek.

DIRECTIONS

To get to the Rock Creek check station from Dahlonega, take U.S. 19 north 9.3 miles to Stone Pile Gap. Go left at the gap on GA 60. After 18.7 miles, you will reach the junction with F.R. 69. Turn left on the forest-service road and go 2.8 miles to the check station.

To get to the Jones Creek check station from Dahlonega, go 9 miles west on GA 52 to Grizzle's Store. Turn right and go 2.4 miles. Turn right on the dirt road. You will reach the check station after another 2.4 miles.

BROAD RIVER WILDLIFE MANAGEMENT AREA
ELBERT COUNTY   **1,500 ACRES**

13

Deer, turkeys, small game, foxes, bobcats, raccoons, opossums and doves are hunted at this area, where no check-in is required.

From Elberton, go east on GA 72 for 11 miles to the junction with GA 79. It is 8 miles on GA 79 to the Broad River. The area can be reached from Lincolnton by going north on GA 79 for 20 miles to the Broad River. The WMA is on both sides of the Broad River west of GA 79, as posted.

BULLARD CREEK WILDLIFE MANAGEMENT AREA
JEFF DAVIS COUNTY   12,966 ACRES

14

Deer, turkeys, small game, foxes, bobcats, raccoons, opossums and feral hogs are the game hunted at this area. Special dates are set aside for deer hunting with primitive weapons and for parent/child deer hunting.

DIRECTIONS

Go north from Hazelhurst on U.S. 221 for 6.5 miles. Turn right at the entrance sign and drive to Philadelphia Church. Turn left at the church onto the dirt road and go a mile to the check station.

CEDAR CREEK WILDLIFE MANAGEMENT AREA
OCONEE NATIONAL FOREST
29,000 ACRES

15

Deer, turkeys, foxes, bobcats, small game, raccoons and opossums are hunted in this area of Oconee National Forest. Parent/child deer-hunting dates are set aside each year.

DIRECTIONS

From Monticello, take GA 16 east for 0.7 mile and go right at the fork on GA 212. It is 12 miles down GA 212 to the sign for the check station. The station is 0.5 mile off the main road.

CHATTAHOOCHEE WILDLIFE MANAGEMENT AREA
CHATTAHOOCHEE NATIONAL FOREST
24,000 ACRES

16

Deer, bear, turkeys, small game, foxes, bobcats, raccoons, opossums and feral hogs are hunted in this section of Chattahoochee National Forest.

DIRECTIONS

From Cleveland, take GA 75 north to Robertstown. Turn left on U.S. 75 Alternate, then turn right at the first road. It is 2.8 miles down that road to the check station.

CHESTATEE WILDLIFE MANAGEMENT AREA
CHATTAHOOCHEE NATIONAL FOREST
25,000 ACRES
17

Deer, bear, turkeys, small game, foxes, bobcats, raccoons, opossums and feral hogs are hunted in this section of the national forest.

FISHING

Waters Creek Trophy Trout Stream is located in this WMA. Size limits are 18 inches for brook trout and 22 inches for brown and rainbow trout. All anglers must check in and out. A valid WMA stamp is required for anglers over 16 years of age, except for holders of honorary licenses. Special regulations are posted at the creek.

In keeping with trout-stream management, there are no developed amenities at Waters Creek. The Georgia Department of Natural Resources strives to maintain a high density of trout in a 2.5-mile section of the stream, but this effort didn't prove productive in 1994 and 1995, with blame pointed at poachers and otters. Hopefully, this fine stream will rebound.

DIRECTIONS

From Cleveland, go north on U.S. 129 for 10.5 miles to Turners Corner. Turn left at the junction with U.S. 19 and go 0.5 mile to the first right. The check station is across from the campground.

CHICKASAWHATCHEE WILDLIFE MANAGEMENT AREA
BAKER COUNTY   21,767 ACRES
18

Deer, quail and doves are hunted at this WMA. Quality-buck regulations are in effect, and there is a quota for hunters using firearms. No pre-hunt scouting or camping is allowed. Feral hogs may not be hunted at this area.

DIRECTIONS

Go south from Albany on GA 91 for 4 miles. Turn right on GA 62 and go 8.2 miles to the check station.

CLARKS HILL WILDLIFE MANAGEMENT AREA
MCDUFFIE COUNTY   12,703 ACRES
19

Deer, turkeys, small game, foxes, bobcats, raccoons, opossums and doves can be hunted at this area on Clarks Hill Lake. Special deer-hunting dates are set aside for archers, hunters using primitive weapons and honorary-license holders.

From Thomson, go north on U.S. 78 for 10 miles. Turn right on the dirt road at the WMA sign and go 2.5 miles to the check station.

CLYBEL WILDLIFE MANAGEMENT AREA

JASPER COUNTY   6,000 ACRES

20

Deer, turkeys, small game, foxes, bobcats, raccoons, opossums and doves are hunted at this area. Parent/child dates are set aside for both deer and turkey hunts. A deer hunt for honorary-license holders is also reserved. Other than these special hunts, there is a deer quota. Turkey quotas are in effect for all hunts, and a special permit is required.

DIRECTIONS

From Mansfield, go south on GA 11 for 2.7 miles. Turn left at the WMA sign and follow the signs for 2 miles to the check station.

COHUTTA WILDLIFE MANAGEMENT AREA

CHATTAHOOCHEE NATIONAL FOREST
95,265 ACRES

21

Deer, bear, turkeys, small game, foxes, bob-

cats, raccoons, opossums and feral hogs are hunted in this section of the national forest. Primitive-weapon dates are set aside. For those hunts, all deer harvested must be checked out at the Holly Creek check station.

DIRECTIONS

From Ellijay, go west on GA 52 for 9.2 miles and turn right on F.R. 18 at the sign for Conasauga Lake. Go 3.5 miles to F.R. 68 and turn right. It is 2 miles down F.R. 68 to the Holly Creek check station.

From Chatsworth, go north on U.S. 411 to Eton. Turn right at the traffic light onto Holly Creek Road and go 11.6 miles to the check station.

From Cisco, follow GA 2 for 3 miles to the junction with West Cowpen Road. The check station is at the junction.

COLEMAN RIVER WILDLIFE MANAGEMENT AREA

CHATTAHOOCHEE NATIONAL FOREST
11,000 ACRES

22

Deer, bear, turkeys, small game, foxes, bobcats, raccoons, opossums and feral hogs are hunted at this area within the national forest.

DIRECTIONS

Take U.S. 76 west from Clayton for 8 miles. Turn right on Persimmon Road and go 4.5 miles to Coleman River Road, a gravel road. Turn left and go 1.2 miles to the check station.

COOPER CREEK WILDLIFE MANAGEMENT AREA
CHATTAHOOCHEE NATIONAL FOREST
30,000 ACRES
23

Deer, bear, turkeys, small game, foxes, bobcats, raccoons, opossums and feral hogs are hunted at this WMA.

DIRECTIONS

From Dahlonega, go north on U.S. 19 for 9.3 miles to Stone Pile Gap. Drive north on GA 60 for 17 miles. Turn right on F.R. 236 and go 0.5 mile. Turn left and drive 4 miles to F.R. 4. Turn right. You will reach the check station in another 0.5 mile.

COOSAWATTEE WILDLIFE MANAGEMENT AREA
MURRAY COUNTY   6,060 ACRES
24

Deer, bear, turkeys, small game, foxes, bobcats, raccoons, opossums and waterfowl are hunted at this area. A quota is set each year for deer hunts with firearms. The area offers a handicapped hunt for wheelchair hunters; apply for a handicapped hunting permit by letter to the United States Army Corps of Engineers, Carters Lake, P.O. Box 96, Oakman, GA 30732.

DIRECTIONS

From the traffic light at the courthouse in Chatsworth, go south on Old U.S. 411. Turn left at the Carters Lake Powerhouse sign and go 1 mile to the check station.

From Ellijay, go west on GA 282 to Old U.S. 411. Go south 3.8 miles to the powerhouse sign and drive 1 mile to the check station.

CROCKFORD-PIGEON MOUNTAIN WILDLIFE MANAGEMENT AREA
WALKER COUNTY   15,824 ACRES
25

Deer, turkeys, small game, foxes, bobcats, raccoons, opossums and doves are hunted at this area. Quality-buck regulations are in effect, and there is a quota for firearms and primitive-weapons dates.

DIRECTIONS

From LaFayette, go west on GA 193 for 2.5 miles to Chamberlain Road. Turn left and go 3 miles to Rocky Lane Road. Turn right and drive 0.5 mile to the check station.

DAWSON FOREST WILDLIFE MANAGEMENT AREA
DAWSON COUNTY · 17,600 ACRES

26

Deer, bear, turkeys, small game, raccoons, opossums and doves are hunted at this area. Quality-buck regulations are in effect. Primitive-weapon hunt dates are set aside, in addition to the archery season. Squirrels may not be hunted on the Amicalola and Wildcat tracts, and hunting foxes and bobcats is prohibited on all tracts. No waterfowl hunting is allowed at the managed waterfowl impoundment.

DIRECTIONS

Go west on GA 53 from Dawsonville for approximately 6 miles. Turn right onto the check-station access road just before crossing the Amicalola River.

DI-LANE WILDLIFE MANAGEMENT AREA
BURKE COUNTY · 8,100 ACRES

27

Deer, turkeys, quail, small game, foxes, bobcats, raccoons, opossums and doves are hunted at this WMA. Quality-buck regulations are in effect, and there is a quota on hunting deer with firearms. Quotas are in effect for quail hunting as well; a special permit is required.

Hunters interested in bird-dog field trials need to apply by letter to the Georgia Field Trial Association, P.O. Box 87, Cedartown, GA 30125.

DIRECTIONS

From Waynesboro, take Herndon Road south for 6 miles and follow the signs to the check station.

DIXON MEMORIAL FOREST WILDLIFE MANAGEMENT AREA
WARE COUNTY · 38,464 ACRES

28

Deer, small game, raccoons, opossums and doves are hunted in this forest just north of the Okefenokee Swamp. Primitive-weapon dates are set aside for deer hunting.

DIRECTIONS

Go south from Waycross on U.S. 1 for approximately 6 miles to GA 177. Turn left and follow the signs to the check station.

DODGE COUNTY PUBLIC FISHING AREA
DODGE COUNTY · 104-ACRE LAKE

29

Largemouth bass, bluegill, redear sunfish and channel catfish are among the species in this public fishing area. There is a nature trail along the lake. Dodge County Public Fishing Area is open sunrise to sunset daily.

FACILITIES

All of the facilities here are handicapped-accessible. They include a concrete boat ramp, a fishing pier, restrooms and picnic tables.

DIRECTIONS

From Eastman, it is 3 miles on U.S. 23/U.S. 341 to County Road 49. Turn left. You will reach the lake after 0.6 mile.

DYAL PASTURE WILDLIFE MANAGEMENT AREA
APPLING COUNTY   9,625 ACRES

30

Deer, turkeys, small game, raccoons and opossums are hunted in this WMA. Hunting foxes and bobcats is prohibited.

DIRECTIONS

From Baxley, go east on U.S. 341 for approximately 9 miles. The WMA is on the north side of the highway behind Union Camp Headquarters.

ELBERT COUNTY WILDLIFE MANAGEMENT AREA
ELBERT COUNTY   1,722 ACRES

31

Deer, turkeys, small game, raccoons and opossums may be hunted at this area, located on Corps of Engineers land along Lake Richard B. Russell. No camping is allowed on any of the four tracts that make up this WMA.

DIRECTIONS

To get to the Beverly Tract, go east from Elberton on GA 72 for 5 miles and turn north on Pearl Mill Road. It is 1.5 miles to the area.

To get to the Elbert Tract, follow GA 72 east from Elberton for 10 miles to Bobby Brown State Park Road. Turn south; the area is on the east side of the road.

To get to the Heardmont Tract, follow GA 72 east from Elberton for 5 miles. Turn north on Pearl Mill Road, then bear to the right on Heardmont Road. The area is on the right at the junction.

To get to the Pickens Tract, go north from Elberton on GA 77 to GA 368. Go north for 15 miles, then turn south on Gregg Shoals Road. Follow the dirt road to the area.

EVANS COUNTY PUBLIC FISHING AREA
EVANS COUNTY
EIGHT-ACRE, 30-ACRE AND 84-ACRE PONDS

32

These ponds offer largemouth bass, bluegill, redear sunfish, channel catfish, crappie and brown bullhead. The area is open from sunrise to sunset daily from March 1 to October 31.

FACILITIES

Concrete boat ramps, fishing piers, restrooms and picnic tables are available.

DIRECTIONS

From Claxton, it is 8.5 miles east on U.S. 280 to a junction with Old Reidsville–Savannah Road. Turn right and go 1 mile to Old Sunbury Road. Turn left on this dirt road. You will reach the area after 0.3 mile.

FISHING CREEK WILDLIFE MANAGEMENT AREA
WILKES COUNTY   2,903 ACRES

33

Deer, turkeys, small game, foxes, bobcats, raccoons, opossums, doves and waterfowl are hunted at Fishing Creek. No check-in is required

for any species. Within the safety zone, only waterfowl hunting is allowed. Waterfowl hunting is not permitted on the Morris Creek marsh impoundment.

DIRECTIONS

Take GA 44 east from Washington. Go through Danburg and take the first road to the right to Jones Chapel. Turn left to enter the area.

To get to the waterfowl area, take GA 79 from Lincolnton and go 8 miles to Midway Church. Turn left onto the dirt road and drive 1.5 miles to the sign.

FLINT RIVER WILDLIFE MANAGEMENT AREA
DOOLY COUNTY   2,500 ACRES

34

Deer, turkeys and small game are hunted at this area. Quality-buck regulations are in effect, and a special permit is required for turkey hunting.

DIRECTIONS

Take GA 27 west from Vienna for 10 miles. Turn right on GA 230 and go 1 mile. Veer left on River Road and drive 6 miles to Pleasant Hill Church. The WMA is on the left.

GERMANY CREEK WILDLIFE MANAGEMENT AREA

MCDUFFIE COUNTY	1,200 ACRES

35

Deer, turkeys, small game, foxes, bobcats, raccoons and opossums are hunted at Germany Creek. No check-in is required at this area, which is accessible by boat only.

DIRECTIONS

The nearest boat ramp is at Raysville Bridge, 12 miles north of Thomson on GA 43. The area is east of the bridge.

GRAND BAY WILDLIFE MANAGEMENT AREA

LOWNDES COUNTY	9,416 ACRES

36

Deer, small game, raccoons, opossums, doves and waterfowl may be hunted at Grand Bay. Fox squirrels may not be hunted. Outboard motors are limited to 10 horsepower or less in the waterfowl impoundments. Within the dove-field safety zone, only doves may be hunted with firearms.

DIRECTIONS

From Valdosta, go north on U.S. 221 for 10 miles to the entrance sign. Turn left through the gate to get to the check station.

HANNAHATCHEE CREEK WILDLIFE MANAGEMENT AREA

STEWART COUNTY	5,640 ACRES

37

Deer, turkeys, small game, foxes, bobcats, raccoons, opossums and doves are hunted at this area. Check-in is required for deer hunting but not for other game.

DIRECTIONS

From Richland, take GA 27 west toward Lumpkin. Go 4 miles and turn at the first paved road on the right. Drive 3 miles and turn left. After another mile, turn right on the first dirt road and proceed to the check station.

HART COUNTY WILDLIFE MANAGEMENT AREA

HART COUNTY	1,000 ACRES

38

Deer, turkeys, small game, foxes, bobcats, raccoons, opossums and doves are hunted at this WMA, where no check-in is required.

DIRECTIONS

Go south from Hartwell on GA 77 for approximately 1.5 miles. Turn left onto Liberty Hill Road and go about 4 miles until the pavement runs out. The area lies south of the road.

HORSE CREEK WILDLIFE MANAGEMENT AREA

TELFAIR COUNTY   21,000 ACRES

39

Deer, turkeys, small game, raccoons, opossums and feral hogs are hunted at Horse Creek. Quality-buck regulations are in effect. There are special primitive-weapon deer-hunting dates, in addition to the archery season. You can check in at Longhorn Country Store or the WMA check station.

DIRECTIONS

From Jacksonville, go east on GA 117 about 5 miles and turn right at the sign for the check station. Longhorn Country Store is 5 miles farther on GA 117.

JOHNS MOUNTAIN WILDLIFE MANAGEMENT AREA

CHATTAHOOCHEE NATIONAL FOREST
27,989 ACRES

40

Deer, turkeys, small game, foxes, bobcats, raccoons and opossums are hunted in this section of the national forest. The check station is at The Pocket, which is listed in the National Forests section of this book.

DIRECTIONS

Take GA 136C north from Calhoun for 6 miles to Sugar Valley. Turn left and go 6 miles to Lake Marvin and the WMA.

KEG CREEK WILDLIFE MANAGEMENT AREA

COLUMBIA COUNTY   800 ACRES

41

Deer, turkeys, small game, foxes, bobcats, raccoons and opossums are hunted at this small WMA.

DIRECTIONS

From I-20 near Augusta, take GA 104 north for approximately 16 miles. The WMA is west of the road on both sides of Keg Creek.

KING TRACT WILDLIFE MANAGEMENT AREA

BACON COUNTY   9,671 ACRES

42

Deer, turkeys, small game, raccoons and opossums are hunted on the King Tract. Primitive-weapon dates are set aside, in addition to archery season.

DIRECTIONS

From Waycross, go north on U.S. 1 for 10.7 miles and turn west on Bickley Highway. Go 2.4 miles to the Old Dixie Union School. The area is on both sides of the road.

LAKE BURTON WILDLIFE MANAGEMENT AREA
CHATTAHOOCHEE NATIONAL FOREST
12,600 ACRES
43

Deer, bear, turkeys, small game, foxes, bobcats, raccoons, opossums and feral hogs are hunted in this section of the national forest along Lake Burton.

DIRECTIONS

From Clarkesville, go north on GA 197 for 21 miles to the Lake Burton Fish Hatchery on Moccasin Creek Road. Turn left across from the hatchery and go 0.3 mile to the check station.

LAKE RICHARD B. RUSSELL WILDLIFE MANAGEMENT AREA
CHATTAHOOCHEE NATIONAL FOREST
17,300 ACRES
44

Deer, turkeys, small game, foxes, bobcats, raccoons, opossums and doves are hunted at this

area on Lake Richard B. Russell. Dates are set aside for ladies-only and parent/child deer hunting. There is a quota for deer without antlers.

DIRECTIONS

Go north from Gainesville on GA 365. Take the Toccoa/Lavonia exit and stay on GA 365. Drive 1.8 miles and turn right on Rock Road. Go 0.7 mile and turn left on Old U.S. 123, then drive 2.4 miles and turn right on Ayersville Road by the Milliken Plant. Go 0.9 mile and turn left onto Check Station Road. It is 0.5 mile to the check station.

LAKE SEMINOLE WILDLIFE MANAGEMENT AREA
SEMINOLE COUNTY   16,895 ACRES
45

Deer, turkeys, small game, foxes, bobcats, raccoons and opossums are the game hunted at this WMA, where no check-in is required. Small game can be hunted with shotguns only.

DIRECTIONS

For directions to the tracts in this WMA, contact the Albany game office at 912-430-4254.

LAKE WALTER F. GEORGE WILDLIFE MANAGEMENT AREA
CLAY COUNTY   1,000 ACRES

46

Deer, turkeys, small game, foxes, bobcats, raccoons and opossums are hunted at this area near the town of Fort Gaines. No check-in is required. Deer hunting is for bowhunters only.

DIRECTIONS

Drive north on GA 39 from Fort Gaines to find the three compartments of this WMA. Compartment #1 is near Sandy Creek, Compartment #2 is at Pataula Creek and Compartment #3 is at Georgetown.

LITTLE SATILLA WILDLIFE MANAGEMENT AREA
WAYNE COUNTY   16,934 ACRES

47

Deer, turkeys, raccoons and opossums are hunted at Little Satilla. Special dates are reserved for deer hunting with primitive weapons and with bow and arrow.

DIRECTIONS

The area is 8 miles east of Patterson on U.S. 32. Turn left from the main road into the area at the entrance sign.

MARBEN PUBLIC FISHING AREA
JASPER AND NEWTON COUNTIES
295 ACRES/21 PONDS RANGING
FROM ONE TO 95 ACRES IN SIZE

48

Largemouth bass, bluegill, channel catfish, crappie and redear sunfish are among the species found in this fishing area. There is a minimum size of 14 inches on largemouth bass.

Marben is open daily from sunrise to sunset year-round. Some of the ponds may be closed when you visit; check the information board for a list of the lakes that are open.

FACILITIES

There are four concrete boat ramps at the four lower lakes. Primitive camping is allowed.

DIRECTIONS

Take GA 11 south from Mansfield. After 2.7 miles, turn left onto County Road 229. Follow the signs to the fishing area.

MAYHAW WILDLIFE MANAGEMENT AREA
MILLER COUNTY   4,681 ACRES

49

Deer, turkeys, small game, foxes, bobcats, raccoons, opossums and doves are hunted at this

WMA. Check-in is required for deer and turkeys but not for other game.

DIRECTIONS

The Firetower Tract is 1 mile west of Colquitt on GA 91.

The Willoughby and Oldhouse Tracts are 2 miles northwest of Colquitt. Take U.S. 27 north from Colquitt and turn left at the first paved road. The Willoughby Tract is a mile down this road and the Oldhouse Tract a mile farther.

MCDUFFIE PUBLIC FISHING AREA
MCDUFFIE COUNTY
12 PONDS RANGING FROM ONE TO 30 ACRES IN SIZE

50

Largemouth bass, channel catfish and redear sunfish are among the species found in these lakes. The fishing area is open daily from sunrise to sunset year-round. There is a 14-inch minimum-size requirement for largemouth bass.

FACILITIES

There are concrete boat ramps, restrooms and picnic tables in this fishing area. A small fee is charged for tent and RV camping in designated areas. Call 706-595-1684 for more information.

DIRECTIONS

From Thomson, take GA 17 south to U.S.

278. Turn left on U.S. 278 and go 5.6 miles to Ellington Airline Road. Turn right and drive 2.8 miles to Fish Hatchery Road. It is 0.8 mile down that road to the fishing area.

OAKY WOODS WILDLIFE MANAGEMENT AREA
HOUSTON COUNTY   17,805 ACRES

51

Deer, turkeys, small game, foxes, bobcats, raccoons, opossums, feral hogs and doves are hunted at Oaky Woods. Parent/child deer dates are set aside each year at this area.

DIRECTIONS

From Perry, go east on GA 127 to Kathleen. Turn right. You will reach the Oaky Woods sign after 1 mile. Turn left on the dirt road and go 5 miles to the check station.

OCMULGEE WILDLIFE MANAGEMENT AREA
TWIGGS AND BLECKLEY COUNTIES
31,944 ACRES

52

Deer, bear, turkeys, small game, foxes, bobcats, raccoons, opossums, feral hogs and doves are hunted at most of this WMA. However, the Gun Swamp Creek Tract is reserved for archery deer hunts and the hunting of small game and doves.

DIRECTIONS

To get to the main area, take U.S. 23 south from Macon. One mile after passing the junction with GA 96, turn right at the first paved road and follow the signs to the check station.

To get to the Gun Swamp Creek Tract, take GA 26 east from Cochran to GA 126. Follow GA 126 for 3 miles to Byran Sheffield Road. Turn left. The check station is 0.5 mile down this road.

OCONEE WILDLIFE MANAGEMENT AREA
GREENE COUNTY   4,122 ACRES

53

Deer, doves, turkeys, small game, foxes, bobcats, raccoons, opossums and waterfowl are hunted at the Oconee Wildlife Management Area. Special permits are required for duck and turkey hunts. Parent/child dates are reserved for waterfowl hunting. There are also ladies-only and primitive-weapon deer hunts. No small-game hunting (other than for ducks) is allowed at the waterfowl impoundments, and no hunting at all is permitted on Herndon Pond.

DIRECTIONS

From the caution light in Greensboro, go south on Veazy Road for 7.1 miles. Turn right on Liberty Church Road and go 7.5 miles to the check station.

OGEECHEE WILDLIFE MANAGEMENT AREA
WARREN COUNTY   22,475 ACRES

54

Deer, turkeys, small game, foxes, bobcats, raccoons, opossums and doves are hunted at this area. Primitive-weapon deer-hunting dates and archery hunts are set aside.

DIRECTIONS

This area is southwest of Warrenton in the Jewell community on GA 16 at the Ogeechee River.

OSSABAW ISLAND WILDLIFE MANAGEMENT AREA
CHATHAM COUNTY   8,996 ACRES

55

Deer, turkeys, small game and feral hogs can all be hunted on this barrier island, accessible by boat only. Quotas are set for deer and turkeys, and a limit is set for feral hogs. There are muzzleloader hunts for deer and parent/child hunts for both turkeys and deer. A special permit is required to hunt on the island. Hunters may arrive on the island as early as 9 A.M. the day before the hunt and must leave by noon the day after the hunt. No motorized vehicles or hunting dogs are allowed.

FACILITIES

Limited boat-docking facilities are provided; some boats must stream anchor at Newell Creek on the south end of the island. Hunters must supply their own boat transportation. There is walk-in cooler space for storage of deer only.

DIRECTIONS

The nearest boat ramp is just outside the entrance to Fort McAllister State Historic Park. The park is 9 miles east of Richmond Hill.

PARADISE PUBLIC FISHING AREA
BERRIEN COUNTY
75 LAKES TOTALING 525 ACRES
56

Among the species of fish found in these lakes are largemouth bass, bluegill, brown bullhead, channel catfish, crappie and redear sunfish. There is a minimum-size restriction of 14 inches on largemouth bass.

The fishing area is open daily from sunrise to sunset year-round. The lakes are occasionally drained to be improved or restocked and may not be open at the time of your visit.

FACILITIES

This public fishing area has several handicapped-accessible facilities, including a fishing pier, a boat dock and restrooms. In addition, there are concrete boat ramps and a picnic area. Primitive camping is permitted.

DIRECTIONS

From Tifton, take U.S. 82 east for 8 miles to Brookfield-Nashville Road and follow the signs to the fishing area.

PAULDING FOREST WILDLIFE MANAGEMENT AREA
PAULDING COUNTY   30,000 ACRES
57

Deer, turkeys, small game, foxes, bobcats, raccoons and opossums may be hunted at Paulding Forest. Primitive-weapon days are set aside for deer hunters. Three- and four-wheel ATVs are not allowed in this area at any time.

DIRECTIONS

The check station is on GA 278 some 7 miles west of its junction with U.S. 61 in Dallas.

PAULKS PASTURE WILDLIFE MANAGEMENT AREA
GLYNN COUNTY   17,000 ACRES
58

Deer, turkeys, small game, raccoons, opossums and doves are hunted at this WMA. Dates are set aside for deer hunting with primitive weapons and bow and arrow.

The check station is about 8 miles north of Brunswick on U.S. 341.

PINE LOG WILDLIFE MANAGEMENT AREA

BARTOW COUNTY   **14,913 ACRES**

59

Deer, turkeys, small game, foxes, bobcats, raccoons, opossums and doves may be hunted in this area. Parent/child deer-hunting dates are set aside each year. There is a quota on deer hunts with firearms.

DIRECTIONS

From U.S. 411 in White (located north of Cartersville), turn right on Stamp Creek Road and go 3.5 miles to the check station, on the left.

RAYONIER WILDLIFE MANAGEMENT AREA

WAYNE COUNTY   **20,847 ACRES**

60

Deer, turkeys, small game, raccoons, opossums and feral hogs are hunted at Rayonier. Dates are reserved for deer hunting with primitive weapons and for buck hunting with dogs. Feral hogs may not be hunted on dates set aside for deer hunting with dogs.

DIRECTIONS

From Jesup, go south on U.S. 301 for 19 miles to Hortense. Turn left on GA 32 and go 7 miles to the Satilla Forest Headquarters. Turn left on Fendig Road.

REDLANDS WILDLIFE MANAGEMENT AREA

OCONEE NATIONAL FOREST
31,000 ACRES

61

Deer, turkeys, small game, foxes, bobcats, raccoons, opossums, feral hogs, doves and waterfowl are hunted at this WMA. There is a limit of one raccoon per party. No hunting is allowed on the marsh pond.

DIRECTIONS

The check station is 4 miles north of Greensboro on GA 15.

RICH MOUNTAIN WILDLIFE MANAGEMENT AREA

CHATTAHOOCHEE NATIONAL FOREST
22,061 ACRES

62

Deer, bear, turkeys, small game, raccoons, opossums and feral hogs are hunted in this section of the national forest.

FISHING

Stanley Creek and its tributaries are fine trout streams; only artificial lures are allowed.

DIRECTIONS

Go north from Ellijay on GA 5. After 7 miles, you will reach Rock Creek Road. Turn right. Go 4 miles down Rock Creek Road to the Stanley Creek check station.

RICHMOND HILL WILDLIFE MANAGEMENT AREA
BRYAN COUNTY   3,720 ACRES

63

Deer, turkeys, small game, foxes, bobcats, raccoons, opossums and doves are hunted at Richmond Hill.

DIRECTIONS

From the town of Richmond Hill, go southeast on GA 144 to Oak Level Road and follow the signs to the check station.

RUM CREEK PUBLIC FISHING AREA AND WILDLIFE MANAGEMENT AREA
MONROE COUNTY
6,015 ACRES/3,600-ACRE LAKE

64

Deer, turkeys, small game, foxes, bobcats, rac-

coons, opossums, doves and waterfowl are hunted at this area on Lake Juliette. Special permits are required to hunt turkeys and geese.

Largemouth bass (minimum six inches), striped bass, hybrid bass, bluegill, redear sunfish and crappie are the species of game fish found in Lake Juliette. This area doesn't have many of the rules that apply at other public fishing areas. There is no limit on the number of poles or lines used by one person; commercial fish baskets may be used in the impounded portion of the area; and live bait may be used. In addition, swimming is permitted. Boat motors are limited to 20 horsepower (the restriction is 10 horsepower at other large lakes managed as public fishing areas). The fishing area is open daily year-round.

FACILITIES

Two Georgia Power–operated areas here have concrete boat ramps, restrooms and picnic areas.

DIRECTIONS

The area is 15 miles north of Macon on U.S. 23.

SANSAVILLA WILDLIFE MANAGEMENT AREA
GLYNN AND WAYNE COUNTIES
15,526 ACRES

65

Deer, turkeys, small game, raccoons and opossums are hunted at this WMA. Dates are reserved for deer hunting with primitive weapons and bow and arrow.

DIRECTIONS

From Brunswick, go north on U.S. 341 for 20 miles to Mount Pleasant. Turn right and cross the railroad tracks into the area.

SAPELO ISLAND WILDLIFE MANAGEMENT AREA
MCINTOSH COUNTY   8,990 ACRES

66

Deer, turkeys, small game, foxes, bobcats, raccoons, opossums and doves are hunted on this barrier island. Quotas are set for deer hunting with firearms. Primitive-weapon deer hunting and archery have special reserved dates. A special permit is required for deer hunting.

Hunters may check in after 9 A.M. the day before the hunt and leave by noon the day after the hunt. They are required to stay outside the safety zones, and no motorized vehicles are allowed.

DIRECTIONS

Hunters must access the island by boat through the Moses Hammock Dock at the head of the Duplin River. Limited transportation for deer, fox, bobcat, raccoon and opossum hunters is available on a state-operated boat. You can make transportation arrangements through the McIntosh County Chamber of Commerce by calling 912-437-6684. Hunters using their own boats may be required to stream anchor.

SHEFFIELD WILDLIFE MANAGEMENT AREA
PAULDING COUNTY   2,800 ACRES

67

Deer, turkeys, small game, foxes, bobcats, raccoons and opossums are hunted at this area. Deer hunting is limited to archery hunts.

DIRECTIONS

From Dallas, go north on GA 61 for 6.2 miles to Braswell Mountain Road. Turn left and go 2.4 miles to Lee Road. Turn right and continue 1.2 miles to the area.

SOAP CREEK WILDLIFE MANAGEMENT AREA
LINCOLN COUNTY   1,050 ACRES

68

Deer, turkeys, small game, foxes, bobcats, raccoons and opossums are hunted at Soap Creek.

DIRECTIONS

The area is 4 miles north of Lincolnton on GA 79.

SURVEYOR'S CREEK WILDLIFE MANAGEMENT AREA

CLINCH COUNTY   22,263 ACRES

69

Deer, bear, small game, raccoons and opossums are hunted at Surveyor's Creek. No dogs may be used to hunt bear.

DIRECTIONS

From Waycross, go west on U.S. 84 for 21 miles to Argyle. Turn left at the caution light onto a paved county road. The area is 12 miles ahead on the left.

SWALLOW CREEK WILDLIFE MANAGEMENT AREA

CHATTAHOOCHEE NATIONAL FOREST

19,000 ACRES

70

Deer, bear, turkeys, small game, foxes, bobcats, raccoons, opossums and feral hogs may be hunted in this section of the national forest.

DIRECTIONS

From Cleveland, go north on GA 75 to Robertstown and continue to the junction with GA 180. One mile past that junction is the sign for the WMA.

TREAT MOUNTAIN WILDLIFE MANAGEMENT AREA

POLK COUNTY   5,400 ACRES

71

Deer, turkeys, small game, foxes, bobcats, raccoons and opossums are hunted at Treat Mountain, where no check-in is required. No camping is allowed at this WMA.

DIRECTIONS

From Tallapoosa, go north on GA 100 for 11.2 miles to Treat Mountain Road. Turn left and go 0.25 mile to the area.

From Cedartown, take GA 27 south for 3.5 miles to GA 100. Drive south for 3.5 miles on GA 100 to Treat Mountain Road. The check station is 0.25 mile down that road.

TREUTLEN COUNTY PUBLIC FISHING AREA

TREUTLEN COUNTY   189-ACRE LAKE

72

Largemouth bass, bluegill, brown bullhead, crappie, flier, redear sunfish and warmouth are among the species found in this lake, which is open daily from sunrise to sunset year-round.

FACILITIES

There is a concrete boat ramp at this area.

From Soperton, go north on County Road 166 for 4.5 miles and turn right at the Wildlife Resources sign onto the dirt road for the public fishing area.

TUCKAHOE WILDLIFE MANAGEMENT AREA

SCREVEN COUNTY   **10,950 ACRES**

73

Deer, turkeys, small game, raccoons, opossums and feral hogs are hunted at this area. Parent/child and primitive-weapon hunts are offered at Tuckahoe.

DIRECTIONS

From Sylvania, take East Ogeechee Road for 2.2 miles to the junction of Buck Creek and Brannen's Bridge Roads. Take Brannen's Bridge Road. After 3.4 miles, you will cross GA 24. The check station is 5.2 miles beyond GA 24 on Brannen's Bridge Road.

To get to the Hiltonia Tract, take GA 24 west from Hiltonia for 2.4 miles to Hurst Church Road. Turn left and go 0.7 mile to Mount Pleasant Road. Follow Mount Pleasant Road for 1.2 miles to the junction with Sandy Ridge Road. Turn left, staying on Mount Pleasant Road, to enter the area.

WARWOMAN WILDLIFE MANAGEMENT AREA

CHATTAHOOCHEE NATIONAL FOREST

15,800 ACRES

74

Deer, bear, turkeys, small game, foxes, bobcats, raccoons, opossums and feral hogs are hunted in this section of the forest.

FISHING

Trout fishing on Hoods Creek, Walnut Creek and their tributaries is limited to artificial lures only.

DIRECTIONS

From U.S. 441 in Clayton, turn right at the Heart of Rabun Motel onto Warwoman Road. Go 3.5 miles and turn left on Finney Creek Road. The check station is 0.25 mile down this road.

WEST POINT WILDLIFE MANAGEMENT AREA

HEARD COUNTY   **9,999 ACRES**

75

Deer, turkeys, small game, foxes, bobcats, raccoons, opossums, doves and waterfowl are hunted at this area. Quality-buck regulations are in effect. Special hunt dates are reserved for honorary-license holders, hunters using primitive weapons and bowhunters. A special permit is required for the quota firearms deer hunt; no other hunting is allowed during this hunt. No gasoline outboard motors are allowed on the waterfowl ponds.

DIRECTIONS

Go north from LaGrange on GA 219. The check station is 2 miles north of the Chattahoochee River.

WILSON SHOALS WILDLIFE MANAGEMENT AREA
BANKS COUNTY   2,800 ACRES

76

Deer, turkeys, small game, foxes, bobcats, raccoons and opossums are hunted at Wilson Shoals. No check-in is required.

DIRECTIONS

From Gainesville, go north on U.S. 365 past Exit 7. After 11 miles, turn right on Mud Creek Road. Drive 1 mile to Old Cornelia Highway. Go 0.1 mile on Old Cornelia Highway, then turn right on Yonah Road. It is 2.1 miles down Yonah Road to the entrance to the area, on the left.

YUCHI WILDLIFE MANAGEMENT AREA
BURKE COUNTY   7,800 ACRES

77

Deer, turkeys, small game, foxes, bobcats, raccoons, opossums and feral hogs are hunted at this area. You must sign in for deer and turkey hunting. The sign-in boards are located on Ebenezer Church Road, on River Road a mile south of the Georgia Power boat ramp and at the junction of River Road and Brigham Landing Road.

DIRECTIONS

From Waynesville, go east on GA 80 for 8 miles to the Shell Bluff community. Turn right onto GA 23 and drive 7 miles to the WMA, on the left.

SEMIPUBLIC LANDS

The clubhouse at Jekyll Island was once the center of activity for the world's most exclusive club.

Jekyll Island, Stone Mountain and Lake Lanier Islands are state-owned, independently managed attractions. Callaway Gardens is a privately owned , nonprofit attraction similar in character and amenities to these three state-owned lands.

These four resort areas are more fully developed than Georgia's state parks. Though much of their scenic beauty is still intact, visitors are equally attracted to their hotels, restaurants and shops. Because none of these areas receives public support through federal, state or local taxes, ParkPasses and historic-site passes are not accepted.

CALLAWAY GARDENS
PINE MOUNTAIN

Threadbare cotton fields and a coral-red flower led to the birth of the 14,000-acre Callaway Gardens. While on a family outing in July 1930, Cason J. Callaway set out for a walk

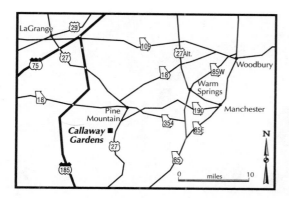

in the woods. His path led him over Pine Mountain Ridge and to the valley and its depleted cotton fields below.

Surely, Callaway thought, this must have once been a lovely and fertile valley. Could it be brought back to its original condition? As he hurried back to his family, the idea germinated. Perhaps he could purchase the land and return it to its natural state—a home for native trees, plants and wildlife. Suddenly, amidst the green of the summer growth, he spotted a shrub with bright, coral-red flowers. The long-stamened blossoms were growing wild in the woods, yet he couldn't identify them. Neither could his wife, Virginia, who was an amateur wildflower buff.

They soon discovered that the blossom was the rare prunifolia azalea. Native only to the area around Pine Mountain, it was then nearly extinct. At that point, they decided they must buy the land around Pine Mountain, propagate the rare azalea and other native flora and build a garden.

For many years, the Callaways worked to restore the land and improve it. They created 13

The Sibley Horticultural Center at Callaway Gardens features seasonal displays of live plants and flowers.

The state butterfly of Georgia, a tiger swallowtail, in the Day Butterfly Center at Callaway Gardens

lakes, propagated plants by the thousands, and finally, in 1952, opened the Ida Cason Callaway Foundation. Over the past 40 years, the number of visitors to Callaway Gardens has grown to three-quarters of a million a year. From the John A. Sibley Horticultural Center to the Cecil B. Day Butterfly Center to Mr. Cason's Vegetable Garden, there is something at Callaway to delight everyone.

Among the gardens' highlights is the Cecil B. Day Butterfly Center, the largest glass-enclosed tropical conservatory for the display of living butterflies in North America

The John A. Sibley Horticultural Center is the most advanced garden greenhouse complex in the world. This five-acre garden features 18 major floral displays each year in its main conservatory.

Mr. Cason's Vegetable Garden is the setting for a PBS television show, *The Victory Garden*. This 7.5-acre garden produces more than 400 varieties of vegetables, fruits and herbs.

The Ida Cason Callaway Memorial Chapel is an English Gothic building designed by Cason J. Callaway in honor of his mother, Ida Cason Callaway. It is built of native materials and was completed and dedicated a year after Cason J. Callaway's death in 1962. A place for quiet meditation and worship, it hosts organ concerts throughout the year.

The Pioneer Log Cabin is an authentic 18th-century structure featuring demonstrations on the life of Georgia's pioneers.

The Discovery Bicycle Trail is a 7.5-mile trail weaving through the gardens' woodlands and interpretive areas, as well as all other major attractions.

The gardens also feature walking trails and roadways that showcase the world's largest display of hollies, more than 700 varieties of azaleas and many varieties of wildflowers. A per-vehicle entrance fee is charged, although resort guests and gardens members are admitted free. Callaway Gardens is open daily; hours vary by season.

ACCOMMODATIONS

There are three places to stay at Callaway itself. Callaway Gardens Inn has 350 rooms, including some with suites and parlors. Callaway Country Cottages feature 155 two-bedroom units available for sale or rent. Each unit has a full kitchen, a screened porch, a grill and a fireplace. Mountain Creek Villas feature 49 two-, three- and four-bedroom units available for sale or rent. The luxury villas have a full kitchen, laundry facilities, a deck and a fireplace.

RESTAURANTS

There are seven restaurants at Callaway, some of which operate seasonally: The Georgia Room, The Plantation Room, The Country Kitchen, The Gardens Restaurant, The Veranda, Champions and The Flower Mill. Their offerings range from burgers and pizza to five-star dining.

CONVENTION FACILITIES

Callaway Gardens has three separate meeting facilities: the Convention Center in Callaway Gardens Inn, the 36,000-square-foot Conference Center and the Cottage Meeting Center, which features 30 meeting rooms, the largest encompassing 10,000 square feet.

SHOPPING

There are 10 stores within the gardens. Food products, horticultural and decorative items, apparel, educational materials and more are available. Callaway Gardens also has a catalog, "Country Flavors," which features its famous muscadine products, speckled-heart grits and bacon and ham.

RECREATION

The gardens feature three 18-hole golf courses and one nine-hole executive course. The Mountain View course is home to the PGA Tour's Buick Classic.

There are 17 lighted tennis courts that feature both rubico and plexipave surfaces. There are also two racquetball courts.

Mountain Creek Lake offers sailboats, canoes and pedal boats for rent. Pedal boats are also available at Robin Lake Beach during the summer.

The 175-acre Mountain Creek Lake offers boats and fishing equipment for rent. The lake is home to bass, bream and other fish. A fly-fishing program is taught by Callaway's own professional fly-fisherman.

Callaway Gardens has a state-of-the-art fitness center with exercise equipment and a sauna. There is also a 20-station fitness trail around Robin Lake Beach.

Swimming is offered at Robin Lake Beach and at the pools at Callaway Gardens Inn, Callaway Country Cottages and Mountain Creek Villas. Robin Lake Beach features the largest man-made white-sand beach in the world. From June through August, shows by Florida State University's Flying High Circus are presented at the beach. On the lake, Callaway presents riverboat rides aboard the *Robert E. Lee* paddle-wheeler. Miniature golf, rides aboard the miniature trains and other entertainments are also available at Robin Lake Beach.

Playground equipment is available at Callaway Gardens Inn and near the Children's Activity Center at Robin Lake Beach.

The Summer Family Adventure Program consists of planned educational and recreational programs for families, sponsored by Callaway from June through August.

SPECIAL EVENTS

Throughout the year, Callaway sponsors a number of events for the public.

In the winter, its most popular event is Fantasy in Lights, during which visitors can take a trolley, sit back and enjoy a journey through a sparkling, light-filled world; visitors can also drive their own vehicle. Winter also sees the New Year's Eve Dinner and Dance, the Southern Gardening Symposium and the School of Needlearts.

In the spring, you can attend the Easter Sunrise Service at Robin Lake. The Spring Celebration Volunteer Plant Fair and Sale and Five Hats Weekend are other popular events.

Summer is the busiest season, with the Masters Water-Ski Tournament, the Summer Family Adventure Program, the Fourth of July Celebration, Florida State University's Flying High Circus and Discovery Programs.

Fall sees the return of the Autumn Adventure, the PGA Tour's Buick Classic, the Harvest Festival of Wine and Food, the Steeplechase at Callaway Gardens and the Chrysanthemum Display.

DIRECTIONS

Take U.S. 27 off I-85 or I-185. Callaway Gardens is 70 miles southwest of Atlanta and 30 miles north of Columbus.

FOR MORE INFORMATION

Callaway Gardens, P.O. Box 2000, Pine Mountain, GA 31822 (800-CALLAWAY)

JEKYLL ISLAND
GLYNN COUNTY

Located 6 miles off the coast of Georgia, Jekyll Island is a golfer's paradise on an island steeped in history. Jekyll was known as Ospo by the Guale Indians, who were living here when Spanish missionaries arrived in the late 16th century. The Spanish mission of Santiago de Ocone was built on the island, only to be abandoned with other missions on the Georgia coast after pressure from pirates, Indians and the English forced the missionaries out.

When General James Edward Oglethorpe named the island for his friend and benefactor Sir Joseph Jekyll, both the Guale Indians and the Spanish were a distant memory. One of Oglethorpe's officers, William Horton, built a plantation on the island. Though it was destroyed by the Spanish in their retreat after their 1742 loss at Bloody Marsh on nearby St. Simons Island, Horton stayed on and rebuilt. The ruins of Horton's second home can still be seen today.

The island changed hands several times and was still in use as a plantation until the Civil War. In 1858, the last large group of slaves transported to America was unloaded on this island.

From 1887 to 1942, Jekyll Island won fame as "the richest, the most exclusive, the most inaccessible club in the world," according to a 1904 edition of *Munsey's Magazine*. A group of some of the country's richest men, including William Rockefeller, J. P. Morgan, Joseph Pulitzer and William K. Vanderbilt, formed the Jekyll Island Club and built a large clubhouse and "cottages" for summertime use. During the Depression, the club floundered, as many members saw their wealth diminish. It closed during World War II and was never reopened.

In 1947, the state of Georgia purchased the island from the club and formed the Jekyll Island Authority to manage the property. In 1954, the causeway linking Brunswick with the island was completed, and the island was reborn as a public vacation spot. With its 63 golf holes, it is the largest public golf resort in the state. The nine hotels along the beach were built from the 1950s through the 1970s and complement the convention center on the island. The old clubhouse in the 240-acre historic district was reopened as a resort in 1986, and many other buildings in the district are being renovated now. The water park and the tennis center were added in 1988.

The island was mandated to be self-sufficient in 1978. It does not use any tax funds for its maintenance or operation. The parking fee the island charges is per car, not per person. ParkPasses are not accepted, as the island is not a part of the state parks system.

LODGINGS

A complete list of accommodations is available at the welcome center on the causeway. The center is open daily in the summer from 9 A.M. to 10 P.M. and in the winter from 9 A.M. to 5 P.M. Call the center for further information.

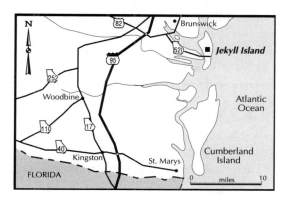

JEKYLL ISLAND NATIONAL HISTORIC LANDMARK

The 240-acre historic district was named a national historic landmark in 1978. Tours are given daily except for Christmas and New Year's; a fee is charged, but children under six are admitted free. The tour begins at the Museum Orientation Center on Stable Road. The center also offers a free photographic exhibit of images from Jekyll's historic past. Call 912-635-2762 for more information.

GOLF

The island's three 18-hole courses and one nine-hole course were designed to be dramatically different from each other. The historic Oceanside Nine was laid out in 1898 for the Jekyll Island Club. This authentic links course was built following the natural lay of the land. It was remodeled in the 1920s by well-known designer Walter J. Travis. The Oleander and Pine Lakes Courses were designed by Dick Wilson and the Indian Mound Course by Joe Lee. Each course has different characteristics to challenge golfers. Water comes into play on nearly half the holes on the Oleander and Indian Mound Courses.

A driving range, a pro shop and a clubhouse with a restaurant round out the island's amenities for golfers. Special winter packages are offered by island hotels and realty companies. Some of the island's hotels offer golf packages year-round. Call 912-635-2368 for more information.

BEACHES

Jekyll's 10-mile-long beach is popular for swimming, sunbathing and seashell collecting. Public bathhouses are located between the Comfort Inn and the Beach Deck at about the midpoint of the beach. At the south end of the island just north of the 4-H camp is a pristine section of beach used for the climactic finish of the movie *Glory!*

FISHING

Surf fishing is popular on the beach. The best fishing is at St. Andrew Picnic Area on St. Andrew Sound, at the south end of the island. Freshwater fishing is also permitted at the lake across from Villas by the Sea on North Beachview Drive and the lake beside the outdoor amphitheater in the historic district. All persons over age 16 must have a valid Georgia fishing license to fish in the freshwater lakes.

BOATING

Two marinas are located on the island. Jekyll Harbor Marina features short- and long-term rates for either wet slips or dry storage. For more information, call 912-635-3137. Jekyll Historic Marina is located on the club's wharf. Private and group charters are offered. You can also take a two-hour tour in a shrimp boat and split the catch with your fellow passengers. Jekyll Historic Marina also rents Jet-Skis. Call 912-635-2891 for information.

There is a public boat ramp next to Water-

Ski Park on Riverview Drive. The ramp offers access to the Intracoastal Waterway.

BICYCLING

A bike offers perhaps the best way to explore Jekyll Island, with its 20 miles of paved trails. Bring your own bike or rent one at any of the many rental outlets, which include the miniature golf course, the campground, Jekyll Harbor Marina and the hotels.

CAMPING

The 18-acre campground on the north end of the island has 200 sites, with a mix of tent sites, electric-only sites and pull-thru sites with full hookups, including sewer. Restrooms, showers and laundry facilities are all located in the campground. There is a camp store with food and other supplies; the store also rents bicycles. Monthly rates are available from November to February. During the remainder of the year, a 14-day maximum stay is in effect. Call 912-635-3021 for information or reservations.

PICNICKING

The island's picnic areas are Clam Creek, near the pier at the north end; St. Andrew Picnic Area, on St. Andrew Sound at the south end; and the Beach Deck, with handicapped access near the convention center. South Dunes Picnic Area has facilities for group gatherings. There are uncovered group areas, covered shelters and a screened-in serving shelter with elec-

tricity. These are available for rent. Call 912-635-3400 for information or reservations.

WATER PARK

Still looking for something to do? On South Riverview Drive, you'll find Water-Ski Park and Summer Waves Water Park. This 11-acre park offers several flumes, a wave pool and the Pee Wee Puddle, with slides and waterfalls. The water park is open daily from Memorial Day through Labor Day, but cable water-skiing is open year-round. In winter, there is a wet-suit season. For more information, call 912-635-2074.

TENNIS

The 13 clay courts at the Jekyll Island Tennis Center led to its selection as one of the "25 Best Municipal Tennis Facilities" by *Tennis Magazine*. There are seven courts lit for play at night. This full-service tennis center offers equipment rentals, lessons and clinics. Call 912-635-3154 for more information or to reserve a court.

OTHER FACILITIES

Two lighted 18-hole miniature golf courses are located on Shell Road near its intersection with South Beachview Drive.

The airport, located on Riverview Drive, can be used for private transportation to the island. Car and bike rentals are offered at the airport. Airplane tours for up to three people can also be arranged here. Call 912-635-2500 for more information.

NEARBY ATTRACTIONS

Cumberland Island National Seashore
Fort Frederica National Monument
Hofwyl-Broadfield Plantation State Historic
Site
Okefenokee National Wildlife Refuge

DIRECTIONS

The island is reached by way of the Jekyll Island Causeway, which branches off GA 17 at an intersection 2 miles south of Brunswick.

FOR MORE INFORMATION

Jekyll Island Welcome Center, P.O. Box 13186, Jekyll Island, GA 31527 (800-841-6586 or 912-635-3636)

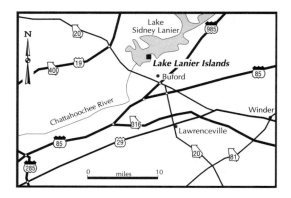

LAKE LANIER ISLANDS
BUFORD

Lake Sidney Lanier's "islands" were mountain peaks before the lake was impounded. Today, they are home to a state-owned resort offering championship golf and resort hotels on the 38,000-acre Lake Sidney Lanier. The lake, the hotels, the water park, the shops and the restaurants pack wallet-tempting fun into a beautiful package. Since this is a public-owned resort, there is no gaudy commercialism. The islands are a worthy attraction for the Corps of Engineers' most-visited lake.

There is an entrance fee/parking fee to enter the islands. You can purchase a day pass or an annual parking decal. Buses and church, government and school vans can park for free. As this resort is run without federal, state or local tax support, ParkPasses valid for Georgia's state parks are not honored here.

LODGINGS

Lake Lanier Islands offers a number of choices when it comes to overnight accommodations, among them the Lake Lanier Islands Hilton Resort. Open since 1989, the Hilton features 224 rooms with views of the lake or forest. It also has 11,000 square feet of meeting space, tennis courts, a health club, a sauna, a pool and a restaurant. For reservations, call 404-945-8787.

Renaissance PineIsle Resort offers 250 guest rooms, three restaurants, an indoor/outdoor pool, a hot tub, enclosed and outdoor tennis courts and a full activities program. For reservations, call 404-945-8921.

GOLF

Lake Lanier Islands Hilton Resort Golf Course is a par-72 championship golf course featuring 13 holes on the water, 75 bunkers and bent-grass greens. There are no parallel fairways at this course, designed by Joe Lee.

Renaissance PineIsle Resort Golf Course is another championship course. It features eight holes on the water and spectacular scenery. This course, designed by Gary Player and Ron Kirby & Associates, hosted the LPGA's Nestlé World Championship from 1985 to 1989.

CAMPGROUNDS

Lake Lanier Islands has more than 300 campsites located lakeside. Open year-round, the campgrounds feature a fishing pier, an outdoor pavilion, laundry facilities, a boat ramp and a dump station. All RV sites have water and electrical hookups. There is a store with food and supplies, and both Good Sam's and Golden Age discounts are available. For reservations or information, call 404-932-7270.

BOAT RENTALS

Lake Lanier Islands rents a number of styles of boats.

Houseboats sleep up to 10 people and are equipped with hot and cold water, a shower, a restroom, a generator, air conditioning, a covered front deck, an open rear deck and a rooftop sun deck. The galley includes a microwave, a refrigerator, a gas grill, sheets and life jackets.

Island Skimmer group boats accommodate up to 20 people; the larger group boats can accommodate as many as 45. The group boats have large interiors, as well as more than 1,000 square feet of exterior deck space. They come furnished with couches, deck chairs, tables, two restrooms, heating and air conditioning, an all-electric kitchen, a microwave, a gas grill, a wet bar with an ice bin, a radio/cassette deck, a ship-to-shore radio, life jackets and a large ice cooler.

Pontoon boats hold up to eight people and can be rented by the hour or day. They are equipped with swim ladders, life jackets and plush seating.

Sport boats seat up to four people and come with a 25-horsepower motor, an electric starter and life jackets.

Ski boats have 90-horsepower motors and seat up to five people. Skis may also be rented.

For more information on boat rentals, call 404-932-7255.

Lake Lanier Islands also offers a sailing academy, which offers sailing lessons, sailboat rentals and charters. Sunfish, day sailers and cruising yachts up to 36 feet in length are available. For more information, call 404-945-8810.

BEACH AND WATER PARK

The entrance fee for the water park covers everything except food, lockers, souvenirs and tube rentals. Among the amusements here are Wildwaves, Georgia's largest wave pool, with more than 850,000 gallons of water and nine different types of waves; Intimidator, a slide that plunges over 30 miles per hour; Triple Threat, a triple-drop slide; the first kiddie pool with waves in Georgia, featuring six- to 12-inch waves, two eight-foot slides and colorful fountains; Typhoon, a tunnel-like slide; Twister, a water slide with six 180-degree turns; Chattahoochee Rapids, an inner-tube ridge that takes you through 725 feet of rapids; Splash Down, a 430-foot twin-flume slide that features twisting turns; Racing Waters, a twin-flume slide that plunges 260 feet at speeds in excess of 25 miles per hour; and Blackout, a 160-foot slide which features complete darkness during the ride.

Pedal boats, canoes and sailboats are available free with paid admission to the park. The park features 1.5 miles of sandy beach with free lounge chairs. Lockers, inner tubes, life preservers and umbrellas are available for rent. The park also offers an 18-hole miniature golf course.

The park is open on weekends only from late April until Memorial Day; the hours are 10 A.M. to 7 P.M. It is open daily from Memorial Day through Labor Day; the hours are 10 A.M. to 6 P.M. on weekdays and 10 A.M. to 7 P.M. on weekends and holidays. The hours during the second weekend in September are 10 A.M. to 6 P.M.

SHOPS AND RESTAURANTS

In addition to the restaurants operating out of the hotels, Lake Lanier Islands offers The Beachside Cafe, with sandwiches and pizza; The Islands Grill, with barbecue, sandwiches, chicken dinners and more; and The Wildwaves Refresher, with snacks and drinks.

The Breakers Gift Shop offers souvenirs, swimwear and beach supplies.

OTHER FACILITIES

Lake Lanier Islands runs a stable that offers horseback riding along miles of scenic trails following the shores of Lake Lanier. Trail rides, pony rides and lessons are available.

There are more than 1,200 acres on the islands that can be explored by bike. Bring your own bike or rent one at Lake Lanier Islands.

Picnicking is available on the islands. Bring your own basket or let Lake Lanier Islands arrange an outing for you. There are three free boat launches on the island, with plenty of parking for cars and trailers.

Finally, Lake Lanier Islands will host your child's birthday party as part of the Islands Birthday Club. The package includes admission to the water park and lunch with ice cream and cake.

SPECIAL EVENTS

Lake Lanier Islands hosts the Memorial Day Beach Music Concert, the Fourth of July Concert, which includes a fireworks show, and the Magical Nights of Lights, to name a few.

NEARBY ATTRACTIONS

Lake Sidney Lanier
Stone Mountain Park

DIRECTIONS

From I-85 north of Atlanta, take I-985 to either Exit 1 or Exit 2, then follow the signs. Or take GA 400 to GA 20, then take Exit 14 and follow the signs.

FOR MORE INFORMATION

Lake Lanier Islands, 6950 Holiday Road, Lake Lanier Islands, GA 30518 (404-932-7200)

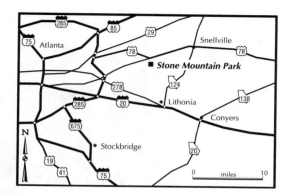

STONE MOUNTAIN PARK
DEKALB COUNTY

A surge of molten lava 300 million years ago gave rise to Stone Mountain. Its base is under half of Georgia and part of North Carolina. It was then sculpted by 200 million years of erosion into the 583 acres of exposed granite seen today.

For the Creek Indians, the granite monadnock was a shrine to be revered. For Spanish captain Juan Pardo, who came through present-day Georgia in 1567, it was "Crystal Mountain." Indian attacks kept the Spanish at bay, and Pardo returned to Spain believing the quartz-encrusted granite to be covered with diamonds and rubies.

In the 1830s, the world's largest mass of exposed granite was bought by Andrew Johnson and Aaron Cloud for $20 and a muzzleloader. Cloud built a 165-foot tower on the summit in 1838; Cloud's Tower had no foundation and was blown away by a storm.

The Georgia Railroad was completed in 1845, paving the way for commercial mining of the mountain's granite. Stone Mountain granite was used to build locks in the Panama Canal, the

Capitol in Washington, D.C., and Tokyo's Imperial Hotel, among other projects.

During the Civil War, the rail line and the town at the base of the mountain were destroyed by Sherman's troops, but no battles were fought at Stone Mountain.

It was the United Daughters of the Confederacy (U.D.C.) who helped turn the 825-foot-tall Stone Mountain into one of the most-visited attractions in the country. In the early 1900s, the U.D.C. first envisioned the mountain as a Confederate memorial. In 1912, Mrs. Helen Plane, a founding member of the U.D.C., proposed a massive carving on the north face of the mountain. In 1972, after two designs, three sculptures and more than four decades, the carving was completed. The horseback-mounted figures of Robert E. Lee, Thomas "Stonewall" Jackson and Jefferson Davis cover three acres of the rockface to form the world's largest bas-relief sculpture. The size of the carving is difficult to grasp from below—a horse's ear or mouth was large enough to shelter the carvers during sudden rainstorms on the mountain.

The Confederate Memorial carving on Stone Mountain is the world's largest bas relief sculpture.

Eventually, the Georgia General Assembly bought the mountain and the surrounding land for development as a park and created the Stone Mountain Memorial Association to develop and run the facility. Under that group's guidance, the park has seen its amenities proliferate to include museums, a sports complex, a conference center and more. The park's master plan calls for four separate districts to be fully developed by 2010.

A per-car fee is charged to enter the park. This state-owned facility is independently managed by the Stone Mountain Memorial Association and is operated without the use of federal, state or local taxes. ParkPasses are not valid for admission. The park is open daily from 6 A.M. to midnight, with the attractions open from 10 A.M. to 8 P.M. in the summer and from 10 A.M. to 5 P.M. the rest of the year, except Christmas.

LODGINGS

The 92-room Stone Mountain Inn and the 249-room Evergreen Conference Center and Resort are convenient to all of the park's amenities. Evergreen has facilities for large indoor events and meetings. The Park Center Inn will replace the Stone Mountain Inn when it is completed. For information and reservations for the

Stone Mountain Inn, call 800-277-0007 or 404-469-3311. For Evergreen, call 800-722-1000 or 404-469-2250.

CAMPING

The lakeside campground has 441 sites, including primitive tent sites, sites with partial hookups and sites with full RV hookups. Call 404-498-5710 for more information.

GOLF

Stone Mountain has two nationally ranked 18-hole golf courses, each with its own unique set of challenges. The championship golf course was named one of the top 25 municipal courses in the country by *Golf Digest*. A new clubhouse complements the golf courses and the Olympic Tennis Center; it is scheduled to be completed for use during the 1996 Olympics. The course is open daily and has a pro shop, a driving range, a putting green and a full-service restaurant. Call 404-498-5717 for information or to reserve a tee time.

SPORTS COMPLEX

An 18-hole miniature golf course, bicycle

A fisheye-lens view of the old grist mill at Stone Mountain Park.

rentals and a multilevel range of batting cages are available at the complex.

TENNIS CENTER

The newest addition at Stone Mountain will be an expansion to the tennis center. The new world-class facility will have 31 lighted courts, including four indoor courts and a 10,000-seat stadium, all in time for the 1996 Olympics.

LAKE ACTIVITIES

The 363-acre Stone Mountain Lake is the center for a variety of activities. You can swim at the beach, camp on the shore or venture into the water on a variety of craft, from the paddle-wheel riverboat *Scarlett O'Hara* to canoes and rowboats. The park also has two stocked lakes for fishermen.

MOUNTAIN ACTIVITIES

To get to the summit, you can take a Swiss-made cable car or hike up the 1.3-mile trail to the top. If you opt for the hike, stay on the trail, as the mountain's plant life is fragile and the cliff edge is lethal. For a tour of the base of the mountain, try the Stone Mountain Railroad, which makes a 5-mile trip to take in both the carvings and the undeveloped side of the mountain.

ANTEBELLUM PLANTATION

To better represent Georgia's pre–Civil War past, a group of buildings was moved to the park and furnished with period furniture. Opened in 1963, the Antebellum Plantation area shows how families of means lived in the period from 1820 to 1860. The main house was moved to its present site from the town of Dickey, near Albany. It was built in the 1840s and occupied by descendants of the original owners until it was moved to the park in 1961. A country store, an overseer's house, a smokehouse, a well, a cookhouse, a barn, a coach house and other outbuildings give a glimpse of plantation life. Every April, a Civil War encampment, period music and living-history exhibits help bring the plantation to life during the Plantation Jubilee.

A separate fee is charged for admission to the plantation.

ANNUAL EVENTS

The park offers an ambitious calendar of annual activities, including the Plantation Jubilee in April; the popular 50-minute Lasershow each night from May through Labor Day; the Fantastic Fourth Celebration; September's Yellow Daisy Festival; the Chili Cookoff and the Scottish Festival and Highland Games in October; and the year-ending Holiday Celebration in December. For special-events information, call 404-498-5702.

NEARBY ATTRACTIONS

Martin Luther King, Jr., National Historic Site
Lake Lanier Islands
Panola Mountain State Conservation Park

DIRECTIONS

Stone Mountain Park is 15 miles east of Atlanta on U.S. 78.

FOR MORE INFORMATION

Stone Mountain Park, P.O. Box 778, Stone Mountain, GA 30086 (404-498-5600 or 404-498-5702)

APPENDIX
GEOGRAPHIC INDEX

NORTHWEST GEORGIA MOUNTAINS

NORTHEAST GEORGIA MOUNTAINS

Amicalola Falls State Park
Black Rock Mountain State Park
Blue Ridge Wildlife Management Area
Bobby Brown State Park
Broad River Wildlife Management Area
Chattahoochee National Forest
Chattahoochee Wildlife Management Area
Chattooga National Wild and Scenic River
Chestatee Wildlife Management Area
Coleman River Wildlife Management Area
Cooper Creek Wildlife Management Area
Dahlonega Gold Museum State Historic Site
Dawson Forest Wildlife Management Area
Elbert County Wildlife Management Area
Fort Yargo State Park
Hart County Wildlife Management Area
Hart State Park
Hartwell Lake
Lake Burton Wildlife Management Area
Lake Lanier Islands
Lake Richard B. Russell
Lake Richard B. Russell State Park
Lake Richard B. Russell Wildlife Management Area
Lake Sidney Lanier
Moccasin Creek State Park
Swallow Creek Wildlife Management Area
Tallulah Gorge State Park
Traveler's Rest State Historic Site
Tugaloo State Park
Unicoi State Park and Lodge
Victoria Bryant State Park
Vogel State Park
Warwoman Wildlife Management Area
Watson Mill Bridge State Park
Wilson Shoals Wildlife Management Area

METROPOLITAN ATLANTA AREA

Allatoona Lake
Chattahoochee National Recreation Area
Kennesaw Mountain National Battlefield Park
Lake Lanier Islands
Martin Luther King, Jr., National Historic Site
Stone Mountain Park

PRESIDENTIAL PATHWAYS

Andersonville National Historic Site
Big Lazer Creek Public Fishing Area
Big Lazer Creek Wildlife Management Area
Blanton Creek Wildlife Management Area
Callaway Gardens
Eufaula National Wildlife Refuge
Flint River Wildlife Management Area
Florence Marina State Park
Franklin Delano Roosevelt State Park
Georgia Veterans Memorial State Park
Hannahatchee Creek Wildlife Management Area
Jimmy Carter National Historic Site
Little White House State Historic Site
Providence Canyon State Conservation Park
Walter F. George Lake
West Point Lake
West Point Wildlife Management Area

HISTORIC HEARTLAND

B. F. Grant Wildlife Management Area
Baldwin Forest Wildlife Management Area and Public Fishing Area

Beaverdam Wildlife Management Area
Cedar Creek Wildlife Management Area
Clybel Wildlife Management Area
Hard Labor Creek State Park
High Falls State Park
Indian Springs State Park
Jarrell Plantation State Historic Site
Marben Public Fishing Area
Oaky Woods Wildlife Management Area
Ocmulgee National Monument
Ocmulgee Wildlife Management Area
Oconee National Forest
Panola Mountain State Conservation Park
Piedmont National Wildlife Refuge
Rum Creek Wildlife Management Area and Public
　　Fishing Area

CLASSIC SOUTH

CS

A. H. Stephens State Historic Park
Clarks Hill Lake
Clarks Hill Wildlife Management Area
Di-Lane Wildlife Management Area
Elijah Clark State Park
Fishing Creek Wildlife Management Area
George L. Smith II State Park
Germany Creek Wildlife Management Area
Hamburg State Park
Keg Creek Wildlife Management Area
Magnolia Springs State Park
McDuffie Public Fishing Area
Mistletoe State Park
Oconee National Forest
Oconee Wildlife Management Area
Ogeechee Wildlife Management Area
Redlands Wildlife Management Area

Robert Toombs House State Historic Site
Soap Creek Wildlife Management Area
Watson Mill Bridge State Park
Yuchi Wildlife Management Area

PLANTATION TRACE

PT

Albany Nursery Wildlife Management Area
Banks Lake National Wildlife Refuge
Chickasawhatchee Wildlife Management Area
George T. Bagby State Park
Grand Bay Wildlife Management Area
Kolomoki Mounds State Historic Park
Lake George W. Andrews
Lake Seminole
Lake Seminole Wildlife Management Area
Lake Walter F. George Wildlife Management Area
Lapham-Patterson House State Historic Site
Mayhaw Wildlife Management Area
Paradise Public Fishing Area
Reed Bingham State Park
Walter F. George Lake

MAGNOLIA MIDLANDS

MM

Big Hammock Wildlife Management Area and Pub-
　　lic Fishing Area
Bullard Creek Wildlife Management Area
Dodge County Public Fishing Area
Dyal Pasture Wildlife Management Area
Evans County Public Fishing Area
Flint River Wildlife Management Area
General Coffee State Park
Gordonia-Alatamaha State Park

Horse Creek Wildlife Management Area
King Tract Wildlife Management Area
Little Ocmulgee State Park and Pete Phillips Lodge
Little Satilla Wildlife Management Area
Rayonier Wildlife Management Area
Sansavilla Wildlife Management Area
Treutlen County Public Fishing Area
Tuckahoe Wildlife Management Area

COLONIAL COAST

Altamaha Wildlife Management Area
Blackbeard Island National Wildlife Refuge
Crooked River State Park
Cumberland Island National Seashore
Dixon Memorial Forest Wildlife Management Area
Fort Frederica National Monument
Fort King George State Historic Site

Fort McAllister State Historic Park
Fort Morris State Historic Site
Fort Pulaski National Monument
Harris Neck National Wildlife Refuge
Hofwyl-Broadfield Plantation State Historic Site
Jekyll Island
Laura S. Walker State Park
Okefenokee National Wildlife Refuge
Ossabaw Island Wildlife Management Area
Paulks Pasture Wildlife Management Area
Richmond Hill Wildlife Management Area
Sapelo Island National Wildlife Refuge
Sapelo Island Wildlife Management Area
Savannah National Wildlife Refuge
Skidaway Island State Park
Stephen C. Foster State Park
Surveyor's Creek Wildlife Management Area
Tybee Island National Wildlife Refuge
Wassaw Island National Wildlife Refuge
Wolf Island National Wildlife Refuge
Wormsloe State Historic Site

INDEX

Halfmoon Creek Park, 236
Hall, Lyman, 111
Hamburg State Park, 42-44
Hannah Clark Nature Trail, 22
Hannahatchee Creek Wildlife Management Area, 273
Harbor Light Marina, 215
Hard Labor Creek State Park, 6, 44-46
Hardley Creek Park, 236
Harris Branch Recreation Area, 204-5
Harris Neck National Wildlife Refuge, 245-46
Hart County Wildlife Management Area, 273
Hart, Nancy, 47, 164, 212
Hart State Park, 47-49
Hartwell Group Camp, 213
Hartwell Lake, 47, 89-90, 212-15
Hartwell Marina, 215
Hawkins, Thomas, 184
Hawthorne Overlook, 89
Hawthorne Pool, 89
Hesters Ferry Campground, 209-10
Hidden Creek Recreation Area, 149
Hidden Pond Trail, 205, 206
High Falls Lake, 49
High Falls State Park, 49-51
High Shoals Falls, 149
High Shoals Trail, 149
Highland Marina, 236-37
Highland Scots, 110
Hiking Trails of North Georgia, 134
Hillsboro Lake Recreation Area, 168
Historic Ruins Trail, 50
Historical Trail, 179
History Trail, 86
Hitchiti Nature Trail, 168, 252
Hofwyl Dairy, 113, 114
Hofwyl-Broadfield Plantation State Historic Site, 102, 113-116
Hog Hannock, 253
Holcomb Creek Falls, 165

Holiday Campground, 237
Holiday Marina, 230
Homestead Trail, 76
Hood, John Bell, 190
Horace King Park, 237
Horse Creek Wildlife Management Area, 274
Horse Trough Falls, 163, 164
Howard, O. O., 124
Hurricane Falls, 88
Hutchinson's Ferry Landing, 222

Indian Mounds Golf Course, 292
Indian Mounds Trail, 170
Indian Springs Group Camping Area, 237
Indian Springs State Park, 51-54
Indigo Snake, 33
Isle of Hope, 129

J. Strom Thurmond Lake. See Clarks Hill Lake
Jack's Knob Trail, 138, 139
Jack's River Trail, 142
James E. Edmonds Back-Country Trail, 12
James H. "Sloppy" Floyd State Park, 54-55
Jarrard Gap Trail, 154
Jarrell, B. R., 117
Jarrell, John, 101, 116, 117
Jarrell, Mattie, 116
Jarrell Plantation State Historic Site, 101, 116-18, 168, 250
Jarrett, Devereaux, 127, 128
Jekyll Island, 114, 286, 290-94
Jekyll Island Authority, 291
Jekyll, Joseph, 291
Jim Woodruff Dam, 222
Jim Woodruff Lock and Dam, 79, 220
Jimmy Carter National Historic Site, 187-89
John A. Sibley Horticultural Center, 287, 288